Maritime Music Greats
Fifty Years of Hits and Heartbreak

Virginia Beaton and Stephen Pedersen

NIMBUS
PUBLISHING

Nimbus Publishing Limited
P.O. Box 9301, Station A
Halifax, N.S. B3K 5N5
(902) 455-4286

Design: Arthur B. Carter, Halifax
Printed and bound in Canada

Canadian Cataloguing in Publication Data

Beaton, Virginia
Maritime music greats
ISBN 1-55019-015-5

1. Country music—Maritime Provinces—History
2. Folk music—Maritime Provinces—History
3. Musicians—Maritime Provinces—Biography.
I. Pedersen, Stephen. II. Title.

ML3563.B42 1992   781.62'009715   C92-098528-9

When The Sun Says Goodnight To The Prairies, My Faithful Old Pinto Pal, Everybody's Been Some Mother's Darling, all by Wilf Carter, © 1938 by Peer International Corporation, Copyright Renewed, International Copyright Secured, All Rights Reserved. Used by Permission. *My Swiss Moonlight Lullaby*, by Wilf Carter, © 1933 by Gordon V. Thompson, A Division of Warner/Chappell Music Canada Ltd., Reprinted by Permission. *The Capture of Albert Johnson*, by Wilf Carter, © 1934 by Gordon V. Thompson Music, A Division of Warner/Chappell Music Canada Ltd., Reprinted by Permission. *Canada Day Up Canada Way*, by Tom Connors, © Copyright Crown-Vetch Music (a division of Stompin' Tom Ltd.), Used by Permission. *Tie Me Down*, by Allister MacGillivray, © Copyright Cabot Trail Music (c/o Morning Music Ltd.), Used by Permission. *When The Lovin' is Through, Reason to Believe, Working Man, Flying On Your Own*, all by Rita MacNeil, courtesy Big Pond Publishing and Balmur Music. Used by Permission. *And now…here's Max*, by Max Ferguson, used by permission of McGraw-Hill Ryerson Ltd. *Her Own Woman*, by Myrna Kostash, used by permission of the author. The authors would like to thank the Halifax *Chronicle Herald*, CBC, CanaPress, Neptune Theatre, Nova Scotia Tourism and Culture, and Dalhousie University Archives for their generosity in permitting us to use their photos.

Every effort has been made to trace copyright holders, but should there be any omissions in this respect we apologize and shall be pleased to make acknowledgements in any future editions.

Cover credits: Rita MacNeil souvenir folder courtesy of Brooks Diamond Productions; Hank Snow, *Lassoes 'n Spurs*, © 1991 by BMG Music; Anne Murray, *A Little Good News*, © 1983 by Capitol Records Inc.

Contents

Acknowledgements

We would like to acknowledge our gratitude to the people who helped in the production of this book. Special thanks go to Dorothy Blythe, managing editor of Nimbus, and to our editor Tanya Buchdahl.

As well, we would like to thank the following people for interviews, advice and encouragement: Michael Ardenne, Skip Beckwith, George Brothers, Gunter Buchta, John Allan Cameron, Brooks Diamond, Ron Labelle, David MacIsaac, Gene MacLellan, Scott Macmillan, Kenzie Mac-Neil, Peter Power, Dr. Neil Rosenberg, the late Ray Simmons, and Don Tremaine.

For their assistance in locating archival material, we thank Ronnie Pugh of the Country Music Foundation in Nashville, Jane Purves, Ken Jennex, and Alberta Dube of the Halifax *Herald*, and the staff of the Public Archives of Nova Scotia.

For helping us arrive at a clearer definition of what is and isn't country music, we would like to thank Tom and Marla Dorward and Brian Mitton of the Halifax Folklore Centre.

For having the idea in the first place and for her constant encouragement and advice, we owe a special debt of thanks to Nancy Robb.

And finally, we thank the country musicians who made this book possible.

CBC-TV Publicity

Foreword

It has been said of country music that in order to be country, it must be lovesick, homesick, or trainsick! Like all generalities, there is a nub of truth in that.

I was born in 1928, just one year after Jimmie Rodgers and The Carter Family had been "discovered" and made their first records for RCA Victor in Bristol, Tennessee. Jimmie Rodgers drew very heavily on the black legacy or work songs and the blues of his native Mississippi, while the Carter Family had the centuries-old folk songs of the Blue Ridge Mountains as a base for their particular brand of music.

The record companies of the day (the big ones being Victor, Decca and Columbia) didn't know what to call this strange hybrid so the early recordings by Vernon Dalhart (*The Wreck of the Old 97*) and Carson Robinson (*Down in the Little Green*) would identify the artist and then in small print: "Novelty vocal with Orchestra"; two instruments and up was an orchestra then! In Jimmie Rodgers case it was just "Vocal Refrain with guitar."

In the late '20s and early '30s there was a sudden surge of popularity for Hawaiian music, which, thanks to radio, North Americans were hearing for the first time. Jimmie Rodgers jumped on the band wagon and recorded a couple of his best songs with Lani MacIntyre and his Hawaiians *For the Sake of Days Gone By* and *Everybody does It in Hawaii* back around 1931, and in my opinion that was when what was to become country music achieved its identity. The addition of the Hawaiian guitar, or dobro then, steel now, gave country music a distinctive sound that, despite the many side-roads it has travelled since, remains one of the basic ingredients to this day. (At least to us old die-hards!)

I had a favorite uncle then who played the first record I ever saw or heard on one of those famous old floor model Victrolas. It was a Jimmie Rodgers tune, *The Mississippi River Blues*, which was cut at his last recording session in May of 1933. Jimmie was dying of T.B. at the time and in fact was dead two days after the session. My uncle was devastated. It is ironic that two good ol' boys from Mississippi, Jimmie Rodgers and Hank Williams 20 years apart, would have recording careers that spanned a mere five years each, would die before their 35th birthdays, and yet make a bigger impact on country music than anyone else since.

The first Maritimers I ever heard on radio or records were Don Messer and Wilf Carter. Funny, the odd things that stick in your mind from childhood. I distinctly recall my mother saying to me the first time she heard Don Messer on the radio from Saint John in 1934, "That man is the best fiddler I ever heard." If my mother said it, it must be true, so I adopted her opinion then at the tender age of six and never had occasion to change my mind. Messer was the king. Who could have possibly imagined that 25 years later I would be standing in front of The Islanders before a television camera ready to bellow for the first of some 500 occasions "From coast to coast on the CBC, It's Don Messer's Jubilee!" A very happy and rewarding decade followed, and I got to know Don and Marg and Charlie and all the lads very well indeed. As is so often the case, those people of whom you stand in awe, are quiet, ordinary mortals after all, and in Don Messer's case a pleasant, shy, almost retiring gentleman, but with this huge talent that I still think of as awesome.

I first met Wilf Carter in the form of a record (RCA

Marg, Don, Charlie and "Don Messer's Jubilee" pass into folklore in this carving by folk artist Scott Higgins, made in 1991. Though all three are dead, the carving shows how strongly they still live in memory.

Victor Bluebird of course) fairly early in his recording career. The recording was *The Capture of Albert Johnson*, a musical saga from the annals of the RCMP that appeared as a story titled "The Mad Trapper of Rat River." The year was about 1935-36 and Wilf had been recording for only about two or three years. This was the depths of the Great Depression and an old 78 RPM record cost about 50 cents so Wilf Carter was not getting rich, but then again, nor was anyone else.

The Capture of Albert Johnson and the *Rescue At Moose River Gold Mine* were very much in the folk tradition, that is, telling in song the events of an era or a person or place; but Wilf also sang his share of love ballads and novelty songs but was noted from his earliest days for his yodelling. He was far and away the best of the yodellers of the time. Jimmie Rodgers was mediocre and Hank Snow was about the worst, (a fact that Hank laughingly admitted on an interview I did with him once.) No one has ever explained to me why or how the yodel got included in those early country songs but most of the artists felt they had to include it, usually in the middle

and at the end of a song. But I think that Wilf Carter's *Swiss Moonlight Lullaby* is still the standard by which all other yodellers are measured.

Wilf was born in Port Hilford, Guysborough Country, Nova Scotia, and, like so many others, heard the call of the road and ran away from home at quite a tender age. I believe his singing career began when he got a job with the CP Hotel in Banff taking tourists on overnight trail rides through the foothills of Alberta. He was expected to look after the horses, help with the camp and the cooking and then sing to them round the camp-fire at night. Mostly it was the old cowboy and folk songs, but he also threw in a few of his own and when his recording career began he had a number of original songs ready to go. That was a prerequisite then and hasn't changed much since.

I don't think I ever heard a guitar with a better tone than that lovely old Martin Wilf played on all his early recordings. Considering the state of the technological art of the 1930s and the fact that Wilf flailed away at it with a thumb pick, it is still a standout sound. When I met him the first time in the early 1970s on CBC's "Countrytime," I actually got to strum it and I was sorely tempted to steal it then and there! In fact, I should have because the airline baggage handlers managed to trash it when he flew out of here after the show. He told me the story when he appeared a year or so later on "Countrytime," and showed me the new model that the Martin Company made for him as a replacement, and although it looked terrific, it was just another guitar. Wilf is well into his eighties at this writing and is still entertaining his fans. I believe he played a few dates in the summer of 1989 here in Nova Scotia.

Cowboy singers, as they were getting to be called, were beginning to proliferate and a lot of those $5.95 Eaton Special guitars got into the hands of a lot of Maritime boys. One of these was Tex Cochrane, who I seem to recall sang out of Charlottetown in the late 30s, got an RCA Victor recording contract and turned out a few records that I remember were very good. It's been a thousand years since I heard one but I think he sounded a bit like Eddy Arnold. Tex Cochrane, I'm sure, could have made it in the country music field but the war came along and he joined the army and made it a career from which he retired as a Major a few years back and lives quietly in retirement in the Fredericton area. I'd like to meet him.

At about the same time, another out of work Maritimer appeared at radio station CHNS with his $5.95 Eaton Special guitar under his arm and a burning desire to make it big as a cowboy singer. Hank Snow shouldn't have had a chance. By his own admission he was an abused child from a broken home with a Grade five education out of work in the middle of the Great Depression! Usually you're out after three strikes; Hank had five on him then and counting! He had the great good fortune to meet Cecil Landry at CHNS that day who recognized that this skinny little Lunenburger had something going for him. They put him on the air for 15 minutes the next week (at no pay) just to see how the public liked him. They liked him a lot. Mr. Landry recorded him and sent the disc off to RCA Victor, and the rest as they say, is history. Hank's first record was *The Prisoned Cowboy* which he wrote on the train on his way to Montreal for first recording session; the royalties from it were $1.96. His very next record was a hit, by the standards of the time, and was his arrangement of an old folk song called *The Blue Velvet Band*. This was the beginning of a recording career that spanned almost 40 years, and was a record in itself for one artist with one label.

It's interesting that three Maritimers should arrive on the entertainment scene within a couple of years of each other, and despite the inauspicious times, were to eventually have the most tremendous success and to be recognized by their peers and the public as real pioneers in what was to become the music industry's biggest and most consistently appealing idiom. One of Don Messer's fiddles rest in the Country Music Hall of Fame in Nashville, Hank Snow is a member and Wilf Carter was elected to the Cowboy Hall of Fame in Calgary a few years ago. By anybody's measurement that is success! Although many Maritimers since have been "successful" and popular and made good or bad livings from country music, it wasn't until Anne Murray came along with her amazing versatility to be able to sing everything from country to rock, that new generations of fans started looking in their Atlas's for places like Springhill, Nova Scotia, and Blue Rocks, and Port Hilford, and Tweedside, New Brunswick and Charlottetown, P.E.I.

The Maritime contribution to country music has been very large indeed and many people can take some credit. The artists of course, the DJs who played the records on air, and the public who bought them; but another element that should be mentioned is the pride we as Maritimers have felt in the achievements of our musicmakers. Not only the fame of those who "made it big" but of those who only made it halfway or those who should have made it but were denied that benevolent but illusive smile from Lady Luck. Their music has touched us all over the years and they have reflected great credit on all of us. "Long may their big jibs draw!"

Don Tremaine
Dartmouth, N.S.
1992

*Anne Murray, brother Bruce and Carroll
Baker sing out for a 1983 CBC-TV special.*

CBC-TV Publicity

Introduction

This book is about Maritime musicians. It is not really about country music. But country music plays a major part in it. The careers of Wilf Carter, Hank Snow, Don Messer, Stompin' Tom Connors, Gene MacLellan, John Allan Cameron, Anne Murray, Carroll Baker and Rita MacNeil stand as landmarks of a peculiarly Maritime style—country music with a downeast twist. In Canada's Maritime provinces a homegrown mixture of folk music and traditional instrumental performance such as the Scottish, Acadian, and Irish fiddling styles is a living extension of centuries-old traditions. Alongside these exist other widely practised styles—pop music, country and western, rhythm 'n' blues, rock—that are imported, absorbed, and assimilated by performers. The Rankin Family Band from Cape Breton, for example, sing and perform Gaelic songs, step dance to traditional fiddle tunes, and write original country and contemporary folk songs such as Jimmy Rankin's *The Tramp Miners*, a song about Cape Breton miners who circle the globe in search of mines to work. Lennie Gallant's *Man of Steel* and Rita MacNeil's *Working Man* give further proof that this kind of contemporary folk-song writing runs in the veins of Maritime musicians.

Considering that the combined population of Nova Scotia, New Brunswick, and Prince Edward Island is fewer than two million, not quite seven per cent of the Canadian total, the number of Maritimers who have made significant contributions to North American country and popular music is high. Wilf Carter and Hank Snow were both main stream country singers. Carroll Baker sings a hurtin' song with the best. Anne Murray and Rita MacNeil have both won country music industry awards. But here is where the arguments start. If Rita is country, then country means something other than what it meant for Carter and Snow. And Anne, though most of her radio play has come from country and adult contemporary stations, does not like to be called a country singer. Stompin' Tom Connors wears the cowboy rig, the hat, the boots, the black shirt and stovepipe jeans, yet he's really not a country singer in the conventional sense but a balladeer. He is the poet of the small-town, wandering the nation over and making "home-town music" wherever he goes, as he once remarked to New Brunswick poet Alden Nowlan. John Allan Cameron, the first to play traditional fiddle and bagpipe tunes on the guitar in public concert, tried to sing country music in the mid '80s but could not filter out his lilting Cape Breton accent. Don Messer bridled at anyone calling him a country musician.

The problem of finding the right category for Maritime musicians is complicated by the fact that contemporary country music has developed a multiple personality. Ever since World War II, it has sought to enlarge its audience by soaking up stylistic features of related kinds of urban music. The popularity of dance orchestras in the late '30s and the early '40s influenced the development of western swing bands such as that of American Bob Wills. Elbowed aside by rhythm 'n' blues and rock 'n' roll in the late '50s, country music elbowed back by adopting the rock drummer's backbeat. In the early '60s country singer Patsy Cline captured pop music audiences with her torchy renditions of songs like *I Fall To Pieces*, and Willie Nelson's *Crazy*. Country Pop has been around ever since. Without such a hybrid form of country music it would be impossible to account for Anne Murray's appeal to Nashville.

While Nashville is the undisputed capital of American country music, and the headquarters of one of the shrewdest and most successful music business communities in the world, Canada's country musicians seldom fit easily into its formats. In spite of the sweet country sound of *Leave Her Memory*, Rita MacNeil is having difficulty breaking into the U.S. market, not because the record companies aren't interested, but because the radio stations don't know what format to play her in. Lennie Gallant is a startlingly original singer-songwriter from Prince Edward Island who poses similar problems for station managers. Where do you play him? Into what category do you slot the new, young Maritime bands working out of deeply-rooted country traditions of their own, The Rankin Family, or The Barra MacNeils?

In Canada the country music industry is not yet as format-driven as Nashville. It resists definitions which would exclude the best "sort-of" country musicians in the nation. Lennie Gallant's nomination for a 1992 Juno as best country male vocalist was welcome, but it puzzled him. "In this country," he remarked to Tracy Hanes of the *Peterborough Examiner*, "you have a lot of artists who don't fit into categories. What do you call Joni Mitchell or Neil Young? And Murray McLauchlan's won the award several times and I certainly wouldn't call him country." McLauchlan, on the other hand, remarked recently on the CBC television special, "Country Gold," "I'm country as hell!"

This identity crisis in Canadian country music can not entirely be explained by the chronic preoccupation of Canadians with the question of who they are. It lies deep within the early history of country music itself. Country music was born in the southeastern mountain states out of the impact, among other influences, of rural black instrumental music upon rural whites brought up singing the folk songs of the Anglo-Celtic tradition.

Together with New England and the Appalachian region of the south eastern United States, the Maritime region is one of three rich repositories of Anglo-Celtic folk music in North America. English and Scottish ballads, whose texts were collected by James Francis Childs and published in Boston from 1882 to 1898, are found in all three regions. Along with similarly imported dances, and instrumental music, they became Americanized in the southern U.S., and were gradually transformed into the beginnings of country music. It was a complex process of absorbing interest, but it is not within either the scope or the expertise of the authors of this book. Readers would do well to consult Bill C. Malone's authoritative and detailed history, *Country Music USA*, a valuable source of facts and insights.

The music and singing style that emerged in the U.S. in the '20s was first known as mountain music. It underwent a process of commercialization through the agency of radio and gramophone records. It was characterized by high nasal singing, and the string band accompaniment of banjo (borrowed from black country musicians), guitar, and fiddle. In time it came to be named not country music, but hillbilly music, a term that stuck to it even into the early '40s.

In those heady early years, the late '20s and early '30s, country music had not yet defined itself as a recognizable genre. American country music historian Bill C. Malone tells us that a record company was the first to use the term as a description of rural music in 1925. Right up until World War II it was known as hillbilly music, deriving its name from the backwoods inhabitants of the hills in the southern U.S. But Al Hopkins's band was the first to be called "The Hillbillies." The late '20s and '30s were the golden age of hillbilly music. According to Malone it was golden because it was still free from big-city exploitation.

Today that once popular style has almost completely died out except in the form of bluegrass music with its tight harmonies, virtuosic picking of mandolin, banjo and guitar, breakdown fiddle playing, and oompah thump of the string-bass anchoring the roots of its simple harmony chords. The high voiced, yodelling style of Texas railway brakeman Jimmie Rodgers, recorded between 1927 and his death in

1933, is generally regarded as the first historical appearance of the commercial product we have come to call country music.

The yodel was a Swiss import. Malone says it probably appeared in America as early as 1847 in the shows of black minstrels influenced by touring groups of Tyrolean singers. The steel guitar, a standard instrument in the mid-century style known as honky-tonk, was another early import. It was originally a Hawaiian instrument introduced to the United States after Hawaii became a U.S. Territory in 1900. Both these novelties, yodelling and the Hawaiian steel guitar, were popularized in the '20s and '30s by musicians performing on radio stations and in travelling country tent shows. They stand out as two of the earliest and most characteristic expressive devices of country music style. Their adoption exemplifies how much country music was open to imported influences right from the start.

The steel guitar became the distinguishing voice of the honky-tonk style that was immortalized in the short, brilliant career of Hank Williams who died of a heart attack at the age of 29 on New Year's Day, 1953. In honky-tonk the steel electric guitar wailed out the loneliness and desolation of the hard-nosed patrons of the honky-tonk dive. They came to dance, drink, listen to cheatin' songs, and fight. Hank Snow's *Married by the Bible Divorced by the Law* shows that even he was affected by this classic style.

By the '50s, yodelling, except in the delivery of a brilliant practitioner such as Wilf Carter, had all but died out. But the steel guitar, like the country fiddle, became an instrument of war in a seesaw battle of styles as record companies tried to track the changing tastes of urban audiences for a softer, sweeter country sound. Both instruments were unceremoniously dropped as country music yearned toward pop music in the '50s and '60s, only to be defiantly reintroduced a few years later by outlaws seeking to return the style to its most characteristic beginnings.

Maritimers picked up these changes and followed the controversies like good country fans all over North America. But it seemed to affect them peripherally rather than di-

rectly. They are unique among Canadians because they like to sing and play their folk, traditional, and country music rather than just listen to it. These musical skills belong to a longstanding Maritime tradition from a quieter time before radio, the long-playing record, and television made passive listening a way of life. The nature of basic industry in Nova Scotia, Prince Edward Island, and New Brunswick helps these traditional kinds of music-making to hold their own against the onslaught of big-city sophistication and commercialization. Lumbering, mining, fishing, farming, and sailing continue to be traditional Maritime industries for unskilled labor. And most of the music-making, until recent years, has come from the workers in these traditional industries. Anne Murray, the daughter of a Springhill doctor, is the only major performer discussed in this book who comes from the middle class. The relative sophistication of her style and the classiness of her presentation reflect that background.

For many working class people in traditional Maritime industries, acquiring skills continues to depend on a traditional apprenticeship system rather than on schools. Apprenticeships in rural communities come from families and neighbours. Fathers teach sons. Neighbors hire neighbors to help out. Strong bonds of co-operative work also draw people together in leisure hours for home-made pleasures, and the fiddle, the guitar, or the parlour piano is never far out of reach. Musical traditions—tunes and styles—are also still being handed down through a similar apprenticeship system.

The community hall is as important to the dissemination and teaching of country music traditions in the Maritimes as the conservatory system is for classical music. Don Messer played in such buildings every weekend for many years. Eager boys learned from listening to him, or, if they were too young to squeeze past the ticket-taker at the door, found a seat outside in a tree, or on a knoll close by. Today, recordings, songbooks, and competitions where the downeast style is closely adjudicated make learning to play traditional music easier. Yet the community hall still serves both the apprentice system and the sense of belonging. It is a small-town institution sometimes reproduced in big-city social clubs such as Farrell Hall in Dartmouth, which still holds traditional Cape Breton dances on weekends. For other tastes there is the pub, the Doryman in Cheticamp, Johnny Reid's lounge in Charlottetown and others. Thus the traditions survive urbanization. For a while longer, at least.

Wilf Carter, Hank Snow, Don Messer, John Allan Cameron, Stompin' Tom Connors, Gene MacLellan, Anne Murray, Carroll Baker and Rita MacNeil, the chief figures in our study—brought up on Maritime music— are only the tip of a very large iceberg. The guitarists and bass players, the drummers and piano players who serve as back-up musicians in bands across the country and across borders, constitute a small army, though they do not enjoy the prominence of their famous colleagues. They show an extraordinary degree of versatility. They play country, yes, but also bluegrass, downeast fiddling style, rhythm 'n' blues, and rock. Gary Spicer, Nova Scotia-born guitarist based in Ottawa, toured with the then 86-year-old Wilf Carter on his 1990 Eastern Canada spring tour. He says that half of the country bands in Canada are filled with Maritimers. These Maritimers are exported, he maintains, so that the rest of the nation's headliners can carry on.

There are yet other levels of support behind the headliners and the invisible army. There are the weekend warriors who sing and write country songs, and play for local Saturday night dances. And there are the hardcore country fans who can be seen and heard singing and picking in the parking lot at a community picnic, playing for community dances, or singing on cable television in karaoke-style jamborees, where all they need is the encouragement of their friends to grab a microphone and sing along with a taped professional band. A few record and distribute their own home-produced cassette tapes and if style and repertoire is anything to go by, Hank Snow is their hero.

There are still many places in the Maritimes where you can go on a Saturday night for the simple celebration of country values. The community halls in Cape Breton still vibrate with the sound of the Scottish fiddlers, providing place and opportunity for a whole new generation of talented young players and singers to prepare themselves for a national career, as the Rankin Family Band and the Barra MacNeils have done. Live musical traditions survive and will probably continue to survive as long as they serve the community. There are probably as many kitchen parties, weddings, and wakes as there ever were, perhaps even more.

You cannot examine the 50 year period ranging from Wilf Carter and Hank Snow to Anne Murray and Rita MacNeil, without being struck by the way the music business has evolved. The early days were simpler. Instruments were portable, unamplified, and mainly used for background accompaniment and color. The instrumentation of lead guitar, double-bass, fiddle, and steel-guitar served for most of the country styles. These instruments were easy to carry from one small-town community hall to another. Whatever lighting was available was acceptable. People came to dance.

Today the picture has changed entirely. Tons of equipment, dozens of roadies, sound and lighting technicians, stage crews—a whole company in fact. And people come mostly to listen and to run down to the front of the stage to take photos. Technological developments, particularly in the '70s, have contributed synthesizers and sound signal processors which are used to create a style of thick orchestration that recalls the 19th century classical music mega-orchestra. In a concert in Halifax's Metro Centre in September, 1991, Rita MacNeil's band, originally quite simple with guitar, bass, drums, and a single synthesizer, had evolved into a hip and swinging electrified orchestra, heavily influenced by rock and blues, with no fewer than seven keyboards (though of course not all of them were played at the same time).

The history of sound recording parallels that of live performance. In the early days of country music, recording technique was primitive. It usually consisted of one performer, with or without a band, standing in front of a microphone. Today separate bedtracks, rhythm tracks and vocal tracks are recorded in acoustically designed studios equipped with expensive, highly sophisticated digital recording devices. It is not uncommon today for different tracks to be laid down at different times in different cities, and then mixed for the final master tape in a control room in, say, Nashville or Los Angeles. In recent years the necessity of creating music videos as marketing tools has made performers dependent upon producers and upon sources of big money. It is hard to imagine today a Hank Snow being able to pull himself up and into the limelight virtually by his own bootstraps as he did in the '30s. The overall importance of a knowledgeable, industry-smart management company cannot be overestimated in the promotion and development of a musical career in the '90s. It is debatable whether any artist can crack the lucrative American market without one.

Yet there is something in country music which resists change. It keeps seeking out its roots. Even urbanites feel the pull of its basic values, alternately regarded now as corny and now as sentimental touchstones—home, family, honest work, rambunctious helling around, romanticism, heartbreak, and tragedy. The outlaws of the '70s (Willie Nelson, Waylon Jennings), are recapitulated by the new traditionalists of the '90s (Dwight Yoakam, Randy Travis, Ricky Skaggs). The maritime mix has its conservatives and loners too. Don Messer exemplified the former, Stompin' Tom the latter. There are those who left for the big cities to pursue their careers (Snow, Murray, Baker, Connors, Cameron), and those who ran their careers from downhome such as Messer.

The men and women treated in detail in this book have experienced, collectively, more than 50 years of change. Only three of them, Snow, Carter, and Murray, have developed a substantial American market. All of them, except for Snow, have maintained both a Maritime and a Canadian sense of style. Their sense of the tribal values of community and the small town have affected their way of presenting themselves. American audiences, especially those from the regions where small-town values are still intact and where song and instrumental traditions are similar, are drawn to their music. But the majority, cultivated for decades by record companies and radio stations, probably perceive them as foreign. Maritime country and traditional entertainers tend to be modest rather than flamboyant, sincere rather than showy. The women in this book are not glamorous stereotypes. Carroll Baker is a sister and a best friend. Rita MacNeil makes us feel as though we had just been invited into her Big Pond kitchen for a cup of tea. Anne Murray plays the simple small town girl even amid the lights and glitter of Las Vegas. The men, except for the Americanized Snow, also dress conservatively, and project their music more than their personality. Taken together these Maritimers—women and men alike—embody the variety, style, and values of the region itself. And that makes them singularly uncommon and fascinating.

CHAPTER 1

Wilf Carter

At home on the range

Unlike most of the rhinestone cowboys in the music business, Wilf Carter (also known as Montana Slim) can claim legitimate cowboy status. When Carter turned up for an audition at radio station CBS in New York in 1935, he wore his cowboy duds—denim pants, chaps, boots and cowboy hat—not to make a dramatic impression on the executives, but because he was a working cowboy. Used to a rough outdoor life as an Alberta ranch hand, Carter had no city clothes to wear. He was more accustomed to riding, roping and handling cattle and horses than he was to job interviews. But he got the job, which was a 15 minute radio spot each day on the CBS network.

Wilf Carter was the voice of the Depression years. Starting with his earliest recordings for RCA Victor in Montreal, he wrote and sang dozens of simple but extremely popular tunes that made him a recognized country music star across Canada, the United States and Australia. During the '30s, '40s and '50s, anybody who turned on a radio was bound to hear Wilf Carter's voice and his trademark Swiss-style yodelling. He was able to parlay his talent for writing catchy tunes with downhome lyrics into a career that lasted over 60 years. Even today, many songs from the Carter songbook are standard items in legion halls, talent shows, and country music jamborees. It would be hard to find a country guitarist who doesn't know a fistful of Carter's songs: *Prairie Sunset, Swiss Moonlight Lullabye, Yodelling Cowgirl,* and *There's a Love Knot in my Lariat,* to name only a few.

Yet Wilf Carter has avoided many of the trappings of celebrity, preferring to cultivate the image of himself as a fellow who plays the guitar, sings, and likes to reminisce about the simple life back on the ranch. Carter has clung to many of the platform mannerisms common among many performers in his heyday: the folksiness, the corny jokes and especially the exaggerated humility and gratitude to the audience. Yet the audiences who saw Wilf Carter on his Last Roundup tour in 1991 seemed to appreciate his fidelity to the stage personality he developed. Perhaps it was a relief to find a performer so secure with himself and his music that he felt no need to follow fads, or remind people of his status and many achievements. As an example, Carter often tells the story of how he once greeted a concert crowd by saying, "I don't want to be on the top of the ladder. I want to be just one rung up, so I can reach down and shake the hands of all you wonderful people!"

Though Carter is usually identified as a cowboy and western singer, his roots are in the Maritimes. Wilf Carter was born in Port Hilford, Nova Scotia, in 1904 as a son of the manse. His parents were English; his father, Reverend Henry Carter, was an evangelical preacher of the hellfire-and-brimstone variety. With nine children in the family, it was hard to make ends meet on a minister's salary, and by age nine young Wilf was driving oxen teams to earn a quarter a day. Not surprisingly, religion was a strong force in the household. The children were brought up to say grace before meals and family prayers after breakfast. Carter often tells the story of the time he brought the family prayers to an abrupt halt by pulling the tail of one of the cats. The resulting angry meow alerted his parents that one of their sons was inattentive and Wilf received one of many lickings.

Both parents sang well, and encouraged their children to sing too. Carter developed a fondness for hymns which he holds to this day, frequently including an uptempo version of *How Great Thou Art* in his concerts. That early influence of religious music later manifested itself in many of Carter's own songs. The musical structure of many hymns can be detected through Carter's use of a careful rhyming pattern, phrases of regular length, and a relatively simple chord plan requiring only four or five chords.

Carter's first exposure to theatre or music as entertainment came after he saw a poster advertising a show to be held in the upper Annapolis Valley farming town of Canning, near the place where the family was then living. Along with a dramatic presentation of *Uncle Tom's Cabin*, there was to be a performer called the Yodelling Fool. Carter's parents explained to him what a yodeller sounded like, but they refused to let him go to the show. He went anyway, paying with a quarter he'd saved out of his wages. That show, which was to have a profound influence on the boy's life, was probably a version of one of the many touring Chautauqua shows which travelled through Canada from the first part of the century until the middle '30s. Usually held in tents, the Chautauqua shows offered a wide variety of entertainment:

lectures, plays, musical groups of all descriptions, novelty and ethnic acts. Carter was enthralled by the performance of the Yodelling Fool that night and was determined to imitate him, even though he got spanked for attending the show when he got home. More spankings followed anytime Wilf practiced his yodelling while doing his farm chores.

At 16 he had left school and was working as a farmhand. Since his eldest brother had enlisted and was later killed in action during World War I, his family needed all the financial help they could muster to feed and care for the remaining children. Worn out from working long hours, young Wilf occasionally missed evening prayer meetings at his father's church and a quarrel with his father led to a final confrontation. The upshot was that Carter left home, determined never to return. But unlike his fellow expatriate Hank Snow, Carter has rarely demonstrated any bitterness about his early life. He always stayed in touch with his mother, a proper English lady who, though she was proud of his success, sometimes reproved him for what she felt was bad grammar in his songs.

After a few years doing odd jobs, Carter, by then in his early '20s, left Nova Scotia for good. He joined up with one of the harvest excursion trains that travelled regularly from Amherst to Calgary carrying farm laborers to work in the western grainfields. But when he got to Alberta, Carter was less interested in farming than he was in learning about horses. He became a ranch hand and learned to break and train horses and rope calves, eventually becoming good enough to enter rodeos as a competitor. One of his trainers was a former Calgary Stampede champion named Pete Knight, who taught Carter many show riding and roping tricks. Soon the two men paired up to tour on the rodeo circuit. Since earning a living was Carter's primary concern, music for a long time took second place as his hobby.

He did occasionally get a chance to play, mostly at the dances and informal get-togethers organized by neighbors and the other ranch hands. At country gatherings, the entertainment was usually rustled up quickly from local talent. A fiddler, a jawharp player and a guitarist made a reasonable band for square-dancing. Somewhere along the way Carter had acquired a guitar and he found time to practise both his singing and his yodelling. In the bunkhouses where the cowboys lived, Wilf was popular since he could sing and play for dances and singsongs. He sang what his friends requested—*Home on the Range* was a standard—but he also began to make up his own songs. During Stampede Week in Calgary, Carter would often perch on the back of a chuck wagon to sing for the street crowds, who would toss him money.

It was during this time that the basis of Carter's stage personality was created. Naturally friendly, unpretentious and easygoing, Carter simply acted like himself and saw no need to assume any show business mannerisms. Later his stage act would start to seem artificial, as he clung to the patter of bygone years, but in those early days, the sentiments he expressed were shared by most of his listeners. Home, mother, that old-time religion, romance—these were the topics that cowboy and western writers exploited to the fullest. Carter sustained the image of the simple, straight-talking cowpoke with many a "pardner" and "doggone it." There were also strong suggestions of the Victorian values that Carter, as the son of a minister, must have grown up with: the values of loyalty, comradeship, and an exaggerated and sentimental respect for women, who were almost invariably referred to as "sweethearts" or "gals."

The West that Carter wrote about was not necessarily the same Wild West that American cowboy singers wrote about. There was certainly less of the gunslinging, shoot-'em-up attitude. During his years as a ranch hand, Carter maintained that violence and gun battles in the manner of Butch Cassidy and the Sundance Kid were unfamiliar to him. He told journalist June Callwood in 1951, "I punched cattle for seven years and never saw a cowboy with a gun, except maybe a rifle in a saddle holster." Alberta cowboys worked on ranches and sometimes freelanced as rodeo riders, but the life Carter lived during the '20s would seem to have

been one in which cattle drives, bronc busting and hard work had all but replaced the romantic adventures portrayed in the dime Westerns and silent pictures.

Carter based dozens of his songs about the cowboy life on his own experiences. As a boy coming from the east coast, he was naturally impressed by the geographic difference of the prairies: the endless miles of plains, the grandeur of the Rocky Mountains, and the brilliant sunsets. Since he led an outdoor life in those great and often lonely open spaces, Carter wrote about them in songs like *Old Alberta Plains*, *Prairie Sunset* and *Tumbledown Shack by the Trail*. He expressed his feelings in the plain language of an ordinary man, struck by the beauty of the natural world around him. Sometimes the feelings he expressed bordered on cliché, but there was little doubt about his sincerity, as we see in his song *When the Sun says Goodnight to the Prairie*: "When it's sun setting time on the prairies/And its rays kiss the rangeland goodnight/When shadows start creeping around you/The night owl starts out on its flight." Carter noticed the small, telling details of life in the wild. He wrote of the far-off wails of the coyotes, about waking up before daybreak to saddle up, and most of all, about his horses.

Some of his most affecting songs were those he wrote about the horses he worked with and rode, as in *My Faithful Old Pinto Pal*, *He Rode the Strawberry Roan* and *Don't Let me Down Old Pal*. The sentiments expressed may sound corny to city sophisticates, but Carter was familiar enough with life on the ranch to know that not only cowboys but country people in general were dependent upon and deeply attached to their horses—the animals who helped them earn a living and provided companionship as well. In particular, the cowboy and his horse worked as a team. The bonds they developed were sometimes stronger than those formed between people, as Carter wrote in *Pinto Pal*: "Old Pal, I'm giving you freedom/You're dearer to me than a gal/Farewell old boy, I'll miss you/My Faithful Old Pinto Pal." In *Strawberry Roan*, Carter, in a lighter mood, described the speed of a horse that was able to turn on a nickel and give you change.

Other songs, based on real incidents on the ranch, had a comic flavor, as in *Little Red Patch on the Seat of My Pants*. As the song went, Carter had been bending over a well for a drink of water while sporting trousers with a red patch on the seat. He was charged by a bull who was enraged by the gleam of red and in an attempt to escape, Carter leaped into the well.

The songs Carter wrote about his life on the ranch have more vitality and originality than do his songs about romance. In this genre his choice of song titles and topics ranged widely from the maudlin (*I Loved You till You Done Me Wrong*) to the semi-sacred songs that displayed the ex-choirboy's taste for hymns (*There'll be no Blues Up Yonder*). It's interesting to note that while the majority of his songs refer to personal experience and are written in the first person, they don't always convey a strong or original emotional viewpoint. Some songs, especially the ones that deal with mother, home, and memories, bear the unmistakable stamp of the Victorian parlor ballad. Songs such as *Everybody's Been Some Mother's Darling* contain many phrases and images that are key to this style: "A little frail mother sat rocking/in an old broken down rocking chair/Her hair was all ringlets of silver/She was singing this familiar old air." Those lines, plus the exhortations in the chorus—remember your mother and make her your darling—are familiar, indeed standard lyrics and sentiments dear to the hearts of the Victorian middle class. But Carter's versions in basic stanza form, usually with no more than four chords in the song, appealed to the bunkhouse too.

Encouraged by the enthusiastic reaction of his friends and co-workers, Carter approached a Calgary radio station for an audition. After listening critically, the manager told Wilf he'd be better off tending cows. Later, however, Carter won a spot on a weekly hoedown broadcast on station CFCN that paid five dollars per show. He was to find that getting his

Wilf Carter, The Yodelling Cowboy, as he looked after moving to Alberta in the 1930s.

money was not always easy; 20 years later, Carter told writer June Callwood that he often had to chase the station manager all over the golf course in order to collect his pay.

While he was enjoying some local notoriety from the radio show, Carter got a job working for Canadian Pacific Railways. He was hired as a guide and entertainer for city dudes who wanted an authentic trip on horseback through the Rockies. In addition to acting as roustabout who helped with the luggage and hauled campfire wood, Carter sang and played his guitar for singsongs around the campfire each night. He was in many ways a born performer: a good-looking six-footer with a winning 'aw-shucks' manner and if his guitar playing wasn't outstanding, his voice was steady and pleasantly melodious. Yodelling remained his specialty. Riding along the mountain trails, keeping an eye on the city slickers, he practiced his yodels using the Rockies to provide natural echo effects. He became a virtuoso practitioner of this imported art in which the voice oscillates rapidly between falsetto notes and normally vocalized ones. His perfect execution of double and even triple yodels (melodic tremolos following the curve of a melody in two or three harmonized lines), can even today astonish an unsuspecting listener who comes across it on an old Wilf Carter recording.

The popularity of these trail rides was only one expression of the public's interest in anything to do with the Wild West. In Hollywood, film producers were busy churning out what were fondly known as horse operas featuring cowboy stars such as Tom Mix. After talking pictures arrived in the late '20s, westerns became even more popular when singing cowboys such as Gene Autry and later, Roy Rogers and Dale Evans, were featured. Novelists Zane Grey and later Louis L'Amour wrote popular fiction in which cowpokes, gunslingers and Indians battled over the limits of the frontier. It was pure escapism. Especially during the Depression, men who were tied down by families, dull jobs (or no jobs) and financial obligations daydreamed about the liberated life of the cowboy in the midst of all that glorious, open, scenic countryside. And if pulp Westerns or a trip to the movies didn't appease their appetites, they could try a vacation on a dude ranch, or take a trail ride through the Rockies with the likes of Wilf Carter.

Cowboy music, such as that which Wilf Carter played, was at that time distinct from country or hillbilly music. Musicians who played and sang hillbilly music tended to be located in the south and southeast States and the hillbilly, or bluegrass, style was usually characterized as the high, lonesome sound. They sang in high-pitched, rather nasal voices in close harmony and their instrumental style on banjo, mandolin and fiddle was notable for a high degree of fingerpicking virtuosity. Cowboy singers, on the other hand, tended to sing with a flatter, twangier tone and treated the guitar as mere accompaniment for the voice.

Yodelling, by this time, was a regular feature of many songs. One of the earliest singers to popularize yodelling was the "Singing Brakeman" Jimmie Rodgers. A native of Mississippi, Rodgers had grown up listening to black musicians singing the blues, and had incorporated the blues style into his own distinctive blue yodel. Rodgers had enjoyed tremendous success on the vaudeville circuit, and the continuing sales of his records after his premature death in 1933 led many record companies to search for other yodelling singers. In Canada, the RCA Victor company executives began to hunt for a Canadian singer to capitalize on the sales potential for record sales. They found Wilf Carter.

Carter auditioned for RCA Victor in 1932 in Montreal, singing two of his own original songs: *My Swiss Moonlight Lullaby* and *The Capture of Albert Johnson*. They are prime examples of Carter's writing style. The *Swiss Lullaby* was a simple pastoral vignette, in which the yodeller described moonlight in the Swiss Alps. "Strolling along in the moonlight/By a mountain stream/High up a mountain/Lies my golden dream./There lives my sweetheart/Waiting day by day/Watching from the doorway/Of her moonlight Swiss chalet." The lullaby had a simple chordal accompaniment, but there was a tricky descending chromatic yodel in the chorus which, in his recording, Carter tossed off almost without effort.

The second song was a lengthy ballad about Albert Johnson, the Mad Trapper of Rat River. After apparently going berserk in the isolation and relentless cold of Canada's far North, Johnson shot and killed one man and wounded several others. After a 45 day chase across the tundra in the winter of 1931-32, he was killed during a police shootout. Carter, like thousands of other Canadians, had followed the news story and was fascinated by its dramatic impact. He wrote the song as a narrative with numerous verses sung to the same melody, accompanied on the guitar by a basic, folk-song like strum. In the simplicity of its structure, the song is strongly reminiscent of traditional English folk ballads such as *Lord Randal*. Carter's ballad told the "news of the day" with a directness and excitement that made the story far more effective than newspaper or radio reports of the event. Though the Mad Trapper was a murderer and a fugitive from justice, many people had a grudging respect for his endurance, as Carter recognized when he wrote of the chase: "Twas then that the trouble started/And as the story goes forth/ It was the greatest manhunt/In the history of the North./For weeks and weeks they trailed him/Through the snow and the bitter cold/And the hardships that he endured/ We folks will never know." To this day *The Capture of Albert Johnson* stands as an interesting example of the way ordinary people perceived news events. The Mad Trapper was a vicious criminal, but the drama of his flight made him a Canadian folk legend.

The first RCA recording session was to be typical of Wilf Carter's lifelong preference for spontaneity—it was short. Recording techniques of the early '30s were rudimentary compared with today's technology. There was usually one microphone which the soloist might have to share with his sidemen. At that time, with no band but only his guitar to accompany him, Carter usually got a satisfactory take after only a few tries. He once went into the studio to cut two songs, but the session went so quickly and so smoothly he ended up cutting 40. Even after he began working with a backup band, Carter preferred not to rehearse at length or labor over arranging parts for the other players. He has never learned to read or write music, and often tells interviewers that printed music looks to him like a lot of hen tracks on a page.

After the RCA session, Carter was engaged to work as a shipboard entertainer on the S.S. *Empress of Britain* for a crossing to England. He enjoyed the Atlantic voyage but returned broke and out of work. Even with the prospect of future royalties from his RCA recording, it would take time before he had any cash in hand. Carter took to the road as a hobo, crisscrossing the country on foot and by boxcar. He spent nearly three years riding the rails, living in hobo jungles and occasionally busking.

The time spent bumming around provided Carter with a wealth of musical ideas, just as his time working on ranches had inspired him to write cowboy songs. It was a tough life, but he turned the things that happened into songs. Just as he had written *Pete Knight, King of the Cowboys* and *Pete Knight's Last Ride* for his friend and mentor of the rodeo, Carter now wrote about his adventures with the men he called "knights of the road."

Dr. Neil Rosenberg, a folklorist and musician who teaches at Memorial University of Newfoundland, says: "Wilf Carter wrote very engagingly about some of his own experiences as a hobo—*Hobo Song of the Mounties* is a classic—and he also drew on genre. He wrote *The Moose River Gold Mine* which is about the mining disaster which occurred in 1936, and which has become essentially a traditional song. Lots of people have collected it. It's in the mould of early disaster songs." Carter's interest in current events of the time was further demonstrated in songs such as *The Life and Death of John Dillinger*, which chronicled the career of the notorious American bank robber.

Arriving back in Calgary in 1934, Carter heard one of his songs, *My Swiss Moonlight Lullaby*, on a radio broadcast, and was able to get more work on the strength of it. The song was turning into a genuine hit—the first in Canada recorded by a Canadian. Toronto music publisher Gordon V. Thompson began to publish some Carter songs around this time. He had met Carter while on a trip west to look for cowboy singers and writers. Since Carter played only by ear, the cowboy singer had to work out the words and tunes with a copyist who then put them down on manuscript paper to turn into sheet music for the public..

Yet the success Carter was beginning to enjoy—a hit song, a published song-book—never seemed to inflate his ego. Perhaps it was the result of his early life as a clergyman's son, and the lessons of humility and hard work that were doubtless his daily fare, but the easygoing, optimistic personality displayed in Carter's song lyrics was probably the real Wilf Carter. He seemed content to accept good fortune, rather than aggressively chase after it. Carter did not pursue his musical career with the kind of single-minded energy that typified most aspiring performers. Despite the time and energy consumed by personally booking tours and appearances through talent agencies and bureaus, he has never, for example, employed a full-time manager.

Carter was used to a certain amount of recognition around town, especially in Calgary where he was often recognized as the author of *My Swiss Moonlight Lullaby*. The newfound fame gave him celebrity status and often resulted in requests to sing, and occasionally to write, songs on the spot. During one trail ride, a teacher who recognized his name asked him to write a song for her. She even gave him an appropriate title: *My Little Yoho Lady*, referring to the Yoho Valley of the Rocky Mountains where they were travelling. Carter was able to complete the song quickly; it was in waltz time using only three chords, and the verses and chorus had an optional yodel on the repeat of the chorus. In a version which he later recorded, Carter didn't always wait until the chorus to add the yodel. On the word "Yoho," his voice twisted upwards in pitch in a yodel on each syllable, and often the last word of each line had a brief, seemingly improvised yodel. Although he varied the elements of key and lyrics, Carter was writing songs according to a set pattern, which made it possible for him to write dozens of different songs, and write them quickly.

Another chance encounter on one of those trail rides was to send him in a new and important direction. One listener who saw the potential of the singing cowboy was an American millionaire named G.B. Mitchell. Mitchell told Carter that he had so much natural talent as a singer and songwriter that he should set his sights higher. Encouraged by the interest of his new friend, Carter decided to try his luck in New York where Mitchell had good contacts at radio stations. En route, he stopped in Montreal to cut a few more records for RCA.

His patron put him up in the Artists' Club in Manhattan, and Carter walked around town inquiring about talent auditions. He was turned down flat at NBC, but the CBS executives liked his style. Unused to the formalities of big city life, Carter showed up in his western clothes and sang several of his own songs, among them *My Swiss Moonlight Lullaby* and *There's a Love Knot in my Lariat*. He got the job, which gave him a quarter-hour show each morning.

Something about the casual Carter style charmed American radio audiences. He was a CBS star from 1935-37, broadcast over 250 affiliate stations across the country. Fan mail, the ultimate sign of audience approval, poured in. At times Carter received more fan mail—up to 10,000 letters in a week—than did Kate Smith, another prominent CBS singing star. It was around this time that he acquired his stage name of Montana Slim. Stories about the origin of the name vary; one version, circulated by Carter himself, has it that radio executives didn't like the name Wilf Carter and told him so. Carter allegedly retorted, "Mother did." Yet another anecdote in Carter's autobiography recounts that a New York secretary who was typing up some of his songs called him Montana Slim because of his height and because he had mentioned Montana in a song. The name stuck. As time

passed and Carter became better known in the States, several other singers began impersonating him. Bogus Montana Slims appeared on concert circuits in different parts of the country. An Alberta Slim even showed up at the Calgary Stampede in the '40s.

Cashing in on Carter's fame, the Southern Music Company collected three dozen Carter songs in a deluxe edition named *Songs of the Plains and Rockies* and stocked it in music stores, where it sold rapidly. The edition was shrewdly designed to take full advantage of Montana Slim's reputation as a real cowboy. Carter appeared on the cover in cowboy hat and neckerchief, lighting a cigarette. Two inset photos showed Carter playing the guitar while perched on a chuckwagon and another photo showed a cattle drive. In the introduction to the edition, Carter mentioned casually, "Oh, I've tangled up around two hundred songs or more and get a great kick out of doing it."

Aside from his announcer Bert Parks (later to acquire fame as host of the annual Miss America Pageant), the radio show was essentially a one-man operation. Carter often talked to his unseen audience as though they were neighbors sitting in a kitchen together, opening his show with, "Good morning, folks. Thought I'd drop in for a cup of coffee." The folksy manner was typical of radio in the days before television. Carter would chat casually, sing a few songs and sign off for the day. The radio exposure translated into an increasing number of requests for live appearances. Carter was soon earning enough money to marry a young nurse named Bobbie Bryan, and to buy a ranch outside Calgary for a family home.

Then, in 1940, the Carters were involved in a serious car accident while travelling in Shelby, Montana. After being struck by another car, their car rolled over twice. A trunk in the back seat shot forward and rammed into the front seat, and Carter was so seriously injured it was to be nearly 10 years before he was strong enough to make any more live appearances. The couple retired to their ranch outside Calgary to raise cattle while Carter convalesced. They were helped financially by continuing royalty payments from records and from the song folios that the Gordon V. Thompson company published. Often, sheet music for Carter's songs outsold that of better-known songwriters. Thompson once printed a folio of songs by Irving Berlin, at the time one of Broadway's best tunesmiths, and in the accompanying publicity release the company mentioned that they also sold Wilf Carter folios. The resulting orders were for 5,000 Carter folios, and a mere 750 for Irving Berlin.

It was during that recuperation period that Carter recorded the song that may be the one most closely identified with him. A young nurse named Elizabeth Clarke wrote a song about a bluebird that flew into the ward of the children's hospital where she worked. Touched by the children's response to the bird, she called her song *There's a Bluebird on Your Windowsill* and managed to get a version of it recorded. With any royalties earned, she hoped to buy medical equipment. Carter heard the song on the radio and was affected by the disc jockey's tale of the nurse's hopes for her song. He managed to locate Elizabeth Clarke in Vancouver and obtained her permission to record his own version of the song. Carter's rendition of *Bluebird* became a popular hit. Though it was a far cry from the cowboy and country songs he usually sang, its sweetly melodic style and optimistic message suited his musical personality.

When he went back on the road in the late '40s, Wilf Carter added his two young daughters, Sheila and Carol, to the show. The program was billed as "The Family Show with the Folks You Know" and dates were booked across the country. The basis of the show was still Wilf Carter/Montana Slim, but his daughters' contributions of singing and dancing changed the show from being a solo evening of cowboy music to being a variety show. Carter began to add more performers to the bill: a backup band, an old-time fiddler, and even a downhome comedian. The Carter Family Show (not to be confused with Mother Maybelle Carter and her family, who were country musicians from the southeastern U.S.) was one of the biggest draws in the country music field during the

Wilf Carter poses in front of a picture of trailriders in the Rocky Mountains of Alberta. He often led such riding vacations, serenading the vacationers at day's end.

1950s. They appeared in theatres, arenas, country fairs and exhibitions across Canada. Aside from Wilf and his two daughters, the playbill's other popular country performers included old-time fiddling champion Ward Allen, Joe Brown of the Hillbilly Jewels (and later the patriarch of the Family Brown), and fellow RCA recording artist Red Garrett and his Tennessee Pioneers ("direct from the home of hillbilly music—WSM Grand Ole Opry," as the newspapers and posters of the day put it). The Carter entourage put on an entertaining, family-oriented show full of cowboy songs, yodelling, a country joke or two, spirited dancing from the Carter girls, who wore matching cowgirl outfits, and some instrumentals from the band. The early '50s were the heyday of the travelling road show. No country fair or exhibition was complete without a country music act, whether it was a homegrown show such as King Ganam and his Sons of the West, or an imported group from Nashville.

Once it was known that he was back on the touring trail, Wilf Carter and his new show were kept busy by requests for appearances. At the Canadian National Exhibition in 1950, Wilf Carter had perhaps the biggest crowd of his life. The estimates varied, but somewhere between twenty and fifty thousand fans crammed themselves into the CNE Bandshell to hear the yodelling cowboy sing once more. He'd had a long absence from the stage; few careers survive a gap of more than a few years, and Carter had not appeared anywhere for nearly a decade. Rumors had circulated that he was paralyzed, or even dead. When the time came to make his entrance, Carter, ever the relaxed performer, ambled onstage. Just before launching into his first number, the reliable *There's a Love Knot in my Lariat*, he took out his wad of chewing gum and parked it on the microphone. Though he was allotted only a 12-minute set, the audience's cheers brought him back for several encores until, on his fourth trip back, Carter told the crowd, "I'm of Scotch descent and I just came back to get my gum." Later, while signing autographs after the show, Carter even lost part of his shirt to a too-eager souvenir hunter who tore it off his back.

Despite his years of absence, Wilf Carter enjoyed enduring popularity in the Maritimes as a native son. As broadcaster Max Ferguson discovered when he joined CBC Halifax and was made host of a daily program called "After Breakfast Breakdown," Carter and his rival Hank Snow each had a ferociously loyal coterie of fans. In his book *And Now…Here's Max*, Ferguson recounted the occasion when a fan from New Brunswick wrote a vitriolic letter accusing Ferguson of promoting Wilf Carter's records at the expense of those of Hank Snow. Nonplussed by the militant loyalty of both the Carter and Snow fans, Ferguson recalled, "Like a mother striving to avoid sibling rivalry, I meticulously played one record of each singer every single morning, except on one occasion while possibly wool-gathering, when I allowed a second Wilf Carter aria to slip in at the expense of Hank Snow."

A similar rule about equal air time applied across town at station CHNS, where Don Tremaine, later the announcer for "Don Messer's Jubilee," worked as a junior announcer in the late '40s. Tremaine recalls that on another daily country show, "Western Airs," the ironclad rule was that each day they had to be scrupulously careful about balancing their programming: one song by Wilf Carter, one by Hank Snow—and one by Eddy Arnold.

All of this protocol arose from a single fact of maritime life: country music of any kind was immensely popular. People on the east coast had long been accustomed to making their own music, whether it was the folk song tradition, or, with a boost from commercial radio, that of the closely related genre of country and even cowboy music. Native sons such as Carter, Hank Snow and Don Messer had a special claim on their loyalty, but in a pinch, Roy Acuff or Hank Williams would do just fine. The late poet Alden Nowlan once remarked that when he was growing up in the Maritimes in the '40s, country music was the only music in the same sense that cheddar was the only cheese. As soon as radios could reliably pick up broadcasts from the southern U.S., many Maritimers became faithful listeners to major country stations such as WWVA in West Virginia.

Country, bluegrass, cowboy and oldtime music programs could count on faithful listeners, and as a consequence, even more faithful advertisers. Recalling his days as host of "Western Airs," Don Tremaine says, "It used to be 11:45 to 1:00 every day on CHNS when I worked there. And it was the most oversold commercial program we had. Everybody wanted on because of the popularity of the music." Commercial sponsors wanting to connect with the large country music listening audience included sausage makers, farm equipment companies, patent medicines and candy manufacturers. One of the biggest sponsors of country musicians and groups was the ubiquitous Crazy Water Crystals Company, makers of a Texan mineral water concentrate whose laxative properties were advertised widely from Canada right down to the Mexico border.

Maritimers listened to Don Messer and His Islanders, the Bunkhouse Boys, the Girls of the Golden West, and Mother Maybelle Carter, all with the same avidity. They also bought records, the 12-inch 78 rpm shellac discs which abounded in the U.S. and Canada until Columbia Records introduced the Long Playing record in 1948. 400 million 78s of all kinds were sold in the U.S. in 1947. Don Tremaine remembers playing 78s during his tenure at CHNS and later at CBC Halifax, keeping a coin on the needle arm to hold it steady. On his CBC radio show, "Jamboree Junction," Tremaine received requests for songs by Vernon Dalhart, the Carter Family, and of course Jimmie Rodgers—and this was 15 years after Rodgers' death. Tremaine was a country music fan himself, and had a few Dalhart and Rodgers recordings which he filed in the CBC library for future reference. He decided on a whim to ask his radio audience to send in any old country records they might have lying around, which he would then be happy to play once a week on his show.

Tremaine was stunned by the response. Speaking of those days he says, "I was swamped. They came wrapped in shingles. People took shingles off the wall and rammed this old 78 between them with seaweed and whatever." It was a messy job, but after cleaning off scores of the grimy old records mailed to him, Tremaine was disappointed to find that most of them were too badly scratched to play on the air. Over the years, he says, most of the records gradually disappeared from the CBC archives.

Recordings of yodellers were as popular in the maritimes as elsewhere in rural North America. Wilf Carter was not the only Maritimer to achieve success with this technique, though he was the best. Gordon "Tex" Cochrane, an aspiring singer from Sweet's Corner near Windsor, Nova Scotia, admired the double and triple yodels on Carter's early recordings. Cochrane joined George Chappelle's Merry Islanders, a popular P.E.I. group which played at many dances and frequently broadcast over station CFCY in Charlottetown. He wrote much of his own material, including a song called *Echo Yodel Lullaby*, which was recorded by RCA Victor along with 15 other Cochrane songs in Montreal during the middle '30s. His original recordings are difficult to locate now. Cochrane might eventually have been as successful as Wilf Carter but for his decision to join the Armed Forces during World War II. He retired in 1963 after reaching the rank of major.

Despite the appeal of other country singers, most of them Americans, Hank Snow remained Carter's only serious rival as top country artist in Canada during those years. Both men retained bonds with their native province, returning occasionally to visit family members and old friends. Naturally each one had a guaranteed concert audience which was only too happy to support a hometown boy who had made good. Carter in particular was not averse to capitalizing on his local connections, and the fact that his father had been well known as a minister. Don Tremaine says that he can remember one concert in Prince Edward Island at which Carter strode onstage, looked around and proclaimed loudly, "My daddy preached here!" to a roar of approval from the crowd.

Although he worked hard at maintaining his Canadian connections, Carter moved his family to the United States, first to New Jersey and later to Florida where they owned and ran a motel called the Wilf Carter Motor Lodge. After years of travelling, the Carters wanted a more settled life for their daughters. They planned to spend the winters in a warm climate, and tour during the summer when the girls were out of school. RCA Victor now distributed Carter's records around the world, and with record and performance income added to that from the motel, Carter was in a good financial position. He was especially popular in Australia, where his records were circulating as early as the middle '30s. He was not only widely admired in that country, which even today has a reputation for liking Canadian country music stars, but much imitated. Australian singer Frank Ifield recorded an early version of Carter's *There's a Love Knot in my Lariat* some time before he scored with his own major hit on the pop music charts in 1962. His breakthrough song, *I Remember You*, featured some tasteful Swiss yodelling that Ifield probably picked up from listening to Wilf Carter records.

Carter continued to make cross-Canada tours, but it was to be years before he was invited back to his Western home to appear as a guest performer at the Calgary Stampede. One persistent story had it that he was contacted by Stampede promoters during the late 1940s, but negotiations fell apart. Carter, at that time living in New Jersey, quoted a fee of $500 to cover all expenses, taxes and a small profit. The Calgary contact allegedly refused on the grounds that it was too much to pay for a local boy. Carter did eventually return to Calgary in triumph in 1964, as a featured performer at the variety grandstand show which followed the chuck wagon races each night at the Stampede. In honor of the occasion he wrote a tribute song called *Calgary—The Heart of the Golden West*. Aged nearly 60, Carter must have found it a sweet homecoming. For six nights he packed them into the main grandstand and the bleachers on either side of it. *Calgary Herald* columnist Bob Shiels grumbled in his newspaper column: "…there is only one thing wrong with his act—it isn't nearly long enough."

But Carter was aging, and the country music business was changing. Authentic cowboys like him had all but vanished.

The term hillbilly had also more or less disappeared from use during the '50s, since many non-western country singers disliked being labelled with what they took as a pejorative term that implied a primitive, backwoods style. Though they wore Stetsons, the new generation of country singers were gradually taking the western out of country and western as well. They dressed in costumes that grew more and more elaborate, with sequins, spangles and fringes. They sang songs about drinking, cheating, loneliness and other problems of postwar life, and the titles of popular songs reflected the drift: *Slipping Around, Born to Lose*, and *Please Release Me*. Wilf Carter preferred to stick with his plain Western suit with its appliqued designs of longhorn steers or saddles. He also stayed with the music he knew best, and which he knew his audience liked: his repertoire of cheerful songs about home and family, God, Mother, and horses.

The change in mainstream country music was directed by Nashville producers and musicians. The Nashville sound of the late '50s and early '60s set up a new kind of standard: the lush, heavily sweetened backup, and a smoother vocal style. Many of the emerging country stars such as Patsy Cline and Jim Reeves could easily fit into the new country-pop format of easy listening music. Former mainstream singers such as Wilf Carter, with an almost exclusively cowboy or Western identification, found that they were now being shunted off to the sidings of country music.

Carter hardly changed his style since he picked up a guitar and let loose his first "yodel-la-di-hoo" back in the Annapolis Valley of his boyhood. He stayed true to his roots, while admiring some of the work done by new, younger musicians. In a candid interview for *Canadian Composer* magazine in 1971, Carter told writer Richard Flohil: "I have never changed my style—I won't. There are lots of people that will buy my records in the old style; to be honest, I can't change. But I listen to some of these young kids—Bob Dylan, Johnny Cash, and this boy here in Canada, Gordon Lightfoot—and I marvel at the things they do, but what they do is not for me."

He continued to record, but his public appearances were less frequent except for guest spots on shows such as the "Tommy Hunter Show" on CBC television. During Centennial celebrations in 1967, Carter agreed to be part of "The Great Rodeo Show" from Calgary," which was to appear at Expo 67 in Montreal. Twenty-five longhorn cattle were shipped from Texas to Montreal so Carter could show off his prowess as a cowboy. At 63, Montana Slim was still spry enough to perform some of his old rodeo stunts of trick roping and riding. Then, guitar in hand, he sang some of his best-loved songs.

Carter still made periodic visits to the Maritimes to visit his family, keep up with old friends, and occasionally appear as a guest on CBC's "Countrytime." Don Tremaine, one of the show's hosts, recalls a show in Prince Edward Island with Wilf Carter as the star. According to Tremaine, "That afternoon setting up, everything went all to hell. The power went off in the racetrack area where we held the thing. So we all sat around drinking beer and listening to Wilf reminisce, which was just an education really." Tremaine says that he asked Carter about the alleged rivalry between himself and Hank Snow. Carter, ever the Western gentleman, insisted that much of the rivalry had been manufactured by the press, and though they were not close friends, they had toured and done at least one television special together.

If Hank Snow was regarded as one of the pillars of the Opry and the Nashville establishment, Carter was acknowledged as one of the pioneers of cowboy music in North America and the industry showed its respect in the usual way—with lots of honors and awards. He was elected to the Cowboy's Hall of Fame in Oklahoma City, to the Horseman's hall of Fame in Calgary, and in 1972 to the Songwriter's Hall of Fame in Nashville. Along with fellow Maritimers Hank Snow, Don Messer, Marg Osburne and Charlie Chamberlain, Carter was one of the first inductees into the Canadian Country Music Hall of Fame. He was grand marshall of the 1979 Calgary Stampede Parade, fulfilling a dream dating back to his days as a cowboy singing for pennies in the Calgary streets. After many years of accompanying himself on a Martin guitar, he was finally honored by the Martin Guitar Company as Entertainer of the Year in 1981. Artist John Boyle painted a portrait of Wilf Carter which the Canada Council Art Bank now owns: surely a high-toned fate for even an image of the self-described cowpoke and ordinary guy.

In 1983 musical retrospective hit the record stores. A double album, *Fifty Golden Years*, contained a sampling of Wilf Carter's recordings over the past half-century. It was a cross-section of the Carter repertoire—songs about his cowboy days, some of his biggest hits such as *There's a Bluebird on Your Windowsill*, and several songs freshly recorded for the occasion.

Since several songs were re-releases of his earliest recordings, the technical production was minimal. In *The Capture of Albert Johnson*, for instance, it was just Wilf Carter and his guitar in front of a microphone. That 1932 track displayed Carter's voice in its prime; he didn't yodel on this narrative ballad, but his voice was steady, clear, and noticeably higher in pitch than in subsequent recordings. The most recent cuts, for example *Have a Nice Day*, were given a more beefed-up musical production using drums, tambourine, bass, steel guitar, even a chorus and hand-claps. Carter's voice occasionally wobbled in pitch, and he sometimes slid up or down to a note, but for a man of nearly 80, it was a vigorous and impressive performance.

And if the sweet quality and purity of the voice was not as reliable, Carter could still tell a story. In *Strawberry Roan*, he half-sang, half-spoke the tale of the strawberry roan horse, sometimes almost breaking into a chuckle as he retold the familiar story of the balky horse that he broke on a dare. He still had his talent for singing sentimental weepers, as in *Wasted Words, Wasted Times, Wasted Years*, which was as close as Carter may have ever come to writing a tearjerker. But tearjerkers and misery had never been Carter's forte. He was much more at home with positive, upbeat songs such as *When It's Apple Blossom Time in Annapolis Valley*.

Though he gradually reduced the amount of travelling and concert appearances he was willing to accept, Carter did not formally announce a retirement. Since the early '70s, Carter has divided his time between Arizona and Florida, though he has made brief concert tours in Alberta in the summers. Deeply saddened by the death of his wife Bobbie, Carter nonetheless recovered and resumed an active life— fishing, and keeping fit by long daily bike rides. In the spring of 1990, Rocklands Talent Management of Scarborough announced that Wilf Carter would make a brief tour of the Maritimes, Ontario and the West. The tour was deliberately kept low-key. Instead of the arenas and large auditoria where he used to play, Carter now prefers small towns and modest venues. Together with Rocklands president Brian Edwards and his backup band, Carter travelled to several Maritime centers, shunning publicity and relying mostly on word of mouth advertising to get people out to the show. Early on in the tour, Carter had an unfortunate encounter with an Australian journalist, in which the combination of the Aussie accent plus Carter's mild deafness made it hard for him to understand the questions. Consequently he was reluctant to grant any media interviews but such chancy and erratic publicity as he received was mostly favorable.

In Charlottetown in June of 1990, Carter broke his unwritten rule and appeared at Confederation Centre rather than at a small venue. Fiddling champ Graham Townsend opened the show and played for the first half of the concert. Wilf Carter did not come on until after the intermission, but he didn't simply walk out to center stage. Standing in the wings, he stuck his guitar out from behind the curtain, neck first, to the delight of the audience.

Wilf Carter had aged well: a tall man, still wearing the Western suit and Stetson of his working days, his only concession to age being a toupee. After the warm greeting, the band chugged into the first number, *There's a Love Knot in my Lariat*, after which he thanked his audience profusely, saying, "For sixty years I say thank you, I love you." References to his long career and to his age were a recurring theme of the evening. "Eighty-six and full of tricks" was his catchphrase. As always, the songs were interspersed with homey anecdotes about his childhood and his days on the ranch. Leading into *Little Red Patch* he told the timeworn anecdote about the patched trousers. But the audience didn't seem to mind hearing it again; they chuckled appreciatively at the vision of Wilf Carter forced into a well by an enraged bull. He also reminisced about his years in show business, about his father's preaching, and poked a little more fun at his celebrity status. Mentioning a recent concert at an old folks' home, Carter told of one testy resident who told him, "I don't like your singing. You're not going to get very far. Now that Wilf Carter—he can sing, but you, you'll never make it!"

The backup band, with longtime associate Gary Spicer on guitar plus a bassist and a drummer, played tastefully, unobtrusively and sympathetically. Many of the songs were well-known, and obviously favorites of the audience. Carter sang *My Old Canadian Home*, *You Are My Sunshine*, and *Goodnight Irene*—none of which he wrote himself, but which he delivered with his own brand of sweetness and personal charm. Surprisingly, there were few of his earliest cowboy songs, songs such as *Two Gun Cowboy* or *My Swiss Moonlight Lullaby*—omissions which undoubtedly disappointed some fans.

Not all the anecdotes were from cowpoke country. Like many stars, Carter was unable to resist reminding the audience that he had rubbed elbows with plenty of big names in the music business. He told the audience about a conversation with Jim Reeves in which the crooner told him, "The songs that you sing, Wilf, are so much like the songs I like." Carter, ever modest, hastened to add, "I never had a voice that could touch Jim Reeves." Nevertheless, it made an intriguing comparison to consider Montana Slim, with his cowboy twang, yodels and no-frills backup band, in contrast to Jim Reeves—one of the biggest exponents of the mellow country-pop style of Nashville in the early '60s. If Reeves saw any similarity in the songs they both liked, it must have been in lyric themes rather than in the musical vocabulary they chose.

Carter closed the evening with the devotional favorite *Amazing Grace*. Before leaving the stage for the final time, he thanked the audience lavishly, insisting, "I'm not a star— you are the ones who made me. Thanks a million, you've been wonderful." In deference to Carter's age and probable tiredness, the fans, some with tears in their eyes, did not demand an encore.

Many of the people who saw Wilf Carter on the 1990 tour must have realized that the old cowboy would not be playing many more tours and as a result, made a special effort to see his shows. At Fort Edmonton Park that August, Carter headlined the annual Country Music Picnic sponsored by the Country Music Foundation, and drew a crowd of 5,000. His final tour, billed as "The Last Roundup," was planned for the spring of 1991. Kentville was his only stop in the Maritimes, with most of the other performance dates slated for Ontario and the west. In a two-page article and photo spread that appeared in the July 1991 edition of *Country Music News*, Brian Edwards wrote that before each Carter tour, he could count on getting a phone call from his star to check on details. Carter always told him, "Remember, if you're going to lose money on a date, I would rather you cancel it and pay me nothing. I don't want you to lose a cent." On his final Canadian tour, Carter didn't need to worry about cancelling dates or losing money. All nine of the concerts were standing room only, and according to Edwards, there were plans for yet another Carter album on the BMG (formerly RCA) label.

Reviewer John Boyle, writing in *SiteSound* magazine, noted somewhat uncharitably that Wilf Carter received a standing ovation merely for walking onstage. Boyle remarked on "…Carter's now quavering 87-year-old baritone voice," but noted the audience's obvious affection for Carter's self-deprecating humor and unaffected delivery.

Many of Carter's recordings from BMG/RCA Victor are still in circulation, but his fans now have another choice open to them. Late in 1990, Bear Family Records in Germany issued a special tribute—a major re-issue of his recordings in a 30-song compact disc set called *Wilf Carter—Dynamite Trail*. The re-issue contains songs from his Decca recordings made in the middle '50s and produced in Nashville by Paul Cohen and Owen Bradley. Some of Nashville's best session musicians, such as the Anita Kerr Singers and guitarists Chet Atkins and Hank Garland are in the supporting cast.

Carter must be pleased to see the revival of interest in all aspects of western life, from cowboy poetry and history to western music. There's even a resurgence in the number of western singers who exercise their vocal equipment by yodelling. Country torch singer k.d. lang sometimes describes the music on her first records, such as *Angel with a Lariat* as "cowpunk." Alberta-based singer/songwriter George Fox is another working cowboy with a yen to play music. Fox writes songs out of his strong sense of the western countryside, and alternates between tending cattle on his ranch and trips to Nashville or Toronto for recordings and meetings. Western folksinger Ian Tyson, another active cowboy, who has been known to cut loose with a yodel in front of concert audiences, has released a series of albums called collectively *Cowboyography*.

As long as there is a generation of performers such as these who like the idea of open spaces and cherish the image of tired cowboys sitting around a dying fire, one of them softly strumming a guitar and singing, Carter and his simple, straightforward songs will not soon be forgotten.

CanaPress

CHAPTER 2

Hank Snow

Hard times and dreams of glory

Hank Snow celebrated his 78th birthday on May 9, 1992. He still makes his weekly appearance at the Grand Ole Opry in Nashville, and when he does, he is still the quintessential country star he has been for 42 years. With his flashy sequined suits from Nudie's of Hollywood, his hand-tooled leather boots, his chunky rings, and above all, his Tennessee drawl, he epitomizes the country music establishment. He still has the same passion for country music and its traditions that has driven him through a lifetime of struggle to seize fame and then hold on to it. So deep is his love for country music that he has no time for dissenters. He once told an interviewer that if somebody doesn't like country music, "they must be a damn communist or not be from this country."

These are odd words from a man who is himself not a native born American. But they show how strongly Snow identifies with his adopted country. Snow has been an American citizen since 1958, but, as all his Maritime fans know, he was born in Liverpool, Nova Scotia.

The distance from Liverpool to Nashville, Tennessee, is much longer than the 1500 air miles shown on a map, if your only chance to get there is by way of your guitar, a head full

of songs, and a burning ambition to become the Canadian Jimmie Rodgers. It took Hank Snow 17 years to do it. And when he finally got there, he almost blew it. His debut was so unimpressive he thought the managers of the Grand Ole Opry in Nashville's old Ryman Auditorium would never ask him back. But fate lent a hand. Within a few months, a song he recorded over the protests of RCA Artist and Repertoire man Steve Sholes unexpectedly jumped out to the front of the country music charts and stayed there for the next 44 weeks. It was a song he had written four years earlier and had spent two years trying to get Sholes to okay. Hank Snow made country music history with this little 12-bar number, cast in the form of a major blues, a favorite song form with Snow's hero Jimmie Rodgers. It was, of course, *I'm Movin' On*, perhaps his greatest song, and one of country music's greatest classics.

Today most country music fans regard Snow as one of the pillars of the Grand Ole Opry, along with Roy Acuff, Bill Monroe and Ernest Tubb. In a business that thrives on change, new faces and new ideas, he has remained an influential figure for 42 years. After crashing into the Nashville music establishment in 1950 as a virtual unknown, he produced a string of hits over the next decade that still earn him comfortable royalty payments on continuing sales. With his rich, flexible baritone voice and hard-driving, deep-picking guitar style, Hank Snow became one of the most easily recognized and respected entertainers of country music's heyday in the '50s.

But it must have seemed to him at times that he would never make it to Nashville. Ever since he acquired his first guitar, and played his first public recital in a Bridgewater church hall at 16, he had known exactly what he wanted from life: fame, money, big cars, influence and above all, recognition. But the world was a mean place in 1930. Ever a fighter, a feisty survivor from Nova Scotia's rocky, storm-wracked South Shore, Snow had to claw his way up from an abusive childhood, through poverty, depression, and nearly two decades of relentless hard work.

Clarence Eugene Snow was born into a poor family on May 9, 1914. His home town of Liverpool is located near the mouth of the Mersey River on the South Shore of the province, about 75 miles south of Halifax. Although it was not incorporated as a town until 1867, the year of Canadian Confederation, the settlement goes back to the mid-18th century. Populated at first mostly by immigrants from Massachusetts, it grew slowly into a center for fishing, shipping, ship-building, and fish processing. Snow did not live there for long. His parents separated and divorced while their children were still quite young. The family was divided up, two of Snow's sisters were sent to an orphanage, another to work in a factory. Clarence moved in with his paternal grandparents, but it was not a happy arrangement. Little more than six or seven years old, the boy was sensitive, frail, and so deeply attached to his mother that he frequently ran away to visit her. When he was eight, his mother remarried and took him to live with her and her new husband, a Lunenburg fisherman.

Unfortunately, the fisherman took a deep dislike to his new stepson. Snow suffered regular and brutal beatings from his stepfather which he was never able either to forget or to forgive. Years later, recalling the pain, Snow said he still carried the scars across his body from his stepfather's "ham-like hands." The marks left were not just physical. As an abused child, Snow grew up expecting the world to be tough on him. He learned to protect himself by developing a strong sense of determination and ambition. But he never blamed his mother. In those days, a wife was expected to stay with her husband even if he was abusive. But, after one particularly vicious beating, Snow left home for good. He was only 12.

In the retelling, the story would later expand to include more painful details, a blinding snowstorm, Snow and his young sister cast out to fend for themselves, but the essential elements of the story remain unaltered. For all intents and purposes, Clarence Snow was an orphan. He would never complete any schooling past the fifth grade. Looking for work, he went to sea as a cabin boy on a fishing schooner for several years. On shore he had already displayed some musical talent, and now, at sea, he would entertain the other crew members by singing, playing the harmonica, and even tapdancing. On one trip back home, his mother bought him a cheap Victrola record-player and some records by two of the most popular singers of the day, Vernon Dalhart and Jimmie Rodgers. Clarence listened in fascination to the songs about hillbillies and cowboys, to the stories of loneliness, and to the message of the blues. The sentimental songs about mother, sweetheart, and home deeply impressed the teenager who had already ridden a few rocky emotional roads. He bought himself a cheap guitar, a T. Eaton special costing $5.95, and played the records over and over, then learned them by imitating the songs as closely as possible.

Interestingly, Vernon Dalhart was no hillbilly at all. In fact, he was a trained opera singer (his real name was Marion Try Slaughter) who had already made his mark in light opera and popular parlor songs. In the year Hank Snow was born, Dalhart was singing tenor in a New York production of Gilbert and Sullivan's H.M.S. Pinafore.

But Dalhart also understood hillbilly music. He was the son of a prominent Texas rancher and had worked for a time as a cowboy. With his operatic training and flawless ear for dialect, Dalhart was used to shining up a rural accent for his many recordings of popular songs of the day. In the mid-'20s, when his record sales started to fall off, he looked around for something popular to record and found *The Wreck of the Old '97*, *The Prisoner's Song*, and *The Fatal Wedding*, the last a lengthy story-song dripping with pathos. They became runaway hits. Dalhart settled into a career of singing hillbilly music in his cultivated hillbilly accent, delivered so convincingly that many people believed him to be a genuine mountain musician. Between 1925 and 1931, his records sold in the thousands and earned him an international following.

Snow's other idol was Jimmie Rodgers, known as "The Singing Brakeman." Rodgers died in 1933, only 35 years old. But his fame as a composer and singer of country songs had already spread far beyond the southern U.S., and certainly as far as Canada's east coast. Rodgers assimilated the blues of impoverished rural blacks into his knowledge of folk music and cowboy lore. He capped this distinctive blend with his own version of a Swiss yodel, producing his famous blue yodels, songs in blues form on the eternal themes of lost loves, gambling sorrows, and hard times. His specialty was the train song, a restless version of the blues about leaving town, breaking away from the past, and seizing the freedom of the open road or track. It was also about the hurt of leaving loved ones behind.

Rodgers had a great gift for evoking the basic emotions and experiences of rural people. Even today his recorded performances, though sounding tinny compared to modern recording technology, touch a responsive chord. His fans were caught by lyrics that tapped into the deep vein of feelings many of them felt but could not adequately express in words. He sang nostalgically about lost love, old pals, daddy and home, mother, that old-time religion, gambling, hard luck, and the blues. The troubles of his own private life were often reflected in his music: financial woes, a messy divorce, a liking for whisky, and his battle with tuberculosis, the disease that finally killed him. Typical Rodgers songs,

such as *Moonlight and Skies*, *TB Blues*, *Daddy and Home* and *Muleskinner Blues* inspired Clarence Snow to resolve to become a country entertainer himself.

At first glance, there seems to be little common ground between Clarence Snow, growing up on the east coast of Canada, and American country musicians who performed a song literature filled with references to cowboys, tumbleweed, moonshine, and little shacks in the Kentucky hills. But there has always been a bond between the Atlantic provinces and the American southeast. The early settlers of both regions had a common heritage—the English/Scottish/Irish literature of instrumental tunes and folksongs. Though regional and local variants on these traditional tunes are numerous, folklorists and musicologists have recognized their common source in the waves of English, Irish, and Scots who settled along the Atlantic coast from Newfoundland to New England, from the 16th century onward. Others moved Westward into the mountain country of the southeast United States. Though instruments, vocal styles and lyrics differed slightly, fiddle tunes like *Soldier's Joy* were as well known among Tennessee hillbillies as they were among Irish immigrants settled in Prince Edward Island.

The emotional resonances of Rodgers' music rang true to fans all over the poor and rural southwest U.S. To the teenaged Clarence Snow in rural South Shore Nova Scotia,—poor, neglected, and used to more than his share of hard times—it must have seemed like a message aimed directly at him. He was not yet writing his own songs, but the ones he memorized and sang while listening to his Victrola summed up the lessons of his life so far. Music for him was to serve a double purpose. It was an outlet for expressing the pain, joys and frustrations of daily life. But the talented, ambitious and determined youngster also saw it as a way out of poverty and hard times. He was to spend the next 20 years in pursuit of this goal.

Snow promoted himself tirelessly at any talent show or theatre that was interested in a boy who sang, yodelled, and could play the guitar. To keep himself, he worked at a variety of odd jobs—as a worker at a fish plant or a lumber camp, as a stevedore, even selling lobsters from door to door, sometimes throwing in a song, dance or yodel for paying customers. He wrote a letter to radio station CHNS in Halifax requesting an audition, and at the age of 19 hitchhiked up the coast in March of 1933 to try out for his first professional job as an entertainer. The audition for manager Cecil Landry was as short as it was successful. Snow went on CHNS that same evening at seven, with a show billing him simply as "Clarence Snow and his Guitar." He sang and played old favorite songs, as well as songs by Rodgers, Dalhart, and fellow Nova Scotian Wilf Carter, and he did it without pay at first.

The regularity of the radio exposure helped Snow to smooth out his rough edges as a performer. Landry gave him the chance to listen to recordings of himself singing and playing, and to work on his enunciation and stage presentation. But the show, while invaluable as professional discipline, did not pay him enough to live on. He was forced to work for a time selling Fuller Brush products from door to door, and when things were at their worst, he had to sign up for government relief payments. To qualify for relief, Snow was assigned to a work crew to clean the city streets— ironically, right in front of the CHNS station. As he later told his friend Ray Simmons (Don Messer's clarinet player and announcer), he pulled his collar up around his ears and hoped that nobody would recognize him. For anybody it would have been humiliating, but for the proud Snow, it was intolerable. In a 1991 interview with reporter Cathy MacDonald of the Halifax *Daily News*, he told her, "When I got back home I said to my wife 'get me a looking glass' and she said 'why?' I said 'we're going to sit here and watch ourselves starve to death because I'll never do that again.' "

In 1935, two years after his first appearance on CHNS, Snow had married Minnie Blanche Aalders, a pretty girl of Dutch-Irish descent who was working at the Moirs chocolate factory in Halifax. They spent most of their meagre savings on their wedding, and moved into two small rooms in the run-down, poverty-ridden north end of the city. Snow curtained off a part of the room to make a teaching studio. After a year, Snow's only son was born in the charity ward of the Salvation Army Hospital. The name they gave him demonstrated that Snow's dream of becoming a country music star was undiminished by hard times. They called their son Jimmie Rodgers Snow.

Clarence continued to give guitar lessons at the same time he was studying guitar himself, learning to read music and working out his own distinctive guitar style. Many years later in an interview with *Guitar Player* magazine, Snow described his playing: "I developed a unique style of playing which blended the flatpicking of mountain music, the string pushing of bluegrass, and the chord harmonies of straight country music." Snow's mature guitar playing was impressive. He was no mere strummer, but could pick his way confidently through a solo chorus, even swinging the style a bit. Modern guitar players and singer-songwriters such as Vancouver's Roy Forbes pay him tribute. Halifax jazz musician Skip Beckwith, who was Anne Murray's music director during her early years in the 1970s, says that he taught himself to play guitar by copying Snow's licks from records. So did Stompin' Tom Connors.

As Snow continued to support his family with odd jobs such as selling Fuller brushes or jewellery door-to-door, he never gave up on his main ambition of becoming a country music star. His radio program on CHNS proved so popular that he finally landed a sponsor, the Crazy Waters Crystals Company of Texas, sponsors of entertainment programs all over North America, with a special interest in country music shows. They asked Snow to form a band. It was around this time that he started calling himself Hank, and, still under the spell of Jimmie Rodgers, added "Yodelling Ranger" to his stage name. Later on, when his voice deepened, he gave up yodelling, at which he was never better than ordinary anyway, and changed his public name to "Hank the Singing Ranger." Meanwhile, Cecil Landry was urging him to request an audition from RCA Victor. One day in 1936 a letter arrived from Hugh Joseph, manager of the RCA repertoire department, inviting Snow to Montreal to make a test record. When he arrived, Joseph told him that RCA already had enough re-releases of standard tunes, and that new material would be of more interest to them. Snow went back to his Montreal hotel room and set to work writing his first two original songs, *The Prisoned Cowboy* and *Lonesome Blue Yodel*. The recording took place in an old church and though Snow had high hopes, his first royalty check came as a rude shock—a mere $1.96. Also in 1936, Snow began to attract national attention. The infant Canadian Broadcasting Corporation, founded in that year, signed him on to a regular spot on "The Canadian Farm Hour," opening up a national, coast-to-coast audience for him.

Snow's recordings and subsequent exposure on numerous radio stations made it easier for him to line up personal appearances and concerts. These became increasingly important. Snow rehearsed his band and took to the road, appearing at dances, taverns, and schoolhouse entertainments. Minnie became the band's advance worker. She would get to a town early, put up posters, book a hall or theatre, and sell tickets. Snow was learning one of the first lessons of artistic management—to keep his overhead costs down. Even with cheap admission prices, ranging from 15 cents to a quarter, they cleared money each night. Snow even drew his small son into the act. By the time he was two, Jimmie Rodgers Snow was lisping songs such as *Jesus Loves Me*. The audiences were indulgent.

Continuing his relationship with RCA, Snow returned to the studio a year after the initial recording to tape eight more songs. Such sessions were to continue more or less regularly through the war years until 1947. With his first genuine hit, *Blue Velvet Band* in 1938, sales began to pick up across the country and by the time Snow moved permanently to the States and stopped recording at the Montreal studio, his record catalogue contained nearly 100 titles.

With the outbreak of war in 1939, Snow tried to enlist in the army but was rejected after a routine physical. Though tough and wiry, he had suffered from pleurisy while living in Halifax. Local rumor later exaggerated the illness into full-blown tuberculosis. Snow spent most of the war years working in New Brunswick at radio stations in Moncton and Campbellton. For a while he was the on-air pitchman for Wilson's Flypaper Company. At station CKCW in Moncton, his band included some well-known maritime musicians, such as banjo player Maurice Bolyer, who enjoyed a local reputation as "King of the Banjo." Later Bolyer moved to Toronto and was, until his death in 1979, a cast member on CBC's country-music flagship program, the "Tommy Hunter Show." Although it seems incongruous, given the differences in style between country music fiddling and traditional Scots fiddling, Cape Breton fiddler Winston "Scotty" Fitzgerald also played in Snow's country band for a year. By 1942, Snow was well enough known that he and the band could pack a theatre for four shows a day. He'd landed tours with two theatre circuits, the B and L chain, and the Independent Exhibitors chain.

Clarinetist Ray Simmons, then a member of Don Messer's band, met Snow around this time. Secure in his position as a member of the most popular musical group in the region, Simmons took a liking to Snow. When the two men talked, Snow often mentioned his hard times in Halifax, and his plans to make it big in the States. They appeared in a few shows together at the old Capitol Theatre in Charlottetown, and Simmons said, "I always liked Hank. We always got along okay." But not everyone got along that well with Snow. Touchy and sensitive at the best of times, he was known to be belligerent when he drank. Simmons earned his gratitude for protecting both Snow and, more importantly, at least as far as Snow was concerned, his large Cadillac, of which he was inordinately proud, during a tipsy altercation at a local tavern.

During these years, from the mid '30s to the end of the Second World War, Snow began to see himself as a western or cowboy singer. Cowboys were popular figures all over rural North America. There was an undeniable glamor to the cowboy's life—he was his own boss, he travelled light where

there were no roads, he lived outdoors, and he ignored the clock if he felt like it. Cowboy movies showed stars like Tom Mix, Roy Rogers, and Gene Autry who did little more than ride across the lonesome prairie as the cameras rolled, playing their guitars and singing. Snow wasn't the only Maritimer who was fascinated by western fantasy. Wilf Carter specialized in it and even became a real cowboy. Bob Nolan, one of the Sons of the Pioneers, was born in New Brunswick, but moved to Arizona at the age of 14. He wrote many memorable cowboy songs for the Sons, including the classics *Tumbling Tumbleweed* and *Cool Water*.

Snow was now doing better financially, but his success with Canadian audiences on his cross-Canada tours only whetted his appetite. As he told Ray Simmons, it began to look as though he would have to head south to Nashville in order to contact the most influential radio stations, and the best agents and managers. And though his main focus was to be a country music star, he began to nurse another ambition—a career in the movies like those of Autry and Rogers. Hank Snow was confident that he too could make a string of popular films. All he needed to do was to make the right connections. It was time to start moving on.

By now Snow had become an established performer who not only sang the kind of songs country audiences liked, but knew how to get the most out of a public appearance at a country fair or exhibition. He had a band now, The Rainbow Ranch Boys, and, in keeping with his cowboy image, had also acquired a trained horse called Shawnee. For a major Canadian tour in 1946 a tentmaker in Toronto made him a showplace tent large enough to seat 500 people. A large truck carried not only the electricity generator but the grandstand for the audience. With his swinging band, his trained horse, and his cowboy bag of tricks, Hank set out to entertain the folks.

In one crowd-pleasing routine Snow rode in fast on

A typical publicity shot of Hank Snow from the '60s showing him in full cowboy rig, along with his horse.

Shawnee while the band played an up-tempo tune. He doffed his hat, sang a few songs and displayed some trick-riding, such as the "death-drag," in which the horse raced up and down while Snow lay across the animal's neck. Then came comedy routines, the favorite being a pretend meal with Snow sitting on one side and Shawnee on the other, the horse even lifting his front hooves up as though asking Snow to pass the potatoes. Then Snow and Shawnee would go to sleep together while the lights dimmed and the band played slowly. Snow would tug the blanket over to his side, and the horse would reach around with his neck and pull the cover back, exposing Snow. It was corny. But audiences couldn't get enough of it.

Snow's chance to expand into the U.S. came in 1944 when Philadelphia music publisher and promoter Jack Howard invited him to play a number of bookings in the Philadelphia area. Howard owned a record label with a roster of talented songwriters and artists that included Ray Whitley and Hawkshaw Hawkins. He had already sent Snow a few songs. Snow eagerly accepted Howard's offer to spend two weeks barnstorming in the Philadelphia area. He then appeared with a group called the Cackle Sisters on legendary country radio station WWVA in Wheeling, West Virginia, and was featured in a spot on a country show called "Hayloft Hoedown" on the ABC radio network. The warmth of his reception convinced him his future lay in the southern U.S. He returned home, gathered his family and his belongings together, and moved to Wheeling in January of 1945. It was a good move. Snow was soon doing two shows daily on radio station WWVA.

He kept up his connections at home with his summer tours. They made money and built up his confidence. Snow now felt ready to make a stab at another of his long-standing goals. He decided to try his luck in Hollywood. It was a bad move, however—he was too late. The popularity of singing cowboy movies was declining in Hollywood, except for established stars such as Roy Rogers and Dale Evans. Hank Snow and his music were hardly known to west coast Americans. Although he had signed with a booking agency, no movie offers materialized, and he managed to secure only a few scattered concert dates to finance his attempt to break into films. His first two tries, in 1946 and 1947, were unsuccessful. The third, in 1948, was a disaster. Snow lost his savings of $13,000, ran up debts, and eventually had to pawn even Shawnee's silver tooled saddle.

Part of the problem was recognition. Hank Snow was known in Canada, where he could sell records and fill houses wherever he toured, but he was a virtual nobody in the United States. Now in his middle '30s he was not only no longer young but also short, skinny and beginning to lose his hair—a far cry from Hollywood's idea of a matinee idol. He fell back on his strengths, therefore, and they were considerable. After years of playing in roadhouses, taverns and country fairs, Snow knew his audience, knew the kind of songs they wanted to hear, knew how to balance between the slow, sentimental songs and the fast, energetic country tunes with more than a hint of the country swing style. As a vocalist, Snow, with his hearty, nasal voice, could deliver both styles convincingly. He had developed a distinctive guitar sound that combined elements of bluegrass, mountain music and orthodox country harmonies. All he needed, he felt, was a lucky break at one of the bigtime radio stations.

What made recognition difficult for Snow was that his records were not widely distributed in the U.S. Without radio play on the dozens of American country music stations, he was doomed to remain a nonentity, or at the least, be forced to retrace the painful steps of his early years in Halifax. But at least one American fan knew Hank Snow's work. In Dallas, a woman named Bea Terry pestered disc jockey Fred Edwards to play his recording of *Brand on my Heart*. The public began to notice the strong resemblance of Snow's style to that of local hero Jimmie Rodgers. RCA had released some of his Canadian recordings in America in 1948. Sales were good enough to get Snow his first American recording session in Chicago in 1949. He was not completely satisfied with the results, however, because he had to work with session musicians rather than his own band, and ended up recording four songs written by other writers, rather than his own material. But his career started to pick up. He was offered a full time job with radio station KWKH in Shreveport when their main attraction, Hank Williams, left to join the Opry in Nashville, but since the pay wasn't enough, Snow left for another extensive Canadian tour.

His next break turned out to be the one for which he had been preparing for most of his adult life. On tour in Texas, playing in Fort Worth, Snow shared the playbill with popular Grand Ole Opry star Ernest Tubb. Both men were Jimmie Rodgers fans. Tubb liked Snow's style so much he promised to use his influence to get him a booking at the Opry in Nashville. Nashville was not the only city with a reputation for good country singers and pickers—Atlanta and Dallas also attracted large clusters of country musicians. But to the thousands of people who tuned their radios to the half hour segment broadcast each Saturday night from the four-hour live Opry stage show, Nashville was the real capital of Country. It wasn't just the Athens of the South it proudly boasted to be. It was Music City.

Throughout the late '40s Nashville had gradually concentrated more and more musicians, agents, A & R men and recording studios within its limits, all of them dedicated to the commercial exploitation of country music. The Grand Ole Opry, in the old Ryman Theatre in downtown Nashville, fielded a cast of 120 in 1950, including singers, instrumentalists, and comedians. Friends and family of the performers frequently crowded in to the back stage area. The format was informal and homey as it still is today, even though the Opry moved out of the Ryman and into swank new state-of-the-art headquarters in the early '70s. The entertainment was folksy and fun.

Tubb was as good as his word. In early January of 1950, Hank, Minnie and Jimmie Snow drove into the city that was to become their very own city of dreams. Nashville was poised on the threshold of its postwar boom. Signs of de-velopment raised up on every hand. Aside from its growing position as the heartland of the country music business, it was also becoming a significant manufacturing center, with its factories making everything from glass to chemicals. The Athens of the South was becoming crowded and noisy with competition. Minnie Snow is supposed to have commented to her husband that it was also the dirtiest city she had ever seen.

They were making a gamble. Hank Snow was older than the average hopeful country musician. He had a wife and son to support and despite the solid offer from the Opry, he was competing with dozens, perhaps hundreds of aspiring stars. At his first Opry show on January 7 of 1950, his reception was only polite, not overwhelming. He persisted, using the opportunities to meet other Opry performers such as Red Foley and Hank Williams. The two Hanks even went on a few tours together. Williams, who had a longstanding fascination for the bottle, would need reliable backup from his friends when he got too drunk to perform. But at Snow's Opry appearances the fans continued to sit on their hands. "I don't mind telling you that I bombed," Snow was to recall in later years. "The people just sat there while I sang. And sat. No applause, no nothing almost. Just sat. The first three months for me on the Grand Ole Opry, trying to compete with well-known and established artists, was heartbreaking. Harry Stone was going to let me go."

At a Nashville studio session in March of that year, Snow was determined to record more of his original songs. Backed by a new, hand-picked band, he insisted on recording a song he'd written several years earlier. It was *I'm Movin' On*, a pure country tune, complete with a fiddle player imitating a train whistle during the opening bars. It reflected Snow's longstanding interest in trains and train songs dating from his earliest exposure to Jimmie Rodgers. *I'm Movin' On* had a strong bluesy feel with lyrics that combined the yearning for the open road with a rebuke for the unfaithful lover who had done her daddy wrong.

I've told you, Baby, from time to time
But you just wouldn't listen or pay me no mind;
Now I'm movin' on, I'm rollin' on.
You've broken your vow and it's all over now,
So I'm movin' on.

The band was small: fiddle, bass, steel guitar and Snow himself on lead guitar and vocals. In the breaks between the verses, the fiddle and then the guitar take solos, but the real focus of the band's sound is Snow's voice and guitar. The drive of the vocals catches the urgency of a restless, footloose personality about to hop the next freight train out of town. An old hand at the game by this time, Snow knew exactly how to deliver the lyrics for maximum effect. Snow was happy about the song, but after the session producer Steve Sholes expressed little confidence that any of the cuts would be usable. As a result, when *I'm Movin' On* was released in May, neither soloist nor producer was prepared for its runaway success. By the end of June, it had rocketed to the top of the hit parade charts, staying there for nearly a year. *I'm Movin' On* made Snow's reputation, secured his spot at the Opry and with RCA, and established the name of Hank Snow at the forefront of the country music industry.

Popular wisdom in the music industry has it that anyone can have a breakout hit, but the real challenge is following it up with a second successful album or single. Unable to relax with his success, Snow continued to work on new songs. He wasted precious little time. As early as August, another studio session produced two more hits for him, a second train song called *Golden Rocket*, and the swinging *Rhumba Boogie*. Both songs reached the number one position on the country charts and any fears that Hank Snow was a one-hit wonder evaporated. By January of 1951, Hank Snow was named both America's favorite folksinger, by *Folk Music and Its Folks*, and America's number one singer by *Country Song Roundup*—a neat if unintentional acknowledgement of Snow's debts to both folk tradition and country style.

Even today, *I'm Movin' On* is still the song that defines Hank Snow's image and musical style. Dozens of other artists have recorded it—there may be as many as 60 different versions, including a 1984 re-release by singer Emmylou Harris. Whether it was Snow's own talent as a performer, or the strength of the song itself, *I'm Movin' On* captured the mood of postwar America. Hank Snow wrote it out of his own experience, but it was also the experience of thousands made restless by the Depression and a world war. Now they were finally feeling optimistic about life: if your spouse cheated on you, your boss fired you, the factory shut down, or the bank foreclosed on the mortgage, why stay put? Why not try another life in another city, make a break with the past, move on?

Thousands had. The migration of country people to the city to look for work had already begun during the '30s. The flow increased to a flood during the post-war manufacturing boom and its demand for workers. In Canada, rural people moved to Montreal, Toronto, Calgary or Vancouver, in hopes of a good job and a decent education for their kids. In the States, for the same reasons, whole populations shifted off the farms and out of isolated rural areas in the mountains, and resolved to try their luck in Nashville, Boston and Chicago. But they paid a price. Cut off from the network of family, friends and social life that had provided them with a strong support system, many rural folks became heartsore and homesick after a few months of city reality. Dr. Neil Rosenberg, a folklorist at Memorial University of Newfoundland, has studied both the music and the sociology of the south and speculates about the new urbanites: "These people left marginal existences in not very desirable places way back up in the hills where you couldn't farm very much, or you had to work in the coal mines. All kinds of very negative situations, and then they ended up in housing developments in urban areas, working in factories.... At least back home, they could run some good moonshine and hunt."

Sequined suits from Nudie's of Hollywood, chunky rings, toupee and the cigarette were all part of Hank Snow's personal style.

Country music was like medicine for such people. All the things Hank Snow and other country singers sang about—lost loves, loneliness, a sorely missed mother, the little old country church, death—were emotions homesick urban audiences could identify with. But the big unfriendly city was not without its consolations. They could no longer go to hoedowns and barndances where a pickup group played bluegrass and sang high and clean, but a big city like Nashville, for example, offered more variety—clubs, dancehalls, bars, and roadside honky-tonks where the principal activities were dancing, drinking and fighting. And most of those places had live bands that played country music—bouncy dance tunes, or the weepy ballads that were guaranteed to have you crying in your beer after two verses. As defined by performers like Snow, Acuff and Tubbs, country music was setting itself apart from its subcategories of bluegrass and gospel, and was entering the mainstream of American pop culture.

Snow tapped directly into the new, larger, more urban audience for country music. He gradually stopped singing about the staple topics of mountain music—death, orphans and disaster. He modified his style and his image from cowboy singer to all-round balladeer. Unlike many country musicians who make records using a large studio ensemble and tour with a much smaller group, Snow always preferred that when audiences saw him live onstage, the sound was the same one they heard on his records. Even on tour his instrumental back-up remained that of the Saturday night country band—Snow on lead guitar, his sidemen on acoustic bass, fiddle, steel guitar, and drums played with brushes rather than sticks. After years spent playing in bars and other venues where the patrons expected the entertainers to put on a tight, well-rehearsed show with no fumbling, no glitches, and plenty of hummable tunes, Snow knew how to work his audiences.

Possibly he had spent so long dreaming about someday being famous and wealthy, that when it happened he already knew how to handle it. Snow told journalist Cathy MacDonald in 1991, "I wasn't surprised…I had put in many years and, as a matter of fact, I thought I deserved it." He was far from being a smalltown boy who could be preyed upon by the sharks of the industry, and he soon demonstrated that he was nobody's fool about money. In an interview with writer Blake Emmons in 1968, Snow recalled that he had read a book called *Think and Grow Rich* five or six times, and had taken its advice seriously. He informed Emmons that he had established solid relationships with an accountant, a lawyer, and a bank, and had worked closely with them. "This is the secret to the success of many people," he explained. "You leave the business to the businessmen." The musical skills he had worked so hard to perfect, combined with an instinctive shrewdness about the songs people wanted to hear, made him a songwriter and performer who, at least within the country genre, could not go wrong. And he was hot. He wrote 23 Top Ten singles in the five years between 1950 and 1955, and they had staying power. Songs like *I Don't Hurt Anymore*, *I Went to your Wedding* and *Honeymoon on a Rocketship* all roosted on the hit parade charts for 20 or 30 weeks at a stretch. In 1954, only four years after *I'm Moving On*, *Billboard* magazine named him one of the all-time greats.

On visits back home to Nova Scotia, Snow didn't hesitate to let old friends know how well he was doing. Wearing his western suit and cowboy boots, he drove around Halifax in his Cadillac, dropped by station CHNS to see old friends like Dick Fry, and played to packed houses at the old arena on Shirley Street. Sometimes his entourage included other acts from the Opry. A 1953 showbill included not only Snow and his Rainbow Ranch Boys, but also Radio Dot and Smoky, Sleepy McDaniels, and Snow's teen-age son Jimmie Rodgers Snow, who was considering a career in show business himself. The local papers published "local boy makes good" stories, mentioning his part ownership in several American radio stations, and that his yearly income was estimated to be somewhere around $250,000.

Snow was cordial and gracious to his fans and old friends, but there were those who felt that the many years of pushing and relentless struggle to make good had left their mark on the man. One young radio employee who met him on one of his homecomings recalls: "I always thought, he's got sparkling blue eyes, and they were as cold as bloody rocks. Didn't appear to be a lot of warmth in the guy, that was my impression." Ever the genial, folksy and polished performer onstage, the offstage Hank Snow was a hardheaded businessman. In Nashville, he capitalized on his fame, establishing a Hank Snow Music Center, and a Hank Snow School of Music where teachers taught aspiring students to play guitar the Hank Snow way. Publicity photos and songbooks of the time often showed a smiling Hank Snow, mounted on his faithful horse Shawnee and strumming a guitar.

His career was to suffer minor setbacks along the way. A car accident in 1951 left him with a fractured skull. He had gone for a wild ride through Nashville, upset over bad news from a veterinarian who had told him that his German shepherd Pal would have to be put down. Snow was deeply attached to all his animals, from Shawnee on. Distracted by grief, he took off in his Cadillac at high speed, lost control of the automobile, hit a telephone pole, and overturned twice. During his hospital stay fans sent him thousands of get-well cards, and within weeks Snow was not only back in the studio, but heading out on tour again. He received another blow when his mother died in the early '50s. Snow wrote one of his most heartfelt songs, *My Mother*, for her.

Though he trusted Steve Sholes, and later Chet Atkins, with many of the details of musical production, Snow preferred to keep his own hand firmly on the tiller of his business career. He built up a reputation as a shrewd money manager, preferring to book large tours in which he appeared as the headliner and could command top fees, to performing in smaller venues like clubs. But he made a mistake when he appointed as his personal manager Colonel Tom Parker, a former carnival employee. Parker formed an agency called Hank Snow-Jamboree Attractions. Within a year the agency was representing the Carter Family, Slim Whitman and Ferlin Husky as well as Snow himself.

The agency also represented Jimmie Rodgers Snow. But, unlike the agency's other clients, Jimmie was less interested in country than he was in rock and roll, then in its infancy but already showing signs of revolutionary vitality. The energetic, often raunchy sounds of rockabilly and rhythm and blues were already beginning to have an impact on teenage audiences. And then came Elvis Presley.

Both Snow and Parker were aware of the young rockabilly singer who created a sensation wherever he sang. Elvis sang country, gospel and the kind of ballads that Snow favored, but his personal idiosyncrasies—the curled lip and the pelvic gyrations that brought girls screaming to their feet—were not Snow's style. Yet it was impossible to ignore Presley's potential. Despite the fact that he already had a manager, Bob Neal, Parker recruited Hank Snow to talk with Presley's parents, Vernon and Gladys, in order to get Elvis to break with Neal and sign on with Hank Snow-Jamboree Attractions.

Parker could hardly have chosen a more convincing person. Exactly what Snow and Presley's parents talked about will never be known since Snow has always maintained a steadfast silence about it. But there seems little doubt that Hank Snow's public image—clean living, Godfearing and strait-laced—would appeal to the Presleys and reassure them that their boy would not be corrupted by crooked handlers and managers. Snow also used his influence to get Elvis an audition with RCA Victor, through Steve Sholes, the A & R man who dealt with Snow. Elvis even won one guest spot at the Opry, and early in 1955 they booked a large package tour with Hank Snow as headliner and with Elvis Presley as an added attraction.

Sometime after that tour, the partnership foundered and Colonel Parker became Presley's sole manager. The details of the split remain unclear. Whether Parker cut Snow out, or Snow withdrew voluntarily, will never be known since neither has ever spoken publicly about the affair. Presley's musical style was already drifting further from country, and closer to the rock and roll style that would catapult him to stardom with *Hound Dog* and *Blue Suede Shoes*, but he would always retain a fondness for gospel songs such as *How Great Thou Art*. Snow, despite the reservations he must have had about the star who was nicknamed "Elvis the Pelvis," was fond of him. Years later he told an interviewer, "I always found Elvis to be a very fine boy. He's good to his folks and his friends and he's a clean-spoken boy. Nobody's gonna knock him to me."

Snow had become an American citizen in 1958. Jimmie Rodgers Snow had given up show business plans in favor of

the ministry, and the family's assimilation into Nashville seemed almost complete, especially with Snow's outspoken patriotic support of the United States. In addition to his Opry bookings and tours, Snow made many appearances in USO (United Service Organizations) shows, entertaining American troops in Korea and later Vietnam.

But the sound of country music was gradually evolving even as Snow and other conservatives fought to hold the traditional line on style. Many young musicians, like Elvis, started off playing the country music that they heard on the

The cream-colored Cadillac convertible bought by Snow in 1947.

radio at home, and drifted into experimentation with rock and blues as they were exposed to a greater variety in style. Bill Haley, whose group the Comets later had a smash hit with *Rock Around the Clock*, started his musical career by playing western swing and imitating Gene Autry. Hank Snow had even booked a few tours with him. Rock and roll, rhythm and blues and jazz added new elements to the sound of hard country music—basically in the more widespread use of electric instruments, a more prominent bass line, more aggressive guitar solos, and the use of sticks rather than brushes for a snappier sound on the drum set.

And it wasn't only the sound of the instrumental back-up that was changing, but the lyrics and the subject matter as well. Shortly after the war, songs about cheating, such as *Slipping Around*, were regarded as saucy, but just barely acceptable. Country love songs tended to be about being lonely, blue, and left waiting at the altar. Such topics, widely used on radio soap operas as well, could always be counted on for a good cry. Though diehard fans of train songs, cowboy songs, and the music of Jimmie Rodgers were still around, country music was losing its hillbilly, rural connotations and becoming the music of an urban population. Rock and roll, on the other hand, appealed to the younger, urban audience with less experience of life's tragedies, and lots more interest in romance and sex. Singers such as Elvis, Jerry Lee Lewis, Bill Haley and Fats Domino singing *Blueberry Hill* could deliver those thrills, and by the late 1950s, rock and roll music was cutting noticeably into the formerly loyal country audience.

The solution was simple—find a way to make country music more accessible to a bigger segment of the population. Several country singers had already had good luck with songs that crossed over to the pop charts, and more were to follow; Jim Reeves, Eddy Arnold and Patsy Cline appealed to a middle-of-the road audience who weren't keen on the hard-driving, honky-tonk style with its wailing steel guitar, rhythmic strums, and self-pitying lyrics, but liked the gentler emotional delivery and the vocal qualities of the singers.

Little by little, the identifying characteristics of country were modified to make the sound palatable to new consumers. Less fiddle, or no fiddle at all, easy on the steel guitar, and a vocal style that was smoother, sweeter and mellower than the honky-tonk style.

By the early '60s, what is now regarded as the classic, more cultivated, Nashville sound had evolved. Blended in with the guitars were a large cast of backup musicians playing instruments identified with pop and show music—vibraphone, piano, and orchestral strings for sweetening. Often a choral backup of "oohs" and "ahs" was added. Not all country musicians picked up on these new developments. Bluegrass musicians, scorning any adaptation to modern trends, went their own way with their close harmonizations, string-band virtuosity, and the high, nasal vocal style of hillbilly and mountain music. The greatest practitioners of this style, Bill Monroe's Blue Grass Boys, became so closely identified with it that the name of their band came to represent the entire style. Like Monroe's band, the equally brilliant bluegrass duet team of Flatt and Scruggs also kept their audiences and even attracted new fans. In the early '60s, Flatt and Scruggs became widely recognized in the mainstream media for their playing of the *Ballad of Jed Clampett*, the theme music for the popular television series *Beverly Hillbillies*.

One of the major architects of the style change in country music was Hank Snow's longtime record producer Chet Atkins. Since 1957, Atkins had been chief of the country division of RCA in Nashville, and was widely regarded as one of the finest session guitarists in the business. Atkins and Snow had recorded albums of guitar duets together, and Snow trusted Atkins' judgement implicitly. By now Snow's baritone voice had lost some of its edges. He was sounding less like the energetic young man who belted out *I'm Movin' On*, and more like a country crooner version of Bing Crosby.

A re-recording of his first big hit tells the story of Snow's encounter with the Nashville sound more completely. Unlike the first single which had plenty of drive and intensity, the second version, despite the zipped-up production, lacks Snow's early vigor. There is a chorus in the background, harmonizing to Snow's vocal solo, and his guitar playing is less at the center of the sound. A little studio reverberation has been added to his already resonant voice, and a Floyd Cramer slip-note style piano break stands in complete contrast to the fiddle and guitar riffs of his 1950 hit. (Cramer's slip-note technique of ornamenting a melody or harmony note by striking the note a tone below as a kind of lazy grace note, has since become as standard a part of country piano as blue notes are in jazz.) The result, at least for a fan who knew Hank Snow in his heyday, is disappointing. He's an extremely competent stylist who gives all his songs his personal imprint, but some of his energy—the raw, compelling drive of a much younger and hungrier man—is gone.

From his first identification of himself as a western/cowboy singer and player, Hank Snow gradually modified his approach to that of a mainstream country singer. His skill as a guitarist has led him to explore numerous different styles, and from his earliest days at RCA Victor, Snow cut instrumental as well as vocal solos. His instrumental version of *Among My Souvenirs*, recorded on one of of his Collector's Series albums, shows the effects of the easy-listening style on hard country music. The tempo is lazy and the guitar solo part is sweetened by a thick layer of orchestral strings. Yet another instrumental solo on the album is a cover version of Doris Day's pop hit *Sentimental Journey*. Snow's version of *Tumbling Tumbleweeds* is pallid when one thinks of the zestful energy of his days as a cowboy singer. A choir hums and harmonizes over the string ensemble, and a set of Chinese temple blocks, rather than a drum set, imitate the sound of horses' hooves. The album contains his rendition of several country standards—*There Goes my Everything, Today I Started Loving You Again*, and *You're Easy to Love*. But he also dips into the hit parade and the crossover charts, as with his version of Nat King Cole's hit *Ramblin' Rose*. He gives it the studio treatment: a large chorus, a string orchestra with a unison entrance, and a drum set. One cut, a rendition of the theme song from the movie *Dr. Zhivago*, is an out of character choice for Snow. On *Somewhere My Love*, which is originally a sweeping lovesong in triple time, has been altered into a plodding kind of duple time. The vibrato in Snow's voice has widened and become slower, and with the added burden of the string orchestra, the song has become lifeless and is barely recognizable.

Nevertheless, Snow's record sales continued strong and his public appearances were solidly booked. A 1964 special with Wilf Carter on Canadian television received high ratings, but Snow, as did many other high profile entertainers, preferred to limit the number of appearances he made on television. Hank Snow fan clubs thrived as far away as Ceylon. He was so well known that when he appeared on a Japanese version of *What's My Line*, the panel guessed the identity of their mystery guest within 30 seconds. He could sell just about anything he recorded—a Christmas album, gospel favorites, train songs, a Jimmie Rodgers tribute, even a catch-all album titled *Songs I Hadn't Recorded Until Now*, and sell hundreds of thousands of copies. He continued to write new songs and after building a studio at home, could work there at his own convenience. During one spell of reminiscences about Nova Scotia, he wrote and recorded a ditty called *My Nova Scotia Home* which has since become one of the standard crowd-pleasers of any Maritime country band worth its beer.

Royalty payments could probably have guaranteed him a comfortable retirement any time he wanted it, but Snow in the '60s seemed still to be possessed by a restless need to keep moving on. He told Canadian writer Stewart MacLeod, who came to Nashville to write an article for *Weekend* magazine in 1967, "I am sincere when I say that I love the business now as much as I ever did, and if the Lord be willin' I'll just continue the same pace as now. I'd go crazy if I retired." He took some artistic chances—one was a recording of himself reading poems by the frontier Canadian poet Robert Service—long, narrative poems in doggerel rhythm like *The Face on the Barroom Floor* and *Dangerous Dan McGrew*—over a

Resplendent in one of his
trademark jackets, Snow accepts
the good wishes of residents of
Northwood Manor, a senior
citizen's residence in Halifax,
during a 1986 visit to the city.

Halifax Chronicle Herald/Mason

subdued background of appropriate country band music. The *Dan McGrew* recitation begins over a honky-tonk piano playing *Oh Susannah*. There must have been something in the Service material that appealed to Snow's sense of drama, and his feelings about the life in the old west and the frontier. But his voice has an odd quality of distance as if he were trying to make Service's stories over into a personal statement like those in his recorded autobiography. Curiously, both wind up sounding like a minister reading the gospel story instead of a man talking about his own tragic early life.

The ripples in country music style caused by pop and rock and roll music became even wider as the '60s progressed. Not only was the music being invaded by technical elements like louder drumming, but a younger generation, regarded as upstarts or Johnny-come-latelies, were moving in. If the notorious folkie Bob Dylan could record an album like the country-flavored *John Wesley Harding*, and his 1969 effort *Nashville Skyline*, the business was open to almost anybody. Opinions were divided. Some people felt that the influx of energetic and talented young musicians and writers would revitalize Nashville and save it from sinking into the complete homogenization of the studio sound. Others were outraged, particularly when Australian singer Olivia Newton-John won the 1974 Country Music Association's coveted Female Singer of the Year award.

Hank Snow was one of them. He had previously been critical of what he called the "Fifth Avenue bunch" and what he regarded as attempts to citify, dilute or alter pure country music, but this was a chance to act. He joined the fledgling Association of Country Entertainers, a group of concerned country musicians who banded together to fight what they considered to be an invasion of traditional country music by outsiders.

Snow's membership in the association was short-lived, however. He resigned when he recorded an album using Chuck Glaser of the Glaser Brothers as producer. Although Snow had once resisted those of Atkins' ideas that developed into the Nashville Sound, the Glaser-produced record, titled

Still Movin' On, showed him departing from the old Snow style. In acknowledgement that he had modified his original resistance to such changes, Snow gave up his prominent position in ACE but kept his membership.

If the business was changing, so was the city of Nashville itself. Always big, crowded and competitive, Nashville was also becoming prone to the urban violence that was common in many American cities during the '70s. The violence came close to Snow in 1974, when his longtime backup rhythm guitarist Jimmie Widener was robbed and shot to death in a downtown street. Snow had often been troubled by overly friendly and nosy fans hanging around his home, Rainbow Ranch, but the tragedy worried him so much that he installed a chain-link fence around his property. His political opinions, always conservative, now found expression in his support for law-and-order causes. In a way, though, country music, to which he had dedicated years of struggle and ambition, governed his politics as well. He had some associations with Governor George Wallace, and later Governor Jimmy Carter during his presidential campaign. Though both men stood on opposite sides of some of the issues that divided the South, both were outspoken fans of country music and musicians.

When Robert Altman released his 1975 film *Nashville*, some moviegoers and Nashville insiders felt that Haven Hamilton, the aging and autocratic country star portrayed by actor Henry Gibson, was modelled on Hank Snow. Snow apparently refused to see any similarity between his life and that of Gibson's character, and maintained a dignified silence on the matter. In truth, the resemblance of Snow to Hamilton in Altman's remarkable movie is superficial. Altman wasn't talking about Nashville so much as about contemporary American society. But he found ready-made in Nashville an entire modern metropolis filled with strikingly bizarre visual images that he scarcely needed to exaggerate to make his profounder point about the violent and chaotic state of the nation. Snow, with his flashy costumes and the imperial aura bestowed upon him by fans and the country music industry both, was an irresistible icon. But Altman's Haven Hamilton is too cunning and calculating to be confused with this Nova Scotian country boy, no matter how translated into American show business lifestyle he had become.

Snow did score another song hit in the early '70s. *Hello Love*, released in 1974, was an uplifting and, for Hank Snow, a cheerful lovesong about a returned sweetheart. It later became the theme music for the award-winning Public Broadcasting System radio show "A Prairie Home Companion," serving as the signature song for host Garrison Keillor. But as the '70s passed mid-decade, Hank Snow was devoting less of his time to show business and more to the charitable organization he wanted to establish.

It started when he read about the death of a battered and neglected four-year-old girl in Tennessee. Remembering his own experiences as an abused child, he founded the Hank Snow International Foundation for the Prevention of Child Abuse and Neglect and organized a large benefit concert each year with star performers such as Roy Acuff and Bill Monroe. But running such a foundation turned out to be a more complicated and expensive effort than its founders had imagined. The group went through several reorganizations and shuffles and was finally absorbed (in 1985) by the National Exchange Club, a large club that already ran a number of counselling centers around the country. Snow continued as one of the directors.

In many interviews, Snow has sounded pessimistic about the future of country music. "I don't believe real country music will ever come back," he told writer Joe Edwards of the Associated Press in 1985. In the same interview, he spoke of his erratic luck with updated production styles on his recordings, saying, "The last two or three albums we used more "uptown" background and they didn't do [sell] anything." He had teamed up briefly with a young country songstress named Kelly Foxton in 1979 to record a duet album with a stronger pop feel. A single release titled *Hasn't It Been Good Together* appeared on the charts, but the partnership did not endure.

Snow returned to the studio again in 1984 to record a duet album called *Brand on my Heart* with Willie Nelson. Together they shook the dust off a few of the Snow specials: Nelson and Snow with duelling guitars on *Golden Rocket*; a version of *I've Been Everywhere*, on which Nelson harmonizes while Snow does his trademark rattling off of the dozens of place names he's been; plus a few others including *I'm Movin' On*, *I Don't Hurt Anymore*, and *A Fool Such as I*. Nelson's voice, that reedy yet flexible tenor, is played off against Snow's rich baritone for one of the most successful pairings in Nelson's history of duet recordings, which includes records with other country legends such as Ray Price and Roger Miller. Nelson's lifestyle as one of the country outlaws might not exactly have satisfied Hank Snow's image of an upstanding citizen, but he respected Nelson's musicianship. "Willie Nelson has stuck pretty country," he told an interviewer. "Kenny Rogers kept pretty close and Ricky Skaggs is very country. But then a lot of 'em have gone Fifth Avenue."

He is still famous for his occasional squabbles with the country music establishment. In January of 1986, Snow boycotted a CBS special saluting the Grand Ole Opry, because he was asked to sing only one verse of *I'm Movin' On*. The show was a two-hour special with 60 stars including Roy Acuff, Dolly Parton and Loretta Lynn, and Snow told Associated Press writer Joe Edwards, "I felt like the Opry should have done a lot more for me. They should have stepped in and said, 'Give him more than a verse.'" Opry spokesman Jerry Strobel responded that they regretted Snow's absence from the special, but that the show was intended to be a look at the Opry's influence and its cast, both living and deceased. Snow, still feisty after 51 years in the business, told Edwards that he felt no remorse for speaking out, and that he would make his next Opry appearance as scheduled. A year later, he made headlines again when he revealed that he'd asked RCA Victor for an audit of his earnings from 1966 to 1976, and discovered that he was owed over $400,000. In an interview with writer Robert Oermann of *The Tennessean*,

Halifax Chronicle Herald/Len Wagg

Nova Scotia honors her famous son with a state dinner at the World Trade and Convention Centre in Halifax in 1986. Pictured above, left to right, are millionaire businessman Jack Irving, wife Suzanne, Snow, Mavis Buchanan, and former premier of the province, John Buchanan.

Snow advised young musicians to audit their record companies every five years, and added that he figured that because of his blind faith in Music Row executives, he may have lost two or three million dollars in royalties that were due to him.

Despite his irritation with the Opry and other aspects of the music business, one thing has remained constant throughout Snow's long career—the loyalty of his fans. Tributes to Snow's influence have continued unabated by the passage of time. The Canadian country group Family Brown included a reference to Snow in their hit single release *Pioneers* in 1990, and another Canadian country group, the hard-driving Prairie Oyster, recorded a bright new rendition and also shot a video of Snow's 1954 single *I Don't Hurt Anymore*, which climbed to the top of Canadian country charts. West Coast singer Roy Forbes, another Snow admirer, included a version of *A Fool Such as I* on his 1992 album.

Although Hank Snow has never been plagued with the personal scandals associated with many country musicians— messy divorces, bankruptcies, time spent in jail—he has admitted on several occasions that his fondness for the bottle has given him trouble in the past. Talking about the beginning of his career, he told writer Stewart MacLeod in *Weekend*, "I used to play so many beer joints in those old days that the only way you could stand it was to get drunk yourself. Never again. Now I even insist that my band not do any drinking when we're on tour. I don't want to play anywhere where liquor is sold." But he must have fallen off the wagon at least once more, for in a lengthy profile in *Canadian Magazine* in 1975, Snow told author Dick Brown that he had finally quit drinking for good in March of 1970. "I loved to take a drink," he said. "If only I could have stopped after three or four. But I could not." Snow told Brown that after a few drinks with a friend who happened to be a judge, the judge quit in order to go on the bench the next day. But Snow said of himself, "I just started to roar, you know? And I got all tanked up—had a brand new Lincoln Continental Mark III, probably didn't have but two, maybe three thousand miles on it—and I ran into another car." Nobody was hurt in the

collision, but Snow, viewing the damage, vowed that this was it—he was off the bottle forever.

Snow today lives in some isolation in his Nashville home. He has said that he doesn't care for rock music, bluegrass, or many of the newer country singers. He doesn't listen to records or the radio, and doesn't like videos, telling an interviewer, "From what I've seen, I don't care for 'em. They distract the audience from the music…I'm glad my time is done with recording. I got out at the right time." Snow suffered some public embarrassment in 1990, when a national tabloid newspaper revealed that his preacher son, Jimmie Rodgers Snow, had had an extramarital affair with a woman in his church choir.

After several years cooperating with various writers on his autobiography, Snow announced in late 1991 that he was looking for an international publisher for the book, which he promised would settle the truth about his part in Elvis Presley's career.

Trips back home to Nova Scotia have been fewer in the last decade. While his wife Minnie suffered from a rare disease that kept her bedridden, Snow was reluctant to travel far. He played a six-concert tour sponsored by Irving Oil during the summer of 1986, and at a concert held at the Archibald Field in Sydney, more than 12,000 people flocked to hear him.

A number of fans in his native South Shore area of Nova Scotia are in the process of establishing a Hank Snow museum as a lasting memorial to their favorite country singer. To raise money, they advertised a beach barbecue and picnic with live entertainment on a Saturday afternoon in late August of 1991. The parking lot at Risser's Beach quickly jammed up with trailers, campers, cars and recreational vehicles of all descriptions. The usual "parking lot pickers" were out in full force—fans who meet casually and after exchanging a few words, haul out the mandolins and guitars and start to jam.

The beach itself is a stunning natural setting. It can only be reached from the parking lot by crossing along a stretch of boardwalk elevated three or four feet in the air to protect the slender beach grass spiking out of the sand. The walk is worth it as you reach the top of a slight incline and suddenly come upon a broad sweep of clean silvery sand 50 or 60 feet wide to the ocean's edge, and stretching for perhaps half a mile on either side. There are, at most, 20 people on the entire beach. Back at the concert site, a flatbed truck trailer, boxed in on three sides by unpainted plywood sheets, serves as an improvised stage for the performers. But there's no music yet—the gas-operated generator has broken down and there is no power to run the sound system. People have brought their own lawn chairs to sit on the gravelled area in front of the stage, or else they flop on the grass at its edges. Booths sell fresh hot corn on the cob with hot dogs and cold drinks for the kids.

As you wander around, you inspect several improvised displays of Snow memorabilia—well-worn record jackets, photos, thank-you letters from Snow, yellowed newspaper clippings, a fan's Pontiac tiled from hood ornament to tail-lights with more record jackets and garishly tinted publicity photographs. But the center of attention is a beautifully preserved cream-colored Cadillac convertible, a sleek, romantic-looking beauty purchased by Snow in 1947, and currently owned by a New Brunswick man. Polished and lovingly maintained, it looks as though all it needs is a full tank of gas and a key in the ignition for it to purr into life and roll back the decades to nearly 50 years ago.

The generator has been fixed now and the show is about to begin. A hush comes over the crowd when a cheap plastic boom-box is brought forward to the microphone on stage by a wiry middle-aged fan in a blue windbreaker and a peaked baseball hat. He turns the blaster on and holding it high on his chest presses it close to the mike as Hank Snow's taped greetings go out through the loudspeakers to all his friends and neighbors from long ago. And he tells them in that rich, slow-talking, sing-song voice of his, how sorry he is that he couldn't make it today, how grateful he feels for the loyalty of his hometown fans, and how thrilled he is about the planned museum. And judging by the crowd's heartfelt round of applause, it's almost as good as if he were there in person.

CBC-TV Publicity

CHAPTER 3

Don Messer

I let the fiddle do the talking

Don Messer always denied that he was a country fiddler or that the music he played was country, western, or worst of all, hillbilly. In his view, the music he played with the Islanders—the jigs, reels, hornpipes and breakdowns—was as ancient and respectable as anything that classical composers such as Bach or Handel ever wrote. Though he was notoriously shy and reluctant to give interviews, Messer did occasionally speak out on what he felt were misconceptions about his music. In a 1953 profile story in *Maclean's* magazine, Messer told interviewer David MacDonald that the term hillbilly was an inaccurate description of his style. Instead, he said, "It is folk music, the music of the people. Our forefathers brought these hornpipes, jigs and reels with them from the old country—Scotland and Ireland—and kept them alive."

Even before he began appearing on national television in 1959, Messer's radio show, records and personal appearances had earned him a reputation as one of the best oldtime fiddlers Canada ever produced. He played with a skill usually found only in orchestral violinists, distinguished by a high degree of technical polish and a swift, agile bowing style that many have tried to imitate. Flaws that marred the sound of other fiddlers—the squeaking, scratchiness, and occasional sour notes—were rarely heard in Messer's music. His playing inspired several generations of young musicians to take up

the fiddle. Today the numerous categories of non-classical fiddlers include Cajun, Breton, downeast, Metis, Cape Breton, and Western swing—but nobody plays quite as he did.

Some people suggested that Don Messer and The Islanders could have been the Canadian counterpart of Bob Wills and his Texas Playboys if they had been willing to commit themselves to the kind of relentless work schedule that Bob Wills kept up. But Messer had little appetite for the blistering spotlight and scrutiny that accompanies that kind of fame. He was content to live in Halifax, do occasional cross-country tours, and concentrate on improving The Islanders' repertoire. His reputation and the group's weekly television appearances made them a household name. The *Encyclopedia of Music* in Canada described Messer and his Islanders as an "oldtime music group, the most popular in Canada during the mid-20th century."

But The Islanders were not a country group, at least not in the conventional sense. Several Islanders had spent more time playing other styles of music than they had playing country or fiddle music. Clarinetist Ray Simmons had played in dance and stage bands before joining The Islanders, and bassist Duke Neilsen in several jazz ensembles. The band played few of the instruments associated with the classic country or bluegrass sound, such as the mandolin, dobro and steel guitar. Messer preferred a sweeter blend, favoring acoustic over electric instruments for many years. It's probably most accurate to identify the band's style as "oldtime"—meaning that it is the kind of pickup group often heard at barndances, hoedowns and bashes at the Legion hall. The instrumentation consisted of fiddle, clarinet, bass fiddle, piano, guitars, and drum set. They could play country tunes, but also adapt to other styles. However, the band's vocalists, Charlie Chamberlain and Marg Osburne, were more at home singing ballads, folk-songs and nostalgic favorites such as *Danny Boy* than they were with the songs of Nashville.

If by country music one means the music closest to the heart of people who share rural values, Don Messer played country music. "I know what my audience likes," he insisted when others suggested changes to his format, songs or band setup. And from his earliest days touring the back roads of New Brunswick until his final broadcasts from a cable television station in Hamilton, Messer really did know what his fans wanted: peppy, recognizable tunes such as *Turkey in the Straw* or *Soldier's Joy*. They wanted to hear Marg or Charlie sing hymns or oldtime favorites such as *Wild Colonial Boy* that were sure to bring a tear to the eye. But above all, they wanted dance music, lively tunes that made them want to tap their toes and clap to the beat.

Even after many years as a professional entertainer, Don Messer never developed a showbiz manner. He was the same person onstage and offstage. Always dignified, quiet and sincere, he probably couldn't bring himself to utter the fast patter, jokes and snappy intros of the standard bandleader's stage routine. Television audiences knew him as the smiling, silent man who led off each week's "Don Messer's Jubilee" with a rousing version of his signature tune, *Going to the Barndance Tonight*. Though it was his own show, Messer always deputized someone else to be announcer or host. Many urban sophisticates dismissed the show as being hopelessly corny and old-fashioned, but, during its 10 years on national television, "Don Messer's Jubilee" was the last vestige of a rural Canadian entertainment tradition. His music provided a picture of life in small Canadian towns either as it was in fact, or, more likely, as his audiences wished it to still to be, with hoedowns, pie socials, talent shows and vaudeville, all rolled into one.

Messer was a small-town boy himself. He learned to play the fiddle in the southwest New Brunswick town of Tweedside, where he was born in 1909. The youngest of a large family, he was trying to pick out tunes on a brother's fiddle by the time he was five. Through persistence and careful imitation of other fiddlers in the town, he figured out how to play *Haste to the Wedding* and bought a fiddle of his own from a travelling peddler. Before long he was in demand to play for many of the town's events such as the weddings, dances, and concerts at the schoolhouse.

As in many small towns, there was a strong influence of the old country and the not-so-distant Victorian past. Some clergymen disapproved of music in general as being too frivolous, and fiddling in particular, since the fiddle was regarded by some as being the devil's own instrument. Messer's own father was strict in such matters and would not allow any music on Sundays, the day of rest from worldly things.

In small towns, isolated by poor roads and severe weather, entertainment was often limited to what people could provide for themselves. Sometimes there were touring companies of vaudeville or minstrel players who would appear for a week at the local Grand or Capitol Theatre, and in summer the Chautauqua shows travelled to many small centers in the Maritimes, but otherwise, the music was homemade. Local talent shows abounded with people eager to get up on stage: stepdancers, comedians, young ladies who sang ragtime songs or the latest hit from Tin Pan Alley, children who recited and of course, musicians. Many aspiring pianists or fiddlers began their careers sitting in an orchestra pit, improvising an accompaniment to a soprano's shaky rendition of *Home Sweet Home* or *I'm Forever Blowing Bubbles*.

Don Messer did most of his learning on the job. His only formal instruction came during a few years spent in Boston, when a violin teacher forced him to work on scales and exercises and to read music for the first time. That instruction, however brief, helped create Don Messer's characteristic style. He played with a sweeter sound and a more advanced technique than many country fiddlers achieved. Under pressure from his teacher, Messer played scrupulously in tune and learned, as classical players do, to read music exactly as written on the page. While he was studying the violin he took several jobs to earn expense money, but Boston was a large and hostile city for a shy young man. After the stock market crash of 1929 he went back home to New Brunswick.

The Depression hit the Maritimes hard, especially the outlying communities and farming regions. When he returned to Tweedside, Don Messer became one of the hundreds, perhaps thousands of young men who picked up odd jobs and part-time work wherever they could, whether on farms, in coal mines, factories or lumberyards. Messer worked on the railroad. In his spare time he put together a small band which played in the evenings and on weekends. At community dances, playing for several hours of square-dancing, musicians counted themselves lucky to earn a few dollars each night. Messer's knack for keeping a strict, danceable tempo (fiddlers call it "timing") was doubtless acquired during these years. He insisted that the band play the tune as written (meaning no improvisation or ornamentation), because the dancers needed steady rhythms to perform the complicated figures of square sets or step-dancing. As the band's reputation grew, so did the crowds at the dances.

While Messer was developing a following in southern New Brunswick, a lumberjack named Charlie Chamberlain was singing for his buddies in the lumber camps of the North Shore. Like Messer, Chamberlain showed musical talent at an early age; during World War I, five-year-old Charlie stood near the train tracks of his home town of Bathurst and sang for the troop trains that passed through on their way to Halifax. Homesick soldiers flipped him pennies for his renditions of *I'll Take You Home Again, Kathleen*. There was no chance for singing lessons, or even for much formal school-

ing for Charlie. When he was 10, he was working full time in the woods. By the end of his teens, he had picked up a guitar and his singing and playing were often the only entertainment in the camps where he worked. His professional musical career came about almost by accident. During a train trip to Saint John, someone who had heard Charlie singing suggested he look up Don Messer and ask for an audition. He did, and was invited to join the group which Messer was then calling the "New Brunswick Lumberjacks." Messer had by this time bought a half hour of radio time from the Saint John station CFBO. A little later he moved to CHSJ where he named his show the "Backwoods Breakdown."

A year later Julius "Duke" Neilsen joined the band. Neilsen had a colorful background; his father had played cornet for bandleader John Philip Sousa and as a youngster Neilsen had worked for circuses and carnivals before settling down to play the bass fiddle. But the circus fever never fully left him. One of his sidelines was wrestling tame bears as a theater act, and in between shows with the Messer band, Neilsen often filled in with demonstrations of fire-eating. Despite the shenanigans, Neilsen was an accomplished and versatile musician. He toured for a while playing jazz with the Benny Goodman orchestra and always claimed that he had turned down a personal invitation from Arthur Fiedler to play with the Boston Pops. Even when the personnel of the group numbered as many as 19, Neilsen, with his solid playing and penchant for practical jokes, was one of the best-known faces.

The radio show provided a small source of income and in those days, anyone who was heard on the air was treated as a town celebrity. The Lumberjacks were invited to play at more events and began to establish a reputation in the region. They ventured into New England, and even performed on the "Major Bowes Amateur Hour," which was then one of the best showcases for amateur talent. But mainly they played on what Charlie Chamberlain always called the kerosene circuit, so named for the kerosene lamps that still lit the halls in many small communities. Years afterward, Charlie

*Don Messer and four of his Lumberjacks in the studio of radio
station CHSJ in Saint John, New Brunswick in the mid-'30s.
Left to right, Don, Duke Neilsen, Ned Landry, Sammy
Cohen and Charlie Chamberlain.*

and Don reminisced about those days. In a film clip included on the 1992 CBC special *Country Gold*, Charlie talked about hard times, saying, "The mice used to walk across the floor with tears in their eyes." Don Messer quickly added, "Not only the mice. We did the same thing!" Financially the kerosene circuit was slim pickings. But if the payroll came up short, a barter deal could be worked out. At least once the band was paid in cans of sardines.

The show in those days was heavily influenced by the conventions of variety shows and vaudeville. Messer's musical numbers were the focus, but sometimes guest acts included step-dancers, singers, recitations, and the odd comedian. Dialect comedians were always welcome at country shows. The Grand Ole Opry had the Cackle Sisters, Grandpa Jones and Minnie Pearl; Don Messer had Joe LeBlanc. LeBlanc was a fictional character created by Maunsell O'Neil, portrayed as an Acadian woodsman with a repertoire of jokes and tall-tales about life in the backwoods. LeBlanc usually opened the radio broadcasts by saying, "Well, I'll be a son of a gun! This is Joe LeBlanc from the North Shore!" Another element of the stage act was a stunt performed by a very young and fit Charlie Chamberlain. He would take four running steps and leap directly over Messer's head while Messer continued to fiddle away.

The dances they played were often rowdy affairs which lasted until well after midnight. In Woodstock, a verandah once collapsed from the uncontained enthusiasm of the dancers. A fan from another location wrote Messer to tell him with pride: "Last time you played *Redwing* our boys stomped the pine knots through the men's room floor." The Messer band's radio show, broadcast six times a week, drew dozens of fan letters. Only one other show got more mail— the Happy Gang, broadcast from Toronto.

CBC Radio cancelled Messer's show in 1939, but almost immediately he received an offer to be music director of station CFCY in Charlottetown. He already had a strong following on the Island and that, coupled with CFCY's offer of an office, a studio, and a daily show made it a logical decision to relocate the entire Messer operation. With his wife Naomi, their children and his band, now renamed "Don Messer and His Islanders," Messer moved to Prince Edward Island.

CFCY managers had decided from the beginning that Messer's daily show "Outports" was the ideal showcase for playing downeast and country music. The station had already achieved a reputation for playing listeners' requests for Scottish and Irish airs, folk-songs, fiddle music and a mixed bag of songs ranging from music hall favorites to cowboy and western ditties. Messer's first broadcast, in November of 1939, opened with Don and The Islanders playing a Messer original composition called *Operator's Reel*. Almost from the start, the show was overwhelmed with fan mail. CFCY's broadcast signal ranged far across the Maritimes and into the Gaspé peninsula reaching a listening audience that was mainly rural or small town. Broadcast each night between five and six, the "Outports" show was so popular that fans scrambled home from work in time to hear it. Farmers scheduled milking and other barn chores early so that they could get back to the house to listen to the show before or during supper. Families with battery radios rationed their listening in order to save battery power for the nightly Messer show, and in many households, people turned up the volume and rolled back the rugs so they could dance.

The sound of the Messer band during those years was hard to define; it was neither a pure country style, nor a pure Scottish style with only fiddle and piano. Neither was it a big band or swing band in the style of Tommy Dorsey. Both the instrumentation and the style of playing made their music difficult to categorize neatly. When clarinetist Ray Simmons joined in 1940, he was a veteran of dance bands and oldtime bands but when he saw Duke Neilsen wearing a cowboy hat, he had trouble picturing himself in a western group. He stopped worrying when he found out the hat was just another expression of Duke's flamboyant personality.

Gradually other musicians were added: Warren MacRae on drums, Cecil McEachern on guitar or sometimes fiddle

Don Messer and the Islanders in Charlottetown in the late '30s. Left to right, CFCY *announcer Art MacDonald, Cecil Santry, Don, unidentified drummer, Ray Simmons, Charlie Chamberlain, Jackie Doyle.*

and Waldo Munro on piano. Other members came and went: fiddler and harmonica player Ned Landry, Bill LeBlanc, Jackie Doyle and pianist Eldon Rathburn, who was later a successful composer and arranger of film scores for the National Film Board. Few band members had much formal training or dreamed of becoming professional musicians. Ray Simmons said during a 1990 interview that he had worked at a variety of jobs from sawmill worker to coffin builder but until he joined The Islanders, he had not thought he could earn a living playing the clarinet. Since none of the band members except Don could read music, they relied on having enough rehearsal time to pick up the tunes by ear.

The basis of "Outports" was music, with a little humor and a few plugs for the sponsors' products thrown in. Because of his shyness, Don Messer disliked talking to his audiences and so CFCY's Art McDonald became the show's announcer. Ray Simmons succeeded him and held the job until 1963. As music director, Messer chose and arranged the tunes and cleared all programs in advance with the management. They performed the requests that came in for the fiddle tunes, folksongs and oldtime favorites that reflected the heritage of most of their listeners. Charlie Chamberlain, a real barroom singer, liked songs such as *That Long Lost Gold Mine in the Sky* or *The Old Shillelagh* which suited his lusty voice and energetic style. He tended to forget the words to his songs, and although band members didn't mind prompting him, on live radio the results could be disastrous. Like Duke Neilsen, Charlie was given to playing the prankster in the studio. During one studio broadcast, one of Charlie's guitar strings broke with a loud bang. Neilsen laughed heartily, only to see the bridge of his bass fiddle collapse seconds later. Don Messer had to finish playing the tune alone while the two culprits nearly drowned out the sound of his fiddle with their hearty guffaws.

It was the golden age of live radio, and a few flubs were just part of the excitement. CFCY and other stations carried music programs for all tastes, everything from Metropolitan Opera broadcasts to "Your Hit Parade." In the decades before television, the radio was the center of entertainment in many households. A family that owned a floor console model with good reception had lots of choices: comedy shows such as "Fibber McGee" and "Molly, Edgar Bergen and Charlie McCarthy," ballgames, soap operas, boxing matches, hockey, and of course the news. Radio managers, especially at regional stations such as CFCY, believed they had a responsibility to their listeners and tried to give them programs they liked. If the fans wrote to Don Messer requesting *Red River Valley* or *Sailor's Hornpipe* each week, they usually got it.

Messer's mature fiddle style could best be described as middle-of-the-road, well-adapted to the wide variety of tunes the band had to play. He tended to use the upper third of the bow closest to the tip, where he could produce the sweet, lyrical sound he preferred. In up-tempo tunes like jigs and reels, Messer could play quickly and accurately. But his insistence on playing the melody straight and without adornment tended to work against him in slower tunes such as strathspeys, ballads and slow airs. Western fiddlers such as Bob Wills liked to play with a lot of rhythmic swing, showing the influence of big band and jazz music. Appalachian

The name may have changed, but the music was the same. *Messer as an Islander at* CFCY *Charlottetown still wears plaid as he did when he led the Lumberjacks in Saint John.*

fiddlers punctuated melodies by double-stopping (bowing on two strings at once) or treating one string as a drone accompaniment to the melody. Irish fiddlers made lavish use of melodic ornaments—rolls and turns, while Scottish players executed a specialty called "cuts"—bouncing duplets or triplets with the bow, anticipating but played on the same pitch as the melody note. Messer rarely added any personal touches to the melody, choosing instead to play repeated

CBC-TV Publicity

Charlie Chamberlain as he looked in the forties at CFCY *Charlottetown. The plaid shirt proudly speaks of his lumberjack days in New Brunswick.*

sections without any variations to spice it up. Even his accompaniments to Charlie or Marg's vocals were often just arpeggios or quick runs up and down a scale. As he saw it, playing the melody cleanly and keeping strict time were the most important things.

A perfectionist by nature, Messer fussed over his musical arrangements. Though he rarely spoke on the air, backstage there was no doubt who ran the show. Recalling Messer's tenure at the CBC Halifax studio, announcer Don Tremaine said that Charlie Chamberlain was always the first person

out of the rehearsal and Messer was always the last. He was unable to relax and go home until he felt that the timings and arrangements of the pieces were secure. When he was setting up a tune for the band, the first 16 and the last 16 measures always belonged to Messer and his fiddle but in between he tried to make sure that his sidemen had solos.

Many of Messer's own original tunes were recorded by The Islanders on the Apex label, and later published in collections by Gordon V. Thompson. He composed within traditional genres, the set dance forms of jigs, hornpipe, breakdown and reel. But he created his own melodies with twists and turns that struck his fancy. As with most composers of oldtime music, he chose quirky or personal titles, a few examples being *Spud Island Breakdown, Rippling Water Jig* and *Don Messer's Breakdown.*

During the war years, the band began to travel more widely to engagements. Rather than drive long distances by car, the Islanders flew to the mainland using a Gypsy Moth aircraft. They often played for square-dances at the RCAF base in Summerside, and at community dances all over Cape Breton. One young boy in Arichat on Isle Madame would beg his parents to allow him to attend the dances. The boy, Jarvis Benoit, was determined to be a fiddler. Too young to be admitted to the dance itself, Benoit would listen to Messer play for a couple of hours from a tree or a knoll outside the hall, then run the three-and-half miles home and stay up all night practising the tunes on his own fiddle before he forgot them. Benoit eventually played with Fulton Boudreau's orchestra, then established his own group, the Acadian Playboys, and later, in Halifax during the late '70s, the Jarvis Benoit Quartet.

When the CBC International Service was begun in 1945, the Messer show was picked up for broadcast around the world. After the war ended, the group began touring outside the Maritimes. They were highly successful in Ontario and Quebec and across the prairies, but far less so in Newfoundland. Ray Simmons talked about the tour The Islanders made through Newfoundland shortly after that province joined Confederation in 1949. In his view, many Newfoundlanders were still hostile to mainlanders and took out that generalized dislike on the Messer group by staying away from their concerts in droves. In St. John's, Simmons said that a mere 100 people attended the two shows. Certainly if profit margin is any measure of a tour's success, that tour failed miserably. Simmons said that he personally only broke even, saying, "We worked there two or three weeks and I had $100 at the end—the same as when we went there."

Marg Osburne had joined the group in 1947 as a regular vocalist. She was a shy, pretty girl who had called up the radio station on a dare to ask for an audition, and got the job. Quiet and unassuming, Marg was nevertheless a quick learner who was able to sing the standard Messer repertoire and also add newer songs, sometimes from the current Top 40, to the programs. Other musicians joined the band during the early '50s: Cecil McEachern, a guitarist who also played a good country fiddle, and Waldo Munro on piano.

The move to television came in 1956 when The Islanders auditioned for CBC Halifax executives. The producer was an energetic young staffer named Bill Langstroth who had already made a name for himself producing the suppertime news show "Gazette." Langstroth was interested in music and when The Islanders won a place on the regional network, it was up to him to put together the show. Besides the music of The Islanders, and Marg and Charlie's vocals, someone thought that a dance group of some sort would provide a nice balance for a television show which, after all, needed more emphasis on visuals. Langstroth contacted Gunter Buchta, at that time a well-known dancer and instructor working in Halifax.

Buchta, still vigorous today in his 70s, can remember the first time he heard Don Messer's name. Buchta and his wife Irma, a choreographer and designer, had settled in Halifax after the war to teach dancing. At that time, Buchta had little experience of country music or dancing. He was trained in modern ballroom dancing and was only familiar with classical music. At a variety show held in the Halifax Forum

Bill Langstroth, "Singalong Jubilee" host and folksinger from the late '60s, produced Don Messer and his Islanders in 1956 when they first made the move from radio to television.

in 1955, hosted by Max Ferguson, the Messer group played for the dance that was held afterwards and Messer and Buchta were introduced, but the contact was fleeting. A year later when Buchta's dancers auditioned for the show, Messer watched them approvingly and told Bill Langstroth, "That's what I want." Buchta had originally called his dancers the Corte dancers, with a younger group called the Corteens, but Langstroth insisted that Buchta call his students the Buchta Dancers.

When the "Jubilee" show first went to the regional

CBC-TV Publicity

network in 1956, the dancers' contract was at first for only one show. Gradually it was extended to four shows, then to 12 and then for a year at a time. Buchta's association with the show continued for 17 years until Messer's death in 1973. Today, Gunter Buchta believes that the end of the Messer show was untimely. He says, "I would bet that if Don Messer hadn't died, we would still be going on—like Lawrence Welk."

Those early shows were announced by Ray Simmons, continuing in the role he had held at CFCY. Though Simmons was a competent radio announcer, he lacked the flair that the executives were looking for in overall production. When the time came for the show to go to a national television spot, they drafted CBC employee Don Tremaine who, over the next 10 years, became so closely identified with the show that he was considered as much a member of the cast as Messer himself.

The "Jubilee" show first went to the network as a summer replacement for "Country Hoedown" in 1959, but audience response was so strong that it was picked up for the fall season as well. When "Don Messer's Jubilee" made its national debut, the show's producers worked out a format that over the next 10 years, in Tremaine's own words, "never varied a nickel's worth." Each Monday night when Don Tremaine announced, "It's Don Messer's Jubilee!" the viewers could rest assured that for the next 30 minutes there would be no surprises or deviations from the standard script.

Most of the production values that had made the radio show a success were carried over into television. Everything was carefully prepared and timed but there was little glamor and few fancy camera angles or large cast production numbers. Banter between cast members was limited to a couple of lines, and was usually related to whatever song or dance that person was about to perform. The segues were swift and the flow of the show unbroken. Don Tremaine acted as the

The Buchta dancers whoop it up on CBC-TV's "Don Messer's Jubilee."

link between cast and audience. After years of experience working on live radio and television, Tremaine, with his jovial manner and broad smile, sometimes seemed to be the only person who was completely at home with the camera.

Don Messer's shyness occasionally created minor problems. Tremaine remembers that while Ray Simmons was still acting as announcer, representatives from CBC and Massey Ferguson, one of the show's main sponsors, had trouble figuring out which member of the band was Don Messer. As Tremaine recalls it, they were puzzled by Messer's reluctance to act as host on his own show. Tremaine reports the gist of their discussion: "The guy who was talking was the guy who played the clarinet—was that Don Messer? No, that was Ray Simmons. Well, where's Don Messer? He plays the fiddle. Why doesn't he talk? He doesn't like to." The confusion sorted itself out after Tremaine was drafted as the announcer who would introduce Don Messer as well as the various guests, but people would urge him to try to coax a few words out of Messer even if only to name the tunes he was about to play. It wasn't easy. Messer's oft-quoted response was, "I just let the fiddle do the talking for me."

When his fiddle talked, audiences were happy to listen. At times during its 10 year run, the Messer show drew a larger audience—up to 2,500,000—than Ed Sullivan's weekly variety show or "Hockey Night in Canada."

But not everybody liked what they saw. Shortly after the show's debut, Gordon Sinclair wrote a critical column in the *Toronto Star*, scorching "Don Messer's Jubilee" for what he saw as its embarrassing corniness. The article, titled "Don Messer is Stinking Up the Networks," created an indignant backlash among fans who rushed to defend their favorite fiddler. Among them was songwriter Bobby Gimby, formerly of the Happy Gang radio show, who wrote to Messer to point out that Sinclair's sniping was more than offset by a positive article in *Time* magazine called "Hillbilly Hit."

The word hillbilly, with its connotations of bluegrass music, banjos and moonshine, didn't really capture the essence of the show. Given the way that hillbilly or Appalachian fiddle styles evolved out of folk traditions shared by European settlers in the Maritimes, it is easy to see why an American viewpoint might use the term to describe similarities between Messer and southeastern U.S. styles. To aficionados of classical music or jazz, Don Messer's band and Hank Snow's Rainbow Ranch Boys may even have sounded pretty much alike, but to Canadian country fans, they were worlds apart. The Islanders' music was impossible to pigeonhole neatly as country, oldtime, or dance band since they did a little of each. And the Buchta Dancers were far too polished to be dismissed as mere square dancers, even though they danced such country dances as the two-step and the polka. Gunter Buchta's coaching was evident in the sophistication of their dance routines. Square dancers, especially at country dances, sometimes shuffled but the Buchta Dancers glided elegantly across the dance floor, dipping and swaying like ballroom dancers.

Even the show's guest list ran the full musical gamut: everybody from country singers Myrna Lorrie, Stompin' Tom Connors and Tommy Common to folksingers Shirley Eikhard, John Allan Cameron and Catherine McKinnon. Calling "Jubilee" a hillbilly show was inaccurate. "Country" was closer to its spirit, but the musical content was wide-ranging.

Don Tremaine, Gunter Buchta and others think that at some point Massey-Ferguson, the farm implement manufacturer who sponsored the show, may have brought pressure on Messer to change the format. Massey-Ferguson sponsored a similar show in the United States, hosted by singer Red Foley and called "Jubilee USA." Messer refused to make any changes in his repertoire or format, allegedly saying, "I know what my audience likes and I'm going to present it." American audiences, closer to the roots of hard-core country and bluegrass style, preferred string bands, nasal voices, and more twang in the sounds. Messer understood his Canadian fans and their tastes; they were the tastes of a population who lived mainly in small towns and rural areas, liked a sweeter country sound, and clung to a British heritage. According to

Don Tremaine, Messer let his sponsors know that if the show didn't go his way, it wouldn't go on at all. It worked; the *Jubilee* show ran untouched and compared to such country bumpkin shows like "Heehaw," "Don Messer's Jubilee" was the epitome of quiet good taste.

And so the format remained unchanged. The show always opened with Don and The Islanders playing *Going to the Barndance Tonight* with a verse sung by Marg and Charlie, a turn around the floor by the Buchta Dancers, and the introduction of the guests. There were always several instrumental numbers by the group, vocal solos from Marg and Charlie, at least two dances by the Buchta Dancers and solo spots for the guest singer, dancer, or fiddler of the evening. There would be a quiet time featuring Marg or Charlie singing a hymn or gospel tune and finally, a rousing number by the whole cast followed by *Till We Meet Again* while the production credits rolled. But the musical content varied wildly within any one show: anything from a ragtime tune such as *Dill Pickle Rag* to a folksong such as *Flow Gently Sweet Afton*, to a hoedown tune such as *Turkey in the Straw*.

It was country music in the broadest sense of the word: down to earth, nothing arty or pretentious and a straightforward presentation of the acts. Gradually more cast members were added and the musical content became even more diversified. Vic Mullen, an expert fiddler, guitarist and banjo player, joined the cast in the early '60s. Singer and accordionist Johnny Forrest, a Scot, joined the cast in 1966; he specialized in Scottish, Irish and Welsh folk-songs. Catherine MacKinnon became a regular in 1964 and though her first inclination was toward folk-songs, she later became an expert pop stylist as well.

Messer may have been reluctant to become an on-camera personality, but he called the shots backstage. As Gunter Buchta recalls it, the usual procedure was that the two of them would confer with Bill Langstroth to map out a series of shows. Buchta's background was in classical music and ballroom dance; as he puts it now, "I had no idea about country music. I was brought up on music for ballroom dancing. Two-steps and polkas didn't belong to ballroom dancing." He relied on Messer to suggest tunes that Buchta would then choreograph. The Buchta Dancers were so well trained that they usually learned their new routines for each show in only two rehearsals. Buchta says that he and Don agreed that in choreographing any tune, the first section was 96 measures long and the second was always 128. The only stipulation, he says, was that whatever went on in the middle sections—solos on string bass, extra percussion such as the tempo blocks the drummer favored—Don Messer always began and ended the pieces.

Buchta says now, "The most interesting part is, we never had a fight. Never had a disagreement." The closest they came to a tiff was during a discussion about improving the show artistically for better flow. Messer, always conservative, was apprehensive about making any changes, but Buchta explained to him that his main concern was the quality of the show and the reputation of his dancers. "I explained to him, 'I also have to think of my dancers. My dancers were a household name. Music and dance blend together.' And he agreed with this and from there on, clear sailing." Buchta also says that in time, Messer came to regard the dancers as such an essential part of his entourage that he disliked going on tours without them.

As Buchta and others discovered, Messer was cautious about making changes or additions to his musical repertoire. He preferred to stick with music that had passed the test of time, and knew that his target audience shared that preference. Yet he kept in contact with current trends; his music library, donated to the Public Archives of Nova Scotia after his death, contained songbooks by Hank Williams, copies of *Country Song Roundup* and a record collection that included Bob Wills, Paul Whiteman's orchestra and jazz violinist Joe Venuti.

Messer liked to plan shows around special themes and holidays such as Christmas, Remembrance Day, St. Patrick's Day and St. Andrew's Day. On those celebratory shows, the band wore costumes: for a Scottish show, tartan jackets and

Marg Osburne, Don, and Charlie Chamberlain always gave their devoted, nation-wide fans a warm feeling.

ties. The dancers costumes were designed by Irma Buchta and the musical repertoire would also underline the theme. For St. Patrick's Day, the band would play mostly Irish jigs, Marg and Charlie's solos would be airs such as *When Irish Eyes are Smiling* and the set design would feature shamrocks. Whatever the occasion, the sets were always modest and with obvious connections to rural life. The painted backdrops were of cottages, barns and rustic fences. Sometimes the singers used props; Marg Osburne would sit in a rocking chair while she sang *Easy Rocking Chair* while Charlie Chamberlain favored rakish hats and his shillelagh. He brandished it in his fist, leaned on it and danced with it.

Charlie was extremely popular with audiences. He had some shortcomings as a singer; his voice, once a beautiful natural instrument, gradually declined in range and power. Don Tremaine says, "I saw him actually cry one day when he heard a recording of himself done in 1937 and a clearer, more bell-like tenor you would never hear. Pure, natural sound— he was good." Chamberlain was never a polished vocalist in the style of Irish tenor John McCormack, nor was he a

Charlie Chamberlain, part clown, part inspirational singer, in a typical pose from the hey-day of "Don Messer's Jubilee."

CBC-TV Publicity

country crooner like Eddy Arnold. If he didn't sing country or western songs with the appropriate nasal twang, his personality overcame the technical flaws of the voice. When he sang the vaudeville ballad *If You were the Only Girl in the World*, he could sweeten it with so much blarney that people overlooked the unromantic figure he usually cut.

Chamberlain was a born performer, but he gave his colleagues some bad moments. He was reluctant to learn new songs, choosing instead to stick with the ballads he had learned in his childhood, but even with those old standards, his memory was unreliable. It was a source of jokes on the set. Tremaine says that once while preparing an Easter show, a technician had to write up goof cards (prompters) in case Charlie forgot the words to his selection—the *Lord's Prayer*. The technician reached the bottom of the card, ran out of space and was heard to ask, "Charlie, can you ad-lib the Amen or do you want me to make a separate card?" He could never relax with the camera as he had with the radio microphone, except in his occasional bouts of clowning with Tremaine or ad-libbing a spontaneous stepdance during The Islanders' final tune of the show. But his familiar bulky frame, sweet smile and the nods and winks he tossed at the fans made it easy for them to overlook his foibles.

Marg Osburne too preferred the older song repertoire, but Marg had the knack of picking up hit parade songs, country or show tunes. She was a middle-of-the-road stylist, similar to Patti Page. Her voice fell into the mezzo-soprano to soprano range; it wasn't large, but it was sweet and true. She learned new material quickly but it was sometimes difficult to persuade Messer to program different songs. Once, Don Tremaine recalls, he and Marg spent an afternoon together taping a selection of songs which they felt would suit the show's format. But of 15 possible choices, Messer approved only two.

Marg's image on the show was that of the typical girl (or possibly housewife) next door: plump, smiling shyly and possessing the gift of a charming natural vocal style. "Marg was a nice person—one of the nicest I ever met in my life," said Ray Simmons in 1990. Gunter Buchta agreed, adding, "Everybody cared for Marg. Everybody wanted to come near to Marg when we were travelling.... And Marg was as good as gold. You never saw another man around her. She never drank anything." Marg sometimes found it a strain to work with Charlie Chamberlain. She was genteel and quiet while Charlie, fond of a drink, was often boisterous and noisy. Since they were frequently paired off for duets on the show, they cooperated, but it was a partnership with frequent tensions—a fact that might have surprised the many viewers who assumed that since they sang so well together, they must be married to each other.

Don Messer the man remained an enigma, even to the people who worked with him most closely. A devoted husband and father, he was most relaxed at home, but even there he was sometimes preoccupied. He was not known as a great conversationalist. Jack O'Neill, a CBC executive closely associated with the show, told CBC "Mainstreet" in January of 1992 that Messer communicated best through his music. O'Neill recalled, "It was easy to tell when he was upset [by] the look on his face and the way he would bow his fiddle.... He had high standards. The band had to be up to snuff all the time." During rehearsals, O'Neill would go out to the floor to find out what Don thought of the show. The exchange would go somewhat as follows: "How's it going, Don?" "Not bad." Sometimes Messer's answer would be a mere "Hmph." Other times, "We'll do better next time."

The other band members tended to play supportive rather then featured roles. Cecil McEachern, who played guitar and electric guitar, was also a competent fiddler but only occasionally played solos. Duke Neilsen, always smiling broadly, could slap out an energetic bass line for *Five Foot Two* or a gospel tune. Percussionist Warren MacRae had played drums with a Charlottetown band and was adept at producing the kind of percussion sound that Messer needed: easy on the bass drum and snare drum, and lots of the snappy-sounding tempo, especially in the middle section of any piece.

CJC-TV Publicity

Of Waldo Munro, the band's pianist, Gunter Buchta says, "A musician completely without knowledge of music, written music. But pitch? When we had guests on the show, he would ask them, 'What key are you singing in?' Little kids—how do they know what key they're in? They love singing. He said, 'Just start off.' They would start off and after one bar, he was ready. He had such fantastic pitch, even Don relied on him." His talent for quick improvisation came in handy, for Waldo had to invent piano parts for several different musical styles on every show. For Don's solos, Munro usually doubled the melody line in his right hand while making sure that the left hand had the correct chord changes and didn't overbalance the fiddle in volume. For a guest who sang country songs, Munro might toss in a few slip notes, à la Floyd Cramer, and for the hymn or gospel tune at quiet time, he would imitate the dulcet tones of a church organ.

By the early '60s, most of the cast had relocated to the Halifax area, except for Ray Simmons who chose to commute from his Charlottetown home. The show did not provide a full time living for the cast members. Some of them did odd jobs to support their families; Charlie Chamberlain sometimes pumped gas to support his wife Ti-Belle and their children. Gunter Buchta and Irma Buchta taught dance classes and travelled all over the country to run seminars and act as judges at dance competitions. Most of the Buchta Dancers were college students or young working people who treated dancing as a sideline rather than a main source of income. Buchta says that for most of *Don Messer's Jubilee* 10 years on network television, the dancers received only $10 per show.

When the television season ended, Messer and The Islanders went on tours to earn extra cash. Travelling around

"Don Messer's Jubilee" may have ended in 1969, but show favorite Marg Osburne kept right on singing. In 1975 she was a featured performer on the Atlantic Folk Festival at Hardwoodlands Farm near Windsor, Nova Scotia.

and playing at fairs and high school gyms kept them in constant touch with their audiences. Contrary to those who thought that Don Messer's downeast style would appeal only to Maritimers or exiles living in Toronto, he was extremely popular in Quebec, in rural Ontario and in prairie towns.

Don Tremaine went along on one of the national tours sponsored by Massey-Ferguson in the early '60s. Tickets for The Islanders' shows were available free from any local Massey dealership, but Tremaine says that even the lure of free admission couldn't account for the size of the response. He remembers, "We went to Brandon, Moose Jaw, Prince Albert, Lloydminster, Calgary and Edmonton. And I think in those seven places the total audience was around 80,000. With free tickets, why not? But they drove in March, sometimes 300 miles in the snow." The usual routine was to play a concert for the first half of the evening and a dance for the second half so that the audience could participate. Doubts that The Islanders' homespun style might not go over as well in the West soon evaporated. Don Messer knew that the community barndance still thrived in rural Canada. In fact, callers competed for the chance to call a square dance for Don Messer and his Islanders. Uneasy on television, Messer was much more at home playing for dances, where the dancers appreciated both his steady tempos and his encyclopedic memory for dance tunes.

Not all the tours were successful. A trip by the Messer troupe through northern Canada fizzled as the earlier Newfoundland tour had done. The vast distances between concert locations meant the band had to travel by air and since Marg Osburne hated to fly, she didn't go along at all. Northern audiences were disappointed not to see all the faces they expected from watching the TV show, said Ray Simmons later, adding that if he had only known how eager people were to see Marg in person, he would have rented a car and driven her from place to place rather than have her miss the entire tour.

The eagerness of many crowds to welcome the travelling company is something that Gunter Buchta still remembers

CBC-TV Publicity

September 1960. Producer Bill Langstroth, Don Messer, announcer Don Tremaine and dancer/choreographer Gunter Buchta, display awards from sponsor Massey-Ferguson for "The television program viewed by more persons than any other program viewed in Canada."

fondly today. During an early tour to Cape Breton, he recalls that they were slated to appear at a skating rink in Glace Bay. Local transportation had been arranged from a pickup point to the rink, but hospitality interfered with the scheduling. Buchta says that his host, fairly bursting with pride at transporting a television celebrity, insisted on stopping at no fewer than five different homes so that Buchta could accept a friendly welcome and of course, a drink. What should have been a brief trip turned into an hour-long stopover.

The Messer entourage was not the only show on the road during that period in the late '50s and early '60s, but they were certainly the best known. After so many years of playing together, they had developed a smooth, professional act that a reporter for the *Toronto Telegram* once called, "...the best produced, most slickly packaged country variety show in Canada."

Other groups, both Canadian and American, also targeted the country music audience. Country fiddler June Eikhard, mother of '80s and '90s singer/songwriter Shirley Eikhard, and her husband Cecil, for example, had a band called the Tantramar Ramblers who played at many clubs, roadhouses and dances in the Maritimes before moving from New Brunswick to Oshawa in 1963. In her day she was widely regarded as Canada's first lady of the fiddle and in 1959 was the first woman to enter the Canadian Open Old Time Fiddlers' Contest, where she placed fifth in the open class. Another maritime couple who formed the nucleus of a musical group in the Messer genre was Joe and Vivian Brown, originally from Amherst, who belonged to a popular group called the Hillbilly Jewels. After moving to the Ottawa area, Joe Brown formed a group with his three children, calling themselves the Family Brown. They made occasional guest appearances on "Don Messer's Jubilee," and the Family Brown remained one of Canada's premier country music groups until its demise in 1990.

Despite his wild popularity on tour, Don Messer was not having much impact on the largest new segment of the market—the 25-and-under age group. His traditional target audience had begun to age, and their numbers to shrink. Television executives realized that the postwar generation were asserting a newly-acquired buying power to indulge their own preferences in records, films and television programming. Their musical tastes did not run to the fiddle tunes, country songs or melancholy Irish ballads that so many of their parents and grandparents had liked. They wanted to hear the contemporary sounds of country/folk singers such as Ian and Sylvia Tyson or Gordon Lightfoot, and pop groups such as the Beach Boys and the Beatles. Electric guitars and powerful drumming created the hotter, more energetic sound of contemporary hit radio. The homey

sweetness and simplicity of the fiddle and piano now sounded to them both corny and uncool.

Don Messer noticed the changes taking place in the music market. He had already made several alterations in personnel and instrumentation by the late '60s, modifying The Islanders' sound to conform more closely to mainstream country music. One of the most valuable additions was Vic Mullen, a Yarmouth native with an astonishingly easy versatility whether on banjo, guitar or fiddle. Mullen made a name for himself through many bluegrass and country bands he performed with, including that of fiddler Ned Landry. He led the Bluenose Boys on CTV's "Cross Country Barndance" in the early '60s, and his command of styles allowed him to play anything from bluegrass mandolin to Spanish guitar. His versatility and virtuosity helped to update the sound of The Islanders. Gradually newer songs from both the country and the pop hit parades began to appear on the program lineup. Though the band still played oldtime and traditional music, by the late '60s, many of the regular guests were country stars: Myrna Lorrie, the Family Brown, Gene MacLellan. Even Charlie Chamberlain had been persuaded to add the country tune *Anytime* (Eddy Arnold's theme song) to his repertoire and Marg was doing not only cover versions of country hits such as Tammy Wynette's *Stand By Your Man*, but was moving farther into pop music with such songs as *There's a Kind of Hush* and *Little Arrows*.

Several events in 1968 pointed to rough times ahead for the show. It was moved from a safe slot on Monday to a higher profile time on Friday night. The pressure to acquire and hold a younger audience in this hot, prime-time weekend period came at a time when Don Messer was not in the best of health. He suffered from chronic diabetes and had

Photograph following pages: *1960s studio shot of the "Don Messer's Jubilee" band. Left to right, front, Johnny Forrest, Ray Simmons, Marg Osburne, Don, Charlie Chamberlain, Vic Mullen, announcer Don Tremaine, Waldo Munro. Rear, Cec McEachern, Warren MacRae, Duke Neilsen.*

survived two heart attacks. But it wasn't until everybody showed up for rehearsals on April 14 of 1969 that the axe fell. "Don Messer's Jubilee" was to be replaced in CBC's fall lineup by the folksong show "Singalong Jubilee."

Nobody anticipated the storm of protest that followed. Indignant callers to CBC stations around the country wanted to know the reasons for the show's cancellation. They sent hundreds of letters, telegrams and petitions to the CBC board, to members of parliament and to Messer himself. One telegram, from a fan club in Fort William, Ontario, listed 1,300 signatures. Newspaper editorials criticized the CBC both for its unpopular decision and for the corporation's new policy on entertainment programming, described by the program director at the time as an effort to "…inject a fresh new element into the winter time sked…and provide a younger look and orientation." Public objections raged on. Members of Parliament asked questions in the House of Commons. Supporters staged a demonstration on Parliament Hill with square dancers, step dancers and the championship downeast fiddling of Graham Townsend.

Nevertheless, the CBC refused to reconsider. After recording a final show early in May, the band embarked on a farewell cross-country tour, taking along the entire troupe. Posters for the tour stated defiantly: "Don Messer—the People's Choice." Wherever they appeared, they found appreciative, sometimes even tearful crowds. The demise of the Don Messer show on CBC marked the end of a relatively unsophisticated era in variety broadcasting. But it did not finish off The Islanders. The show would continue to appear on syndication, produced through station CHCH in Hamilton, for another four years. The band members travelled to Ontario to work with their longtime producer Manny Pittson, taping entire blocks of shows at a time. As Ray Simmons saw it, they had all worked together for so many years that they hardly needed any help in studio setup and production. "We used to grind the shows out. No problem," he recalled. Gunter Buchta confirms the wealth of experience and repertoire on which they relied, and estimates that during his

long association with Don Messer, he probably choreographed as many as 1,000 dances.

The syndicated show from Hamilton might have gone on longer, but bad luck and ill health intruded. First there was the loss of Charlie Chamberlain. Charlie chronically ran short of cash because of his sympathy for people who were down on their luck. Don Tremaine reports that he couldn't resist lending money to friends and cronies who pleaded with him for a handout. "He was generous as could be. Every payday there was this lineup of derelicts and has-beens waiting for Charlie to come out with his check." John Gray, in his musical "Don Messer's Jubilee," immortalized Charlie's openhandedness in his song *Payday Companions and Fairweather Friends*. Chamberlain took odd jobs to support his family but his health gradually declined. He died in Bathurst in 1972.

The show from CHCH ended for good with Messer's death in 1973. Despite his quiet personality, Messer had long been the almost invisible guiding force of The Islanders. Without him, the group quickly disintegrated. Messer had always taken care of business in choosing and arranging repertoire. Left to their own devices, the individual musicians floundered. They were at a disadvantage in a music industry that had changed drastically. Dance band and studio musicians were now expected to read music fluently, and pull together a show or concert with minimum rehearsal time. Marg Osburne, a devoted wife and mother, kept busy with nightclub appearances for several years and hosted "That Maritime Feeling," a variety television show broadcast from Halifax. Osburne died in Rocklyn, Ontario in 1977. Vic Mullen may have fared the best. He remained active as a bluegrass player and went on to become musical director of CBC's "Countrytime" on television, and "Country Roads" on radio.

The others scattered to various jobs. Waldo Munro drove a cab in Halifax for a time while Cecil McEachern and Ray Simmons moved back to Prince Edward Island. Simmons worked as a salesman and later a handyman for the Wandlyn

Above: *Frank MacKay does an Irish turn as Charlie Chamberlain in Gray's stage production of "Don Messer's Jubilee."*

Inset: *The Buchta Dancers (left to right): Linda Elliot (one of the original Buchta Dancers), Cliff LeJeune, Thierry Richard and Kathryn MacLellan join Jodie Friesen as Marg Osburne, and Frank MacKay as Charlie Chamberlain in John Gray's controversial stage-production of "Don Messer's Jubilee."*

Motel chain until his retirement. At the time of his death in September 1990, Simmons was still playing his clarinet in church every Sunday. Gunter Buchta and his wife Irma continued their busy careers as dance teachers and later retired for a time to a home in the West Indies. After moving back to Nova Scotia, Gunter Buchta helped to establish Dance Nova Scotia. Following his wife's death, he suffered a stroke, but made a full recovery and even began dancing again as part of his post-stroke therapy program. The Islanders reunited once for a concert in Montague, P.E.I., in July of 1987. Duke Neilsen had died in 1986, but the remaining musicians Ray Simmons, Cecil McEachern, Waldo Munro and Warren MacRae were all on hand.

Playwright John Gray grew up watching the Messer show in Truro during the '50s and later wrote a musical tribute to its heyday, called *Don Messer's Jubilee*. First produced at Neptune Theatre in Halifax and later at Confederation Centre in Charlottetown during the summer season, the show drew some fire from fans and critics alike. They found fault in the fact that although the character of Messer was on stage leading the band, he never spoke. Ray Simmons narrated the story. The play also dealt with some of the issues behind the scenes, especially the tensions between Marg and Charlie, unpleasant realities that the fans didn't want to know about. Fault was found in the fact that, with the exception of *Going to the Barndance* and *Till We Meet Again*, none of Messer's original tunes were used. John Gray had written all the rest of the music himself. Some longtime Messer fans felt Gray had slighted Messer by not sufficiently acknowledging his achievements as a musician and longtime director of one of the best-loved shows in the history of Canadian television.

Although the cast of "Don Messer's Jubilee" recorded perhaps as many as 400 half-hour shows, few master-tapes are to be found in the CBC tape library. While no one seems to know for sure, the story that has gained the most currency is that most of them were trashed, and only the quick wits of a cameraman who retrieved a few dozen either from the garbage, or from the back of a truck (depending on the version), saved something of "Don Messer's Jubilee" for archival documentation. Even the costumes were destroyed, much to the disgust of Gunter Buchta, who insists even today, "Somebody in CBC didn't like Don Messer, because they didn't preserve any tapes. Same with the costumes—just threw them out. Other people would have paid good money for them."

In 1985, Bill Langstroth compiled a selection of some of the best moments from the Messer show and released them as a videotape, hosted by Don Tremaine. Tremaine reminisces on tape about his memories of the show: Marg Osburne trying to get him to sing and helping him by beating time against his foot, Charlie's talent for hamming it up, and the contribution of all the other band members. As period pieces, clips from the show make fascinating viewing—the Buchta Dancers swoop and glide across the floor, the women with their hair teased and swept up into beehives, their skirts short and full, and their partners in narrow ties and white shirts. Interspersed with reminiscences from Tremaine are the film clips taken from the best shows on the few remaining tapes from the Public Archives of Nova Scotia.

"Don Messer's Jubilee" had a successor during the '80s. The show was "Up Home Tonight," which ran for several years on the ATV network. As with the Messer show, the theme was rural but the house band was smaller and its musical personality was closer to bluegrass and gospel style. Band leader Gordon Stobbe was and is an extremely capable bluegrass fiddler and mandolin player, and the others were Skip Holmes on banjo and guitar, Bruce Chapman on piano and Alex Reitsma on double bass. The resident vocal trio, three women who called themselves Sugartime, specialized in singing country, gospel and oldtime tunes in close, three-part harmony. The show always began with a shot of a truck rolling up to a country house. The set captured the flavor of a traditional kitchen party. It was furnished with an old-fashioned stove, wooden tables and rocking chairs; and the guests crowded around as they would at a real-life ceilidh. The Boys in the Band, as the house band of accomplished musicians called itself, could play anything from honky-tonk to folk. Their guests, too, ranged through the entire spectrum of downeast musical style. Like "Don Messer's Jubilee," the programs presented traditional Maritime musical activity in all its fascinating variety: there were bluegrass bands, country singers, Celtic acts such as the Rankin Family and the Barra MacNeils, Acadian singers, stepdancers and many others.

Neatly produced and scripted, the show looked tight and professional. Gordon Stobbe made an engagingly genuine and easy-going master of ceremonies, playing lead fiddle, cracking jokes, introducing acts and keeping the pace snappy and flowing. "Up Home Tonight" filled a vacuum in television programming. By the mid-'80s, only one show, "The Tommy Hunter Show," regularly programmed established Canadian country talent on the CBC network. It was also broadcast on the Nashville Network where Canadians had to vie with Americans for a spot. (In 1992, after 27 years, the corporation finally axed "The Tommy Hunter Show.") For musicians trying to establish a career, "Up Home Tonight" was a good place to test themselves in a friendly atmosphere. The Rankins and the Barra MacNeils have become the show's most distinguished graduates. After "Up Home To-night" was cancelled, it went into a few seasons of repeats before disappearing altogether. In the '90s, the hottest, and the only professionally produced, country show in the maritimes is ATV's "Joan Kennedy Show."

It would probably make Don Messer happy to know that the fiddle music he loved best still flourishes. One of his violins was donated to the Country Music Hall of Fame in Nashville and his personal library is held in a collection at the Public Archives of Nova Scotia. But even more important than his personal fame is the fact that the fiddle tradition, which some thought might die along with him, has been born again. Dozens of oldtime fiddling festivals and competitions take place not only in the Maritimes, but around the entire country. Participants include seven-year-olds, octogenarians, and all ages between. One of the biggest competitions is the Maritime Oldtime Fiddling Contest, held each summer in Dartmouth for more than 40 years now. Prizes are handed out in many categories—best waltz, best jig, best reel—but the most prestigious award goes to the fiddler, male or female, resident in the Maritimes, who accumulates the highest number of points overall in the classes. That fiddler wins the highest distinction that the thousands of fans of maritime fiddling can award—the Don Messer trophy.

Halifax Chronicle Herald/Dave Grandy

CHAPTER 4

Stompin' Tom

Hero of the hometown

Don Tremaine can still remember the first time Stompin' Tom Connors appeared on the CBC's television show "Countrytime." A CBC executive, unaware of the wild popularity of Connors's hit *Bud the Spud*, watched the show being taped and came out shaking his head in bewilderment. He told Tremaine, "My God, I've seen it all now. A great big guy comes out with a guitar in one hand and a piece of plywood in the other, and kicks the shit out of both of them."

Connors picked up his distinctive habit of pounding a sheet of plywood with the heel of his boot to keep time when he first started playing in noisy taverns. Subtle effects are wasted on the Saturday night crowds out for a few beers and a good old hell-raising time. The pounding heel soon became a part of Stompin' Tom's image. He never showed the slightest hint of self-consciousness about it, or of wanting to become yet another of the clone acts who sing whatever is on top of the Nashville charts. Connors, a strong-minded individualist, played (and still plays) for people who didn't want to hear about blue moons in Kentucky, or cabins in the Ozarks or Texas cattle roundups. A Stompin' Tom Connors song is aggressively Canadian, and deliberately ordinary. He

writes and sings about common topics that are so much a part of ordinary Canadian culture, the rest of us don't take much notice of them. Hockey. Spuds. Don Messer. Snowmobiles.

Connors may be the closest thing to a country music outlaw that Canada has produced. His outspoken criticisms of the press, the Canadian music industry, radio programmers, and "border jumpers"—the musicians who leave home to find more work and recognition south of the border—have been making entertainment headlines for years. At one point, he was so frustrated with what he perceived as the neglect of Canadian talent that he packed up his Juno awards and sent them back to Canadian Academy of Recording Arts and Sciences as an act of protest. For close to a dozen years he stayed well out of the public eye, defying the common wisdom that without good public relations and carefully managed photo opportunities, a performer's career is as good as dead. His reputation has survived, something that can rarely be said about a musician whose records are infrequently played on major country music stations. In fact, Stompin' Tom Connors's reputation may even have grown during his exile. Jazz singer Holly Cole, in a CBC television interview broadcast in November of 1991, told reporter Laurie Brown that one of her ambitions was to make a record with Stompin' Tom Connors. To prove her dedication to the idea, Cole sang the jingle from the commercial that Connors taped for the P.E.I. tourism department some time in the '70s.

Stompin' Tom is a cultural symbol, a fact that was often commented upon during his comeback 1990 and 1991 tours. In the December issue of the entertainment magazine *Network*, editor Maureen Littlejohn's Christmas wish list included one tongue-in-cheek wish: that "...a coup d'etat led by Stompin' Tom ousts Brian Mulroney and the national anthem becomes *Canada Day, Up Canada Way*."

When Connors appeared on "Countrytime" in the early '70s, it had just been created by CBC television in Halifax as a half-hour country variety show designed to fit neatly into what was called the "suicide slot"—right after the hockey game on Saturday night. It aired between 1970 and 1974. Don Tremaine, co-host of the show along with singer Myrna Lorrie, fondly calls it "the show that never got on the air." If the hockey game went into overtime, which it often did, any devoted fans who stayed up late to catch the show might get only five or ten minutes of it. But after the cancellation of "Don Messer's Jubilee," it became one of only a few remaining opportunities for Maritime country talent to get television exposure. The musical director was Vic Mullen.

"Countrytime" was usually taped in the Dartmouth High School auditorium. The guests ranged from major stars such as Gary Buck, to local or regionally based groups still trying to get a toehold in the business. The menu ranged from cover versions of country chart hits by Merle Haggard and Johnny Cash to bluegrass instrumentals and gospel music. The sets, compared to that of a big-budget productions such as the "Tommy Hunter Show," were embarrassingly simple. The house band was certainly competent, though many of the guests have since sunk into obscurity. Stompin' Tom Connors is probably the most durable performer left over from that particular show.

Connors was born to a single mother in New Brunswick in 1936. His early years were rough and tumble. A children's aid organization finally took him from his mother and placed him in a Saint John orphanage where his life took a turn for the worse. As Connors was to tell writer Alden Nowlan in a profile published in *Maclean's* magazine in 1970, "...they beat hell out of me, and everybody else, with leather straps and bamboo canes and whatever else they could lay their hands on, and if they couldn't find anything to hit you with they grabbed you by the hair and almost twisted your friggin' head off. I ran away from there every chance I got." Unlike Hank Snow, whose early life was also deeply troubled, the memories of that time do not seem to have marked Connors with any lasting bitterness. At seven, he was sent to live with a foster family named Aylward in Skinner's Pond, Prince Edward Island. Though he eventually ran away from there, just as he had from the orphanage, it is the place that he always calls his home.

Skinner's Pond gave him a sense of stability for the first time in his young but already troubled life. At the one-room schoolhouse where he learned to read and write, he began to memorize poetry and then to write his own verses and later a few tunes to go with them. Though he was well treated by his new family, Connors was a restless teenager and finally one of his periodic attempts to run away from home succeeded. He made his way to Saint John, New Brunswick, took a room in a boardinghouse and started to look for a job. In a greasy spoon restaurant called the Silver Rail, Connors ran into another kid who would become his friend and travelling companion—"Stevedore" Steve Foote.

They met, apparently, when Connors asked Foote to play a Hank Snow song on the jukebox. At the time Snow was one of Nashville's biggest stars, regarded with proprietary pride as one of the Maritime region's favorite sons.

Stompin' Tom's dramatic use of black and the slight suggestion of a smile around the corners of his mouth are captured in this publicity photo. Note the words "Proud Canadian" and the maple-leaf on the peg board of his guitar.

Connors and Foote both liked country music; Connors had bought himself a guitar and was teaching himself to play it. He listened intently to the songs his idols played—singers such as Snow, Wilf Carter, Jimmie Rodgers and later, Johnny Cash. But as much as he liked a good hurtin' song and the sound of a good country band—fiddle, mandolin, steel guitar and bass—Connors was more interested in expressing his own ideas than in imitating anybody else's.

At that time, despite the obvious success of hometown boys such as Carter and Snow, the idea of earning a living by playing your own music was only a dream, something that only happened to other people. Connors had already begun on the succession of jobs that would support him, and eventually give him story ideas for his songs. He worked on coal boats running from New Brunswick to Newfoundland, and in logging camps, as a short order cook on skid row in Toronto, and then as a gravedigger. They were the kind of jobs casual laborers take when they need quick money, and don't mind hard work and getting their hands dirty. Connors would stay on the job long enough to save a few dollars and then take off again for the open road, restless as ever. For nearly 10 years, sometimes with his buddy Steve and sometimes alone, he crisscrossed the Canadian countryside, sightseeing, hitch-hiking with truckers or friendly drivers, and when necessary, taking on more odd jobs such as a stint picking tobacco outside Tillsonburg in southern Ontario. Connors always brought his guitar along and occasionally busked for passers-by. Often when he and Foote arrived in a new town, broke and without a place to stay, they sought shelter and a hard wooden bench for the night in the local jail. After Connors sang a few songs for the officers on duty, one of them would even give them a meal ticket for a cheap restaurant, or a handful of coins to buy breakfast.

Sometimes Connors and Foote split to go their separate ways, but they always met up again. They hitch-hiked to Mexico and crossed the border into the United States illegally, heading for Connors's goal, Nashville. Connors made his way to Rainbow Ranch in hopes of seeing Hank Snow, but Snow refused to see him—a snub which rankled for some years. Back in Canada, they split up again, with Connors heading north. By this time, after years of scribbling out his own songs, he had built up a substantial repertoire of original music and had visited radio stations and record companies to inquire about getting work as a performer, though without success. Other Canadian musicians were experiencing similar difficulty in trying to get station managers to listen to their original songs, but in those days before any regulations requiring stations to guarantee a certain percentage of Canadian content in their songlists were in effect, getting a career off the ground took years of effort. Tom Connors was stubborn, but he didn't plan to wait around for a record executive to call him. So he kept moving.

One thing Connors always did on the road was visit libraries. As he told journalist Alden Nowlan, he'd left school early and his time in the orphanage had taught him little about life except that it could be repressive and painful. Sitting in public reading rooms, Connors gravitated to books that could explain things to a curious and intelligent man. When he surprised Nowlan by a random quote from the Koran, Connors admitted "Yeah, I've read it, the Koran, and the Buddhist scriptures and the Hindu scriptures, and a lot of psychology and stuff. In libraries mostly, when I was on the road." Connors writes about things that are real and important to him: the places he's been, experiences he's had, and people he meets or whom he respects. The continuing process of self-education has led him to study Canadian history, simply because it interests him. He has written songs inspired by it such as *Massacre of the Black Donnellys*, about the murderous feuds of the Donnellys of Ontario, or about Wop May, the bush pilot who captured the Mad Trapper, or *Fire in the Mine*, about a mine fire in Timmins, Ontario.

Tom Connors is often called Canada's version of America's Woody Guthrie. Composer of *This Land is Your Land*, Guthrie wrote protest songs during the '30s and '40s about the plight of displaced farmers and laborers who trekked across the American southwest. He observed the lives of the ordinary people he met and spent time with, and turned them into lively social commentaries set to music in songs such as *Talking Dust Bowl Blues* and *Philadelphia Lawyer*. Stompin' Tom may not have been consciously influenced by Guthrie, but like the American folksinger, he created a specifically native body of folk/country songs that reflected the reality he saw around him.

Some critics, even some country music fans, have criticized Stompin' Tom's songs for a variety of reasons—they were too limited musically, they were corny, and frequently ungrammatical. Typically, Connors took these objections in stride. He told the producers of "Country Gold": "I've often been accused that my lyrics are not sophisticated, and they're crude, and this and that. Well, they're meant to be that way. They're definitely meant to be that way because it's in the vernacular of the people whom I'm singing about. If I'm singing about miners, then I have miners' phrases incorporated into the song. If I'm singing about tobacco workers, it's the same thing. Wherever I'm at—if I'm writing a song about Newfoundlanders I'm going to try to sound as Newfie as I damn well can."

On a trip to northern Ontario, Connors arrived in Timmins all but flat broke and went to the Maple Leaf Hotel for a cold beer. But a beer cost 40 cents, and Connors was a nickel short. A waiter noticed his guitar case and offered him a deal: a beer in exchange for a few songs. By the end of the evening Connors had been offered a job singing in the Travel Host Lounge on Friday and Saturday nights. He was paid cash for it with a free room at the hotel thrown in. He spent the next 14 months at the Maple Leaf, supplementing the engagement with other local gigs: radio and television shows, bars, legions, dances, shopping malls—all the places that need live entertainment. At this stage of his career, Connors didn't mind the occasional request for a country standard or something fresh off the hit parade, but he was

Connors and his plywood stompin' board at a Halifax concert in the early '70s.

Halifax Chronicle Herald

gradually working into his songlist more and more of his own songs. The audiences loved them.

It was around then that a few bar owners complained about his habit of pounding the floor with his left foot when he sang. They said that it ripped up rugs and left dents in the wooden floors. The pounding foot was an unconscious gesture. Connors had learned to play the guitar while sitting and vigorously beating his foot to keep time. When he performed standing up, the booted left foot raising high and slamming straight down on the floor became a part of his normal stage routine. To keep the club owners happy, he placed a piece of plywood under his boot to protect the floor. That too became a part of the act, and a waiter in Peterborough soon gave him the name that stuck—Stompin' Tom Connors.

After leaving Timmins, Connors played at the Horseshoe Tavern in Toronto. He moved to Toronto in 1969, and attained a certain amount of notoriety around town when someone put up billboards that said "Stomp Out Stompin' Tom." Connors claimed that he didn't know who did it, or whether the person was genuinely trying to snuff out his popularity or slyly trying to create more sympathy for him. Connors denied that he himself had put up the billboards as a self-promotion gimmick. He told Alden Nowlan, "…damn few people are neutral about me when they hear me sing! I do know it wasn't me, not on the $200 a week I was getting paid then." A happy combination of publicity and public demand finally got him a recording contract with Dominion and his first single for them, *Bud the Spud*, became a national hit.

Bud was written as a salute to Bud Roberts, a friend who drove a potato truck for a living. The song begins with a blast from a truck horn—presumably, it's Bud rolling down the road carting a load of what Connors likes to call "the best darn potatoes that's ever been growed." The grammar is deliberately uncouth. Musically, Stompin' Tom had found his own style—half singing, half reciting the verses, and bellowing out the chorus with great gusto. The song outlines Bud Roberts' journey from P.E.I. overland to the terminal dock in Toronto where the potatoes are off-loaded. Connors sings the chorus, but recites the verse over a backup and at the end of each one, raises his voice to a near-shout on the final line about another big load of potatoes. It's less a song than it is an anthem to long-distance truck drivers, especially those on the long hauls from the Maritimes to Ontario. Its ordinary subject matter, not usually seen as worth singing about, is ironically funny. But there is no mockery of those who make their living delivering P.E.I.'s most important economic crop.

Stompin' Tom was entering the music business at a time when musical categories were beginning to overlap. Folk performers such as Ian and Sylvia Tyson and Gordon Lightfoot were dabbling with country instruments such as steel guitar, and country song topics, as exemplified in Tyson's classic *Four Strong Winds*. Connors used many of the materials of country music—instruments, lyrics and harmonic style—but he used them in a personal way. He has rejected more than once any attempt to label his songs as country music. His own name for them, hometown music, is better because it is more accurate. As he saw it, he was writing for the people in his own hometown, the biggest hometown in the world because it included the entire country of Canada. His hometown people were the average working Joes who drove trucks, worked in the mines or woods, farmed or fished for a living. As with Woody Guthrie, Connors was unabashedly in favor of the common man, and his songs often resembled anecdotes overheard on Saturday afternoon at the Legion— part news, and part entertainment. Connors could walk into a tavern for a cold beer and walk out an hour later with an idea for a song. His attitude to life was often defiantly working-class. He told reporter Gretchen Pierce of the Halifax *Chronicle Herald* in a 1975 interview: "The grass roots, working man's music isn't given enough exposure because the executives don't like country music. They don't understand that a lot of the public wants it."

After the success of *Bud the Spud*, a lot of the public certainly wanted Stompin' Tom and his music. He was booked for dozens of appearances in concert halls and high school auditoriums, and sold records by the bin. At home in Prince Edward Island, his adopted province honored him with a parade, during which Connors rode through the streets of Charlottetown on the back of a truck loaded with potatoes. Civic gestures are rarely so appropriate as the one awarded him at the time. He was given a gold-plated potato as a token of appreciation for the attention he'd drawn to the island.

Stompin' Tom was riding the crest not only of Canadian nationalism, but of regional pride. Instead of pretending to be from Texas or from Nashville, Canadian musicians were thrilling to the discovery that the music they made up themselves and played at home was as good as, and often better than, that which was imported. Connors's songs, by implication, asked why songs about Kentucky and Texas should be considered universally appealing? Why shouldn't Canadians write songs about the places they knew best, such as Saskatchewan, and the Red River? Connors mined the Canadian landscape rather than the Tennessee hills, striking into a rich and unsung vein of Canadian places and stories, and carrying out unrefined but pure gold nuggets of nationalism such as *Movin' on to Rouyn, Algoma Central #69,* and the alltime Connors favorite, *Sudbury Saturday Night.*

One album that contains a cross-section of Connors's work is *Bud the Spud.* The album cover shows—what else?— a dozen potatoes, with a small inset photo of the singer himself. Again one is struck by the humor of ordinariness elevated to art. According to the liner notes, Connors acted as producer as well as writing all the songs, but there are no credits given to backup players. Presumably, they are the Roving Cowboys, the group that toured with him at that time. Connors takes a no-nonsense attitude to record production. The sound is clear and gimmick-free—no string section, no horn solos, no backup singers, no synthesizer. Both songwriting and delivery reflect an earlier, less complicated style of ballad making. Both are closer to the Wilf Carter songs of the late '40s, than to the contemporary style of a songwriter like Kris Kristofferson in the late '60s.

Structurally, Connors's songs are also straightforward— usually three to five verses, sometimes more in a long story ballad, but nearly always with a chorus between verses. In the lyrics there is always a rhyme scheme and a regular metrical pattern, though sometimes a tormented line is more akin to doggerel than to poetry. He loves to use sound effects— sirens, whistles, surf sounds or wind—to heighten the drama. The words and melody are supported by the naive triadic harmonies beginner guitarists learn to use to accompany singalongs. In the key of D, for example, Connors will stick to the unaltered tonic, dominant and sub-dominant chords of D, A and G. All of these devices make his songs easy to sing and his lyrics easy to remember.

After *Bud the Spud,* as a timely garnish, the *Ketchup Song* relates the tale of a guy from P.E.I., whose nickname is "potato," who marries a "tomato," and produces two spuds and one tomato. Somehow Connors can bring off this corny stuff with high-spirited good humor, applying the art of slapstick to songwriting. *Ben in the Pen* is a jail song—a boy goes wrong and kills his girl and a policeman in the course of a robbery. On top of the refrain, the sound of a hammer hitting a spike sharply suggests both the violence of the encounter and its likely consequence, contrasting the crime of passion with the flat eternity of meaningless hard labor on the prison rockpile. It is a good example of the way Connors can introduce a special effect to intensify the tragedy of a song, with cartoon-like simplicity. *Rubberhead* is a kiss-off song—a sendup of the conventional farewell scenes depicted in many country love songs. She cheats, he asks her to stop, and after breaking up they insult each other like children on a playground with taunts of "rubberhead." *Luke's Guitar* is vintage Connors. It begins with Stompin' Tom jigging the tune with a little mouth music ("Twang, twang a diddle dang.") The lyrics are about a demanding wife who makes her husband sell nearly everything they own so that she can keep buying clothes. By the end of the song the beleaguered husband has hocked his watch, ring, stove and other worldly goods, but draws the line at hocking his guitar.

Connors, in the woodsman's plaid, at a concert in Truro during his 1990 cross-country tour.

My Brother Paul is another recitation in which Connors indulges his fondness for dramatic verisimilitude. He narrates the song in the shaky, infirm voice of an invalid who, it turns out, has been sponging off his long-suffering brother Paul. The final cut, *The Old Atlantic Shore* combines two ideas: it celebrates the docks, seagulls and tides of the seashore, and, as an afterthought, also mentions the girl who is, naturally, waiting there.

Stompin' Tom's canvas is the entire Canadian landscape just as much as his subject is popular Canadian history. On the second side of *Bud the Spud*, *My Little Eskimo* and *Reversing Falls Darling* exemplify the former. His acknowledgement of bilingualism and cross-cultural romance in *She Don't Speak English*, the latter. And in *The Canadian Lumberjack*, Connors draws on his own experience to write a blue-collar working man's song. Connors once worked in a lumber camp in northern Quebec where he acquired a reasonable command of the language spoken by one-fifth of Canadians, judging by the three verses he sings in French. In all these songs, typically, the instrumental arrangements are unremarkable for the most part—bass, lead guitar and steel guitar solos in the breaks. Connors is fully capable of introducing a limbo beat as he does in *T.T.C. Skedaddler*, for example. But the drum and percussion parts remain in the background and serve mainly to keep the song moving along briskly, as they do the next song *I'll Be Gone with the Wind*.

The other notable song on the album, perhaps his second most famous one (or the first, if you come from Ontario), is *Sudbury Saturday Night*. It is another anthem for the working man, written specifically about the INCO (International Nickel Company) workers in Sudbury, but it could have been written about any employee of any factory, mine or industrial complex anywhere in the country. The rhymes shatter some poetic rules—Connors rhymes "bingo" and "stinko" in the very first stanza—but he captures the weekend mood of people who work hard on long shifts, and regard Saturday night as an opportunity to party. The rhythms are rollicking and joyful to suit the occasion. Songs such as *Sudbury Saturday Night*, *Fire in the Mine* and *Horseshoe Hotel Song* made Stompin' Tom a kind of folk-hero among people who weren't used to perceiving the everydayness of their lives as something to sing about. Some years later, Connors told Alden Nowlan, "I guess they were tired of hearing about the stars falling on Alabama and about people waltzing in Tennessee. They wanted to hear some songs about the north country. Their country."

Above all, Connors writes in the language of the itinerant laborer, the hired man on the farm living in the bunkhouse, the truckdriver known to the waitresses at the truck-stop. He neither makes use of the starry-eyed conventions of romance, nor does his language rise above the ordinary. Its greatest virtue is that it is common, and therefore recognizable, and that quality gives his songs a sense of realism.

Tom Connors worked not only on his own career, after his initial successes, but on those of other aspiring musicians. In 1971 he and his then manager Jury Krytiuk formed Boot Records to help promote new talent. Boot was at first an outlet for Stompin' Tom's own recordings, but it soon began to add a few other country and folk artists. Some came from the Atlantic provinces—Newfoundland singer Dick Nolan, Stevedore Steve Foote, and in 1975, a shy young singer from Cape Breton named Rita MacNeil.

Though he spent up to six months of the year touring around and playing concerts, Connors showed little interest in conquering Nashville. For many years in his concerts he told the story of how people ask him why he doesn't do "some of them nice Nashville songs." His retort is that he'll be happy to do some of them nice Nashville songs as soon as some of those Nashville folks sing some of his songs, about his country. The emphasis he puts on the last three words make an ironic commentary on country songwriting in general—though it's not difficult to find Canadian country songs that refer to Texas or California, you would have to be a musical detective to find Canadian references in songs by American writers.

Connors's bristly attitude towards the dominance of Nashville would become more pronounced in time, but for a while he enjoyed a honeymoon with the public and the media. From 1970-1974 he annually won the Juno Award for best male country singer, and in 1973 his album *To It And At It* took the Juno for best country album. In 1972 he made a television special called "This is Stompin' Tom," and another, "Across This Land with Stompin' Tom," made in 1974, featured a journey across Canada with Connors as guide, and included an excerpt of him performing live with his band at the Horseshoe Tavern. By 1977, at the age of 41, he had already written more than 500 songs, conferring immortality through song upon Canadian places and events, and thereby stirring national pride. Thus he endeared himself not just to the working class alone, but also to many members of the middle class with liberal sympathies for those who live by honest toil.

He became something of a media darling, his face and his distinctive voice ("full of gravel and beer" as broadcaster Peter Gzowski once called it) becoming as instantly recognizable as that of Prime Minister Pierre Elliott Trudeau. Even people who didn't follow country music could hardly avoid Tom Connors; for several years in the '70s, he introduced CBC's popular weekly consumer show "Marketplace" with the theme music he wrote for the show, *The Consumer Song*. He also wrote and recorded a song as a tourism promo for Prince Edward Island. His fans, far from being country and western rednecks, included homesick Maritimers, cultural nationalists and just plain folks. Numbered among them were writer Alden Nowlan and New Brunswick Premier Richard Hatfield. At a 1973 concert in Toronto's Massey Hall, Connors's master of ceremonies was none other than the mayor of Toronto, David Crombie.

Connors, a longtime bachelor and loner except for his buddy Steve Foote, got married around this time. He had met his future bride, Lena Welsh, while she was waitressing at the Prince Edward Lounge in Charlottetown—a lounge that is better known to country musicians and patrons simply as "J.R.'s," named after owner Johnny Reid. The couple decided to get married on television and when they tied the knot on Elwood Glover's "Luncheon Date" in November of 1973, it was the first nationally televised showbiz wedding in Canadian history. Some cynics dismissed it as a pure publicity stunt, but Stompin' Tom was, as usual, just being himself. He figured that all the people who bought his records were as close to him as his kin by birth, and as he told his audience in the television studio that day, "What a good way to give everybody a piece of my happiest moment." The occasion was also a chance to return favors to some of the people who had helped him along the way. One of the guests was Gates Lepine, the bartender from Timmins who had asked Tom to sing when he was a nickel short of a beer. Best man was lounge owner Johnny Reid, and Premier Richard Hatfield coordinated the guest list. Both Gates Lepine and Bill Lewis, a guitarist who played backup in the Connors band, sang songs. Connors didn't sing, but he did write a song to commemorate the wedding, called *We're Trading Hearts*. The television audience for the marriage of Stompin' Tom and Lena Welsh was later estimated by CBC to be approximately 2.5 million. The wedding was notable for at least one other reason—it was one of perhaps only two times the public has seen Connors without his trademark black cowboy hat. The other time may have been when he was introduced to the governor-general.

At the same time as Connors exchanged the life of a roaming bachelor for that of a happily married man, his disenchantment with the music industry was growing. He told Halifax *Chronicle Herald* reporter Gretchen Pierce in a 1975 interview that, in his opinion, the Canadian music industry faced too much competition from the bigger, richer, and far more strongly established American industry. He added, "If it weren't for the CRTC ruling on Canadian content [the Canadian Radio and Television Commission, Canada's broadcasting regulator, ruled in 1971 that Canadian AM radio stations would have to broadcast 30% Canadian content], then the stations would have continued to play 90% American music.... I believe the ruling greatly helped a lot of careers to take hold. We do need the stimulus of foreign talent but not in such great concentrations. I suggest for at least five years that Canadian content be pushed to 60% of air time. That will give us a fair chance to get an industry going." Putting his money where his mouth was, Connors continued to use Boot Records to help new young talent get that first break into the business, trying to help them avoid the exhausting struggles he had known on his own way up.

Connors's dissatisfaction with the industry came to a head in 1978 when he suddenly withdrew from the Juno Award nominations, and later returned his earlier awards. He was unhappy about the Juno nomination practices of CARAS, the Canadian Academy of Recording Arts and Sciences. Without naming specific names, Connors let it be known that he disagreed with the practice of nominating for awards the musicians he called "turncoat Canadians" or "border jumpers." (Musicians such as Joni Mitchell and Paul Anka lived and worked in the United States, but still returned home to collect Junos). Connors felt they should stick to the American Grammy awards and leave the Junos, as he put it, "to those who are living in Canada and conducting business in Canada." Connors also disagreed with some of the award categories, and with the fact that musicians were being nominated for awards in categories to which their musical styles did not correspond.

But the flawed Juno award system wasn't his only gripe. Connors had once refused to play at the Canadian National Exhibition after an argument over headliner status and fees. He had learned that American country star Charley Pride would earn a whopping $35,000 for singing only six songs, while Stompin' Tom would earn a mere $2,500 for a two-hour set. By the time Connors's various grievances—humiliating fees, lack of recognition for homegrown talent, the Junos—came to a head, he had already written hundreds of

songs, and made 29 albums. He, his wife and their small son Tommy could live comfortably off his royalties for a while. In one of the most dramatic stories of contemporary Canadian showbusiness, Stompin' Tom simply disappeared, dropping out of sight at the height of his career for the next 11 years, steadfastly refusing to perform, to give interviews, or even to tell the world where he was living.

How legitimate was his complaint about the difficulty of Canadian musicians achieving recognition at home? The story of Michael T. Wall is instructive. Wall moved to Toronto from Newfoundland in 1961 and was an instant hit with homesick expatriates who went to the various downeast and country music clubs such as the 300 Club on College Street, and the Gold Guitar Club on Parliament Street. In an open letter printed in the November 1991 issue of *Country Music News*, Wall described many thwarted efforts he made to interest a Canadian record company in his special brand of downeast country music. "They all turned me down because I didn't sing those Nashville songs!" Wall wrote. He finally went to Nashville where he managed to interest the owner of independent country music label K-Ark Records into signing him. "K-Ark Records opened a lot of doors for me," he wrote with apparent bitterness, "and John Capps gave me the break that I couldn't get here in Canada." Obviously nothing succeeds like success. Wall said that after his records got U.S. radio play, he was deemed more acceptable as a performing act back home and eventually made half a dozen albums for Rodeo Records before starting his own Downhome label. His story is, unfortunately, only too typical of the attitude of Canadian audiences towards their own. That Yankee seal of approval means everything.

Only a few can get it, however. Canadian country music often fails to appeal to American fans in anything like the numbers deemed marketable by music-industry corporations. Eddie Eastman, like Wall a country singer from Newfoundland, recorded 20 charted singles and several hit albums, and captured two Junos as best country male vocalist before he moved on to Nashville to approach the big markets. But in 1991, Eastman told editor Larry Delaney of *Country Music News*, "It's like starting your career all over again.... All the groundwork we laid in Canada to become established in the music industry is pretty much lost here. I have to start from scratch and bang on all the doors again." Eastman's story confirms Stompin' Tom's point. Canadian talent relies on national support, and needs to have its own market protected if it is not to be completely swamped by American culture. It is an argument often made, and even given lip-service by Canadian politicians. But the siren call of the global market and its North American instrument, the Free Trade Agreement with which the Canadian government inaugurated the '90s, is seen by most Canadian artists, not just Stompin' Tom, as a serious threat to the national cultural industries.

Connors remained stubbornly silent through the '80s. Some people claimed to know where he was. Some said he was living on the Magdalen Islands, another source believed he had returned to P.E.I., while still another claimed he owned property in Balinafad, Ontario. By the end of the decade, several prominent Canadians had begun pestering Connors to play concerts again. Singer k.d. lang, actor Dan Ackroyd and broadcaster Peter Gzowski all pleaded, publicly as well as privately, for Connors to come out of hiding. Gzowski finally coaxed Connors into a lengthy radio interview broadcast on CBC's "Morningside" in 1989. During their chat, Connors admitted that he still played occasionally for friends at house parties, and even that he had taken up the fiddle (which he proceeded to demonstrate with only modest success), but he still hedged about where he was living and what his plans were. That soon became clear; in July of 1989, Capitol-EMI released *Fiddle and Song*, the first Stompin' Tom record for more than a decade.

Fiddle and Song has a lengthy dedication in the liner notes to Connors's wife and son, to a P.E.I. couple named Keefe who were celebrating their golden wedding anniversary, and to five young people who had been drowned in a shipwreck off the Magdalen Islands in 1987. The back-up band is small with only four sidemen, Lena Connors doing a little work on the jaw harp, and Connors playing guitar, rhythm guitar, mandolin and fiddle as well as acting as album producer. In the notes, Connors explains that he took up fiddling a few years earlier and had written a few instrumental tunes (included on the album).

The instrumental arrangements are more elaborate than on earlier albums, but there is still no synthesizer or electric keyboard. Compared to other contemporary country recordings, the album is still a model of technical simplicity—the kind of straight-up, unvarnished country music that is rarely heard on commercial radio any more. A casual listener, even someone who doesn't know Stompin' Tom, would never mistake it for pop, rock or any other kind of music. For example, in the tribute song, *k.d.lang*, Connors's strongly nasal voice plus the combination of dobro and steel guitar make for a twangy sound more reminiscent of a 1930s barndance than a 1989 record. *Fiddler's Folly* is Stompin' Tom's public debut as a fiddler. The tune resembles *The Irish Washerwoman* set in 4/4 time, but the lyrics are original Connors, with Lena Connors in the background on jaw harp. As well as singing lead, Connors is overdubbed playing unison with the vocal line on the fiddle. His fiddle playing is spirited but he tends to saw back and forth on the bow and the doubling with the voice reveals some uncertain tunings. *It's All Over Now Anyhow* is the lament of a farmer whose wife has run off with another man, and who is about to lose his farm in an auction. Next is a version of *Quand le Soleil dit Bonjour au Montagne*, better known as *The French Song*. A pure country intro on steel guitar sets up the vocals, which Tom and Lena Connors sing together, and while their French is adequate, Lena Connors wanders slightly off pitch during her solo verse.

Stompin' Tom doesn't write many lovesongs. Possibly something about such expressions of sentiment doesn't appeal to him. But *I Never Want to See The World Again* qualifies as a hurtin' song. It's a slow ballad about an abandoned lover who stays up past midnight drinking and watching television. It's not the kind of lyric Connors does best; the song is shorter than usual—a brief four verses—and he sounds ill at ease. The following cut, *Morning and Evening and Always*, returns to a brisk tempo that serves as an antidote to the gloom of the previous song.

Hillside Hayride, another of Connors's new fiddle solos, shows him working with a traditional instrumental form, in this case a jig. Nothing personal or unusual strikes the listener about the style or the arrangement; the fiddle plays the melody over guitar accompaniment, with the guitarist occasionally doubling on the picked melody. *Return of the Sea Queen* draws on the supernatural, as do a whole genre of traditional Maritime folk ballads. It tells of the crew of a ship called the *Sea Queen* who ride out a ferocious storm, only to be turned to stone statues the next morning. It's in a minor key, which is unusual for Connors's work, and the mood is echoed by sound effects imitating thunder and the tumult of a storm at sea.

Canada Day, Up Canada Way is probably one of the few cuts that got any radio play. Here Stompin' Tom waves the flag, singing "…Where maple trees grow maple leaves/when the northern sun is high/We're Canadians and we're born again on the first day of July." In keeping with the patriotic mood, the fiddle quotes briefly from both *O Canada* and *The Maple Leaf Forever*. (Stompin' Tom either knows something about the Quebecois working man that the rest of us don't, or he is insensitive to Quebec nationalism—*The Maple Leaf Forever* celebrates in verse the victory of the British General Wolfe over the French General Montcalm on the Plains of Abraham in 1759). *Jolly Joe MacFarland* is another comic song, the kind at which Connors excels because he can associate the most outrageous ideas while in search of rhymes. In one verse, Joe falls in English Bay and catches "pneumoneeay," and falls for a mermaid. *Skinner's Pond Teapot* tells the story of a teapot given away as a gift and 50 years later returned to its original owners as a golden anniversary present. Connors treats it as a story, reciting the verses and singing the choruses.

The *Teardrop Waltz* is another fiddle solo. It's a more challenging tune than the jig, and Connors even throws in some double stops to harmonize the tune, to the accompaniment of guitar, bass and steel guitar. *Entry Island Home* is another slow ballad, this time about an expatriate Prince Edward Islander longing to leave his job in Ontario and head back home. *I Am the Wind*, a slow ballad with lots of wind sound effects and a lonely harmonica, has Connors doing a voiceover as the wind, the faceless character. It's as close as Connors gets to philosophy. The aspect of nature he usually deals with is simple and direct: rocks, mountains, roads and other tangible objects. The final song is *Wreck of the Tammy Anne*, the tale of a 1987 shipwreck in which four young people drowned off the Magdalen Islands.

In October 1989, following the release of *Fiddle and Song* Connors made his second debut before the media, the music industry and the public with a show at the Matador Club in Toronto—the first time, officially, that he had been on a stage in a dozen years. The response was so warm that Connors was pushed to play a second set. Later that fall, he appeared as guest of honor on k.d. lang's television special "Buffalo Cafe." When Connors was introduced, the burst of enthusiasm from the audience was unmistakable. Before he had sung a note, they were on their feet cheering, clapping and yelling to welcome him back. Together with his band, Connors played some of his signature tunes, including *Gumboot Cloggeroo* and the new song he had composed for lang herself, *Lady k.d. lang*.

Connors began to make arrangements for a national tour beginning in the spring of 1990, coordinated by Rocklands Talent and Management in Peterborough, Ontario. Rocklands' president, Brian Edwards, booked appearances into 70 venues coast to coast and at the first concert, held in Sudbury in early May, Connors's teenage son, Tommy, watched his father onstage for the first time. The tour was also an opportunity to pay back some friendly debts. When he appeared at the Mariposa Folk Festival in Barrie, Ontario, that June, Maritime singer/songwriter Tom Gallant opened

for him. A fervent admirer, Gallant had written a tribute song called *Hero Stompin' Tom*, and Connors, never one to forget a friend, was returning the favor.

The tour turned into something of a national love-in. Discouraged by the failure of the Meech Lake Accord and fed up with politicians, Canadians, especially college-age males, flocked to Tom Connors's concerts to cheer for the man who seemed to be about the only person left with no mixed feelings about his patriotism. Sellout crowds were common. At Hamilton Place, Connors remained after the concert to sign autographs for nearly two hours. Brian Edwards told a *Country Music News* reporter that over half the audiences in Western Canada consisted of university and college students who thought that Stompin' Tom was the greatest Canadian in the country and should run for political office. At many concerts, Connors received rousing ovations merely by walking onstage, and audiences stood on their chairs, waved Canadian flags and shouted out the lyrics to the songs.

Maritime stops on the Connors tour included Summerside, Charlottetown, and the Centre 2000 in Sydney. The newspaper ads pointedly described the show as "100% Canadian entertainment" and though Connors was wary of giving media interviews, attendance at most events was high. In Halifax, he appeared at the Halifax Forum in August. His backup band billed themselves as the Merry Mick-Ray—the personnel consisting of Mary MacIntyre on fiddle and keyboard, Ray Keating on lead guitar, Mickey Andrews on steel guitar, and J.P. Cormier on fiddle, guitar and mandolin.

The stage, rising to chest height from the Forum floor, occupied the north end of the Forum. The modest set featured a large Canadian flag with a fleur-de-lis centered on it. Rows of chairs on the floor, as well as the seats at the side, filled up rapidly with excited patrons. When the Merry Mick-Ray band came on, they were minus fiddler J.P. Cormier,

Stompin' Tom publicity photo for Boot Records, advertising his first album marking his return from ten years of self-imposed exile from the Canadian music scene.

who was competing at an old-time fiddling contest that night. The band played a couple of warm-up tunes—a rousing honky-tonk number called *Cape Breton and You*, and one of Connors's own tunes, the *Maritime Waltz*. By the time they got around to a real crowd-pleaser, *Sonny's Dream*, the audience was already fidgeting in anticipation. When Stompin' Tom finally strode on stage in his familiar black cowboy boots, dark stove-pipe pants, leather vest and black cowboy hat, the applause and cheering drowned out the announcer.

Carrying his guitar and the inevitable piece of plywood, Connors appeared to have changed very little. His face, seen from a distance, was still lean, his cheekbones high, his skin perhaps a little more weathered. It was impossible to see if his hair had greyed or gotten thin, concealed as it was by his cowboy hat.

The band tore into *Bud the Spud* and the cheers hardly let up during the song, sometimes even drowning out Connors's penetrating voice. But none of the commotion seemed to distract him; if anything, he seemed pleased that the response was so rambunctious. The band was well-coordinated, obviously well rehearsed and used to following his leads. Though the audience's clapping to the music was usually out of time, Connors never allowed it to either drag or speed him up, and he punched out the words with machine-gun clarity.

Between songs, Connors took swigs from a glass placed strategically within his reach. Saying, "You all know how a Newfie takes a drink?" After pouring some liquid into the glass, Connors drank directly from the pitcher. He followed it up by saying, "Drunks are better off than alcoholics because they don't have to attend all those meetings, " and topped off the succession of booze jokes by telling the one about the Newfoundlander who staggers up to a cab waiting outside a Toronto tavern and asks, "Got room for twenty-four beer and a pizza?" When the cabbie says yes, Connors pantomimed the drunk throwing up into the cab. Groans, as well as laughter filled the Forum; these were not new jokes or even particularly good ones, and they were shamelessly ethnic, but Connors clearly knew his audience, and he told them with such gusto the audience was helpless. After the next song, Connors apologized for his slightly raspy voice by saying, "I worked in the northern Quebec woods—that's how I got this frog in my throat." Nobody dares tell such jokes any more, but for the crowd that night, Connors could do no wrong. His blue-collar humor was even liberating. He was preaching to his constituency.

Like most country music fans, the Halifax crowd was demonstrative. Some sang along, others ran down to the area in front of the stage to snap photos, and a few couples even danced at the back of the arena. During *Tillsonburg*, the singing turned to bellowing, as some of the rowdiest participants shouted out the word on each chorus. You were sitting in a hockey arena, but the atmosphere was that of a Saturday night pub. After a few more songs, *Luke's Guitar* and *Mukluk Annie*, the crowd showed definite signs of getting unruly. Most of the songs so far had been uptempo, high-energy numbers which accelerated the general noise level, but Connors seemed unflappable. Just before intermission, he made a more serious interjection. Several times during the tour, he had spoken out in public about his concern for Canadian culture and about the country's fate in the wake of the collapsed Meech Lake deal. He roared now, "If we're ever gonna get this country together we're gonna have to wake it up. The rest of Canada should join Quebec and we'll all separate together!" Amidst applause, and cries of "Tom for Prime Minister!" he started *Gumboot Cloggeroo*.

With the lights up at intermission, it was easier to get a good look at the crowd—yuppies, seniors, couples towing small children and surprisingly large numbers of young men around college age or in their early 20s. Many wore T-shirts with Canadian flags, or carried small flags around with them. Down in front of the stage, manager Brian Edwards supervised a brisk trade in T-shirts and Stompin' Tom cassettes. When asked about the number of young adults present,

Edwards said it was like that everywhere on this tour. In his opinion many of the university students he talked to regarded Connors as a combination of father figure and patriot. Edwards may be right; several of the groups of young men carried large, unfurled Canadian flags which they held up proudly during the show.

After intermission, Connors returned to the stage for a second set. He kept up the patriotic mood with *Cross Canada*, which spells out many of the geographic glories of the country, and followed it with a song about the Bluenose, then one about the Miramichi, and one about Cape Breton. He had apparently decided to include a song about every region of the country—a suspicion later confirmed when, introducing a song about the Magdalen Islands, he said "I try not to forget anybody." Next came *Mufferaw Joe*, then *Sudbury Saturday Night*. By this time, the cheering had become continuous and members of the audience started dancing in celebration. Earlier, Connors had commented that what began as a concert was turning into a party but when the more enthusiastic dancers moved into the aisles or headed for the stage, they were politely but firmly turned away by security guards. People bellowed requests, or wrote them down on slips of paper to be passed up front. Connors accepted them readily enough, even studied one or two a bit and wise-cracked about the "University of Skinner's Pond."

At one point, a young man walked down to the front of the stage carrying an oblong piece of plywood about two feet long, with a small Canadian flag stuck in it at one end. As any other autograph-hunter would do, he handed it to Stompin' Tom. Connors grabbed it, immediately threw it to the floor at his feet and promptly stomped it two or three times before handing it back to the fan. The grinning young man headed back to his seat accompanied by a wave of delighted applause and laughter. The rapport between singer and fans had now gone completely beyond the need for words.

As the concert headed into the home-stretch, Connors introduced a song he had recently written for Rita MacNeil.

It was a sweet, surprisingly gentle waltz, a slower and softer ballad than most of the other songs in the show. Just before his last tune of the night, Connors made a pitch for Canadian music and performers, urging the fans to encourage their children to learn an instrument and make music, so that when Stompin' Tom quits, they can take over. He also pointed out that the performers onstage are dedicated to 100% Canadian music as they moved into the song that had so far been the theme of the summer's tour—*Unity*. As expected, the audience called him back to encore *Bud the Spud*. There was no second encore, but when it was announced that Stompin' Tom would be coming out front shortly to sign autographs, a long, happy line formed within seconds.

The tour continued into the fall, ending with an appearance at the National Arts Centre in Ottawa in October. Capitol Records gave Connors an award at the end of the tour; he had sold 165,000 units, much of it re-released material. Another album was released in the spring of 1991, called *More of the Stompin' Tom Phenomenon*. It included, among others, a new song about J.R.'s Bar and Grill. Another tour was scheduled for 1991, but this time there were no bookings on the east coast. The response was as rapturous as ever; if he wanted to tap into patriotic impulses, Connors could hardly have planned a better time to make a comeback. Publicity again was scarce, but friendly coverage by sources such as *Country Music News* indicated that attendance figures were as high as ever. At Lulu's Roadhouse in Kitchener, Ontario, for instance, Connors sold out for the second year in a row, and the smash singalong hit with the crowd was his single release *Margo's Cargo*.

But anyone who expects to hear Stompin' Tom's music on the radio will probably wait in vain. Because of the many comments he's made about Canadian radio programmers and disc jockeys and what he perceives as their refusal to present more native talent on the airwaves, Connors has been effectively blacklisted from most of the commercial radio stations across the country. Some of the smaller regional stations still play his material faithfully, but the largest commercial stations, especially in urban areas, have largely cut him from their playlist.

In "Country Gold," broadcast early in 1992, Connors talked about his ambiguous relationship with radio broadcasting. He told the unseen interviewer, "For some reason, from day one radio has been telling me I don't fit their format. So if I haven't fit their format since 1964, it makes me wonder, do they ever change their format?"

There are a few exceptions to that observation, however. A number of stations in the Maritimes have weekly spots in which they play only listeners' requests, oldtime favorites from the '40s, '50s and '60s, or roots music recorded by musicians who fall outside the usual format of country radio. For five years, musician and record producer George Brothers had such a show every Sunday night on station Q-93 in Charlottetown. Called "The Walter Picott Chev-Olds-Cadillac Jamboree," Brothers's show featured 100% Island music. Regarded as an Islander by adoption if not actually by birth, Connors definitely qualified for membership in the club.

Some of the material Brothers played would not make it to prime time radio because of varying quality in both production and performance. Yet Brothers reports that the show's ratings indicated a large and devoted listenership. Listeners often reminded him of things he'd just said on recent broadcasts, and he believes that the close-knit communities on the Island tend to support one another, and support local talent by buying locally produced cassettes. The format of the show has altered slightly since Brothers left in September of 1991; it features more mainstream artists, both in recordings and in interviews.

Another show which has consistently played Stompin' Tom's music is "Saturday Night Hoedown," hosted by J.P. Goody on station CFCY. Each Saturday night from six until nine, Goody plays vintage country music, despite CFCY's rock

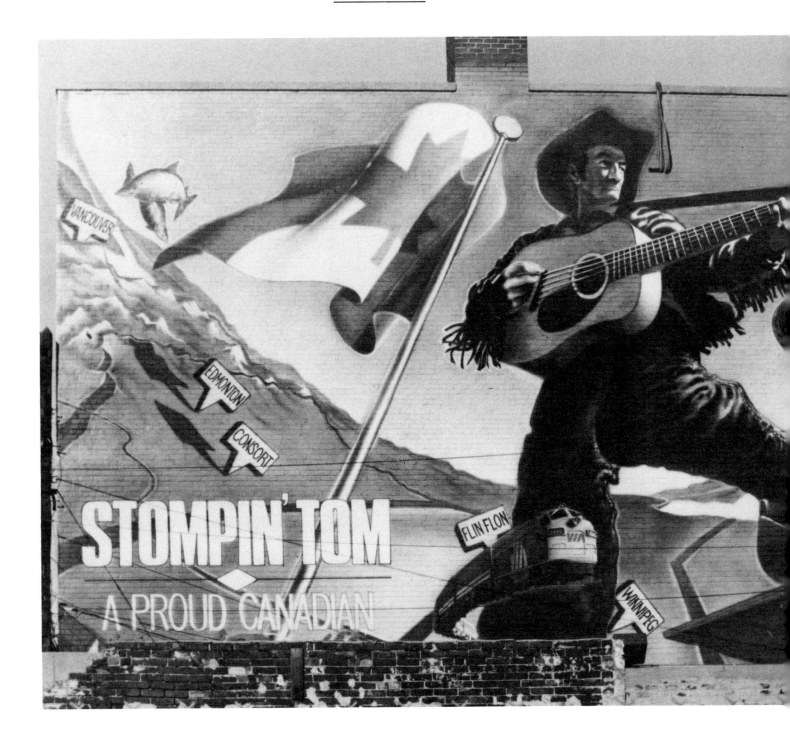

format and according to George Brothers, during that timespot they have the largest listening audience of any show in eastern Canada. "Somewhere around 175,000," says Brothers, adding, "People from the Gaspé, people from western Newfoundland, Cape Breton, northern Nova Scotia would write in requests." The format is eclectic country with current hits by contemporaries like Randy Travis but also a lot of old favorites by Hank Williams and Hank Snow, with a mandatory 15-minute Don Messer segment each week. Of Messer's continuing popularity in the Maritimes, Brothers says "If they took the Messer segment off, they'd have riots on their hands." As George Brothers sees it, Goody's main contribution to sustaining country music in this region is that his program content isn't determined by current record ratings in *Billboard* or by charts made up in Toronto. "J.P. Goody is a real hero to me," says Brothers, "because he's been playing that show for 15 or so years and really giving the audience what they want to hear. And they're telling him what they want to hear, and he puts it on. How much more democratic can you get than that?" Brothers thinks that it's the downhome flavor that keeps people tuning in. "A lot of it is in the style of the show, because he would play requests like, 'To Tammy, who still likes Bobby, who drives a brown pickup truck,' that sort of thing."

Stompin' Tom's public personality as the guy just in town from Skinner's Pond tugs powerfully at the loyalty of many Islanders, yet at both his 1990 concerts on the Island there were empty seats in the house. Ticket prices too rich for Island pockets may well have been the cause. Ticket prices throughout the Maritimes ranged from 15 to 20 dollars a seat—low by central Canadian standards, but quite pricey for Stompin' Tom's blue-collar constituency. Had the tickets been more affordable, Brothers is convinced that the concert would have been standing room only.

Stompin' Tom striding the nation like a colossus on a mural painted on a brick wall.

The release of *Fiddle and Song* and *More of the Stompin' Tom Phenomenon* both resulted in a flurry of media stories reporting Connors to be resolute in his conviction that few members of the press or the country music establishment support his campaign for more Canadian talent on the airwaves.

Though Connors is the most prominent of the Prince Edward Island musicians to achieve national notice, he is by no means the only one. Of all the soloists and groups based on the Island, the Ellis Family has been P.E.I.'s leading country band for at least 10 years. The four Ellis brothers, Rick, Brian, Dave and Steve, plus cousin Greg McDonald, have followed the usual route of regionally based bands; they toured, recorded in Nashville and played gigs in modest venues. Using the traditional country instrumentation of guitars, bass and drums, their trademark is their high vocal style, reminiscent of bluegrass music. Despite having had a dozen or more nationally charted singles, and several nominations as group of the year at the Canadian County Music Awards, the Ellises have gradually scaled back their touring and appearances and kept their day jobs. George Brothers reports that at the 1989 P.E.I. Country and Traditional Music Awards show, the Ellises, much of whose music is original, won in the categories of best album, best single, best country group and entertainer of the year—"everything except best female vocalist." After a number of busy years, the decision to scale down their touring was a sensible one. "To me, they're the epitome of one of the smarter bands. They realized that there was no pot of gold at the end of the rainbow running up and down the Trans-Canada from here to Vancouver, and yet they still put out their singles and make quite good royalties.... They got off while they still had their sanity, and they still get along well." This evaluation by Brothers reflects not only the harsh reality of the music world in the Maritimes, but the enduring love of the style that motivates groups to continue even though the remuneration fails to afford them a full-time career.

The other Island family that has created a musical dynasty is the Matthews family—patriarch Ed Matthews, his sons Neil and Garth, grandson Billy, granddaughters Darlene and Julie, and cousin Gordon. Of the entire clan, Garth and Billy, who work with the country band Urban Outlaws, may be the most familiar to the public.

P.E.I. has also spawned one of the quirkier figures on the Canadian country music scene. The music industry has always had its oddballs, misfits and comedians; country singer Hank Mendoza is one of the oddest. Also known as the "Singing Stranger," he materialized in the early '80s with an appearance in *Country Music News*. As does another well-known country music outlaw, singer David Allan Coe, Mendoza always wears a mask, claiming that he gets a skin rash from camera flash bulbs going off in his face. His projects have ranged from the plausible, such as a rumored appearance on the CBC show "On the Road Again"—to the fantastic, such as his plan to build the Spud Dome, a building shaped like a potato, built almost completely underground, and designed to be the largest country music complex in North America. Mendoza's exact origins are a mystery. His only close contact in the media is George Brothers, who protects his privacy and whereabouts zealously. No one else has ever heard him or seen him, either alone or with his band The Whips—a fact that suggests Mendoza is a fictitious cover. Why it was necessary to invent him speaks volumes about the sensitivity of radio station-managers to criticism. At the outset of their careers few active country musicians care to risk being black-listed for being too out-spoken. Radio play is hard enough to get as it is.

As industry bad boy, Mendoza has frequently pronounced on what he sees as the sorry condition of country music. In a wide-ranging interview with George Brothers, published in the April 1990 *Country Music News*, Mendoza described himself as the only Canadian star who hasn't made it to the "Tommy Hunter Show," claiming that there wasn't enough in their budget to pay The Whips. Mendoza, not the most diplomatic of men, snarled about country radio, saying "I hear Canadian country records being played during the middle of the night, when me and four other people are listening to radio.... One of these days some of these Canadian programmers are going to wake up and find that Canadians actually like Canadian music."

Neither Mendoza nor Stompin' Tom Connors is the first to express outrage about the exposure that Canadian country music gets on radio. CRTC regulations stipulate that between six in the morning and midnight, stations must play 30% Canadian content. Yet when research analyst John Feihl produced his 1989 study *Broadcasting Initiatives for the Development of Canadian Talent*, he reported that many of the Canadian tracks are broadcast between seven at night and six in the morning; prime time tends to be reserved for foreign artists. Some radio employees are openly critical of the Canadian country acts they play on their record shows. In an article called *The State of Canadian Country* published in *Network* magazine in the fall of 1990, radio announcer Dave McCormick, host of the nationally syndicated show "All-Star Country," told interviewer Brenda Whitehall, "Unfortunately, a lot of Canadian artists are getting by on just royalties from airplay with pretty inferior products—off-center 45s when the whole world has gone CD, 1972 technical thinking, 1967 songwriting—some material is pretty passé that they expect us to play."

While homegrown talent still struggles to compete with Nashville expertise, local opportunities to get a start in the business have improved. There are now more independent facilities for producing demo tapes. In a local 16-track studio near Charlottetown, George Brothers is able to create what he calls "market-appropriate productions" for local musicians. Amateurs hopeful of turning pro can air their talent on the "Downeaster Jamboree," broadcast weekly on Halifax Cable television. In P.E.I. local cable television produces "Bill's Country Jamboree." Bill Acorn, host of the show since 1978, is a deputy sheriff who listens to country music tapes while he drives around delivering subpoenas. The production of the show is modest and so is the talent, ranging from semi-pro to definitely amateur, but the performers are like family members held together by an abiding fondness for country music. Occasionally friendships turn into something more permanent, as was the case with regular participants Oren and Cecile White, who met on the show and eventually married.

When groups finally get their act together, they can test the waters of the professional club circuit at J.R.'s Lounge in Charlottetown, arguably the best-known country club in the Atlantic region. George Brothers describes it as a good room to play with decent acoustics, a sympathetic employer and good-tempered patrons. But it's not the best place to break in new songs, he says. "You can get away with some original material, but not a good deal. People want to hear the hits." The room has changed since John Allan Cameron and a brand-new Anne Murray first played there; what was once a small, smoky and intimate space has expanded to accommodate more patrons. A modest dance floor invites, the bartenders expertly decant four beer bottles at a single stroke to accommodate the increased number of patrons, and when the band takes a break the large color television sets play back-to-back country videos.

Every year Island country musicians team up to produce a seasonal cassette called *Christmas on the Island*. The 1991 volume, the third annual issue, was produced by Gilles Godard and contained selections from some of the best of the island's resident players; Maxine MacLeod, Jamie and Neil Matthews, the Ellis Family Band, the Urban Outlaws, and another "come from away" who has been adopted into the island population, songwriter Gene MacLellan.

CBC-TV Publicity

CHAPTER 5

Gene MacLellan

Only from the heart

MacLellan is the only man in the Canadian music industry who is more private than Stompin' Tom. Like Connors, he all but vanished from the stage in the early '70s, at the peak of his popularity as a songwriter. He produced a folder of songs that still remain country classics: *Snowbird, Hard As I Try, Bidin' My Time, Pages of Time, Thorn in my Shoe, The Call,* and *Put Your Hand in the Hand.* MacLellan retreated from the spotlight shortly after the immense success of *Snowbird,* the hit song that may forever define his style. He had worked along quite happily for some years as a solo guitarist and singer in clubs, ending up on "Singalong Jubilee." But the runaway popularity of *Snowbird* was unexpected, and perhaps for him, unwelcome.

He resurfaced briefly several times; he taped an episode of CBC radio's "Swinging on a Star," broadcast in May of 1990, and in the late fall of 1991, broadcaster Charles Duerden interviewed him for CBC radio's "Atlantic Airwaves." MacLellan appeared in public again early in 1992 as a member of a songwriter's panel at the annual Music Industry Association of Nova Scotia meeting. During an interview at the Halifax Hilton, MacLellan seemed mildly surprised but pleased by the friendly reception he'd received at the conference. Greying, neatly dressed in a tweed jacket, with a reserved, slightly shy demeanor, he could pass for a college professor or a civil servant. Friends and colleagues often mention MacLellan's self-effacing manner. He admits that the strain of touring and playing in large concert venues in the old days took a toll on him. But his relatively frequent outings in the early '90s speak of a change. "I feel more like singing now than I ever did.... I felt more at home in more intimate situations, in front of smaller groups of people. Because I'm not really outgoing," he says. He appreciates the stimulation and excitement of change and travel, and acknowledges that fact that his creative impulses often take over his life. "I like to travel. I enjoy the thought of getting over here [to Halifax]. But when I get here, I'm embarrassed to say that what I mostly do is sit in my room and write." A man like this may not be forgotten, but his movements are seldom closely observed. MacLellan moved back to P.E.I. without fanfare after living in Ontario, and it was close to a year before people discovered that he was back.

Though he often speaks of his affection for the Maritimes, and P.E.I. in particular, MacLellan was born in Val d'Or, Quebec, in 1939. He moved to Toronto with his family while still a small child. By age 10, he could play pretty good acoustic guitar. A band he joined later included Jaime "Robbie" Robertson, who was to become a member of The Band. "I was a rock and roll guitar player," MacLellan recalls, "but not a good one. I enjoyed it for a while but it was really an offshoot of the country music." He played with a group called Little Caesar and the Consuls and left home at 18 to travel and take a series of odd jobs that led him around the country. He sang in churches, at outdoor rallies and eventually wound up working with an evangelist named Bud Kern.

By 1964, he had made his way to P.E.I. where he lived with an aunt in Pownal, outside Charlottetown. On one of his occasional jobs working as a backup guitarist, MacLellan played for an aspiring young singer named Lena Welsh—the Lena Welsh who later married Stompin' Tom Connors. In an anecdote related by Betty Large in her book *Out Of Thin Air*, CFCY broadcaster Loman McAulay noted that while Lena Welsh was beautiful, she didn't sing all that well. McAulay is said to have also commented that the guitarist was talented. At any rate MacLellan returned to the studio later to record some of his own songs.

Around that time, MacLellan dislocated his shoulder in a car accident. The injury laid him up for several months, and as he later told broadcaster Charles Duerden, "I decided that it was a sign for me to forsake what I was doing and really get into the music business. So I did, and started playing around the Maritimes. The writing happened after that." His first big opportunity came with an invitation to play on "Don Messer's Jubilee" in 1966, and that exposure netted him several months of work playing for Hal "Lonepine" Breau, father of the extraordinarily gifted Lenny Breau who played in Anne Murray's band in the early '70s. The next offer was to work as a regular cast member and songwriter on "Singalong Jubilee."

"Singalong" was almost a perfect vehicle for MacLellan. It was an ensemble show with slots for anybody who wanted to do solo work each week. Originally conceived in 1961 as a hootenanny, capitalizing on the zooming popularity of folk music, the format subsequently evolved to include other closely related styles such as light jazz, blues, country tunes and the occasional Top 40 hit by the Beatles or whoever else was on the charts. MacLellan's extensive experience in playing rock, country, blues and gospel music made him both a versatile sideman and a soloist on his own tunes.

On camera, he presented an intriguing figure. Thin, with a lean face and high cheekbones, he rarely appeared without dark glasses or an eyepatch, but even with the glasses, he always seemed slightly ill at ease. Georges Hebert, another young guitarist on the show, arrived in Halifax as a cast member around the same time and the two men shared an apartment. Hebert already knew MacLellan's reputation as an up and coming star songwriter and was somewhat awed to find himself in close quarters with him. It was a strange experience. Hebert recalls that MacLellan would disappear for several days without telling anyone where he was going, and on his return, simply explain, "I went to P.E.I. to visit my aunt." The island nurtured MacLellan's creative consciousness; he found solace in the quiet of the island countryside, and several of his best songs were written there.

Snowbird was picked up by fellow "Singalong" member Anne Murray. It was only the second song he'd ever written, says MacLellan. Of the writing process that generated such a smash hit, he reflects, "I tried to analyze it for a long time.... When I started writing, everything I wrote was stream of consciousness. It was really just a lot of images. Then [when] I examine the song later, I find a lot of myself is in there—where I've been, and things I've been connected to." Though he didn't write the song with Anne Murray in mind as its singer, he says that she was his favorite singer at the time. On her second album, *This Way is My Way*, Murray recorded three MacLellan songs, *Bidin' My Time*, *Hard As I Try*, and *Snowbird* as a single release. No one predicted the runaway success of *Snowbird*. It received maximum play everywhere, and the royalties poured in. MacLellan participated in the flurry of tours and concert appearances that resulted, but found the pace and the pressure exhausting. Things were happening too fast for the shy, introverted singer-song-writer. Suddenly there was a demand for his work as a concert soloist. He appeared as a guest on TV shows hosted by Tommy Hunter, Tommy Banks and Ian Tyson, and played in the CNE Grandstand show in 1971. He subsequently recorded three solo albums for Capitol Records; the first called simply *Gene MacLellan*, and two more, *Streetcorner Preacher* and *If It's All Right with You*.

His proven record as a hitmaker earned him a chance to write a song for the movie *Fools* starring Jason Robards. Capitol Records put him up in a hotel room for three days so that he could work without distractions, and sure enough, three days later he produced a song. But the frenetic pace and pressure of life in the limelight began to take a toll on his nerves and his general health. He got married and retreated to a farm in P.E.I. to think things over. Working with his manager, Jack McAndrew, at the time publicity director of the Confederation Centre in Charlottetown, he wanted to continue writing songs but be more selective about the gigs he accepted.

The idyll did not last, however. A Toronto rock band called Ocean recorded his gospel song *Put Your Hand in the Hand*, which sold two million copies in 1971. He was having a hard time getting used to the steady flow of income from royalties. But he had re-evaluated himself, he says now, and changed direction. "I had to figure out what I was—and what I was, was a writer. I wanted to get into other things. I wanted to improve my guitar, so I took classical guitar lessons for six months." He had been listening to records by classical guitarist Andres Segovia, and now chose to play on the wide-necked classical guitar with nylon strings rather than the steel strings favored by many country players. That exposure to classical guitar technique, however brief, became another of the many influences that were to guide his later song composition.

For some years MacLellan preferred to work quietly at home and stay out of the public eye. His first marriage had ended in divorce, but he married again, had three children,

and moved from P.E.I. to Burlington, Ontario. His public appearances were rare except for a session he taped for CBC Radio's *Ocean Limited* in 1984 with Tom Kelly and Marty Reno. Until he materialized again in 1990 on "Swinging on a Star," MacLellan was the invisible man of Canadian music.

On that occasion, MacLellan seemed very relaxed. The backup singers were ex-Maritimers Denny Doherty, formerly of the Mamas and the Papas, and Tom Kelly again, formerly host of "Singalong Jubilee." MacLellan joked with *Star* host Murray McLauchlan, recalling that they had first met in Toronto in 1973. Brian Ahern had booked McLauchlan to play rhythm guitar on a studio gig with MacLellan. Despite the easy atmosphere—at one point, MacLellan made a wry reference to his first wife—McLauchlan was respectful of MacLellan's privacy, and cautious about asking too many personal questions.

His voice has changed little over the years; it's still distinguished by a sweetly soulful quality that hints at the blues and the country-rock music he knows best. MacLellan sang and accompanied himself on guitar for several of his own songs including *Faces* and *Puerto Vallarta*, which he wrote during a Mexican holiday with his son.

A year later, back in P.E.I. with his wife and children, MacLellan told CBC freelancer Charles Duerden that he was busy building himself a writer's studio where he planned to work on songs and do some recording. Unlike earlier interviews, in which MacLellan has often seemed guarded and ill at ease in the public eye, he spoke freely about his career beginnings, his songwriting and his feelings about the island. He told Duerden that he often leaves his studio, takes a guitar with him, and finds a quiet place to play outdoors. He works on new songs now, and mentioned a chance encounter that had startled him. After working late at his studio, he drove to a nearby Tim Horton's doughnut shop for a coffee. "…It's about 12:30 at night and the lady at the drive-through recognized me, which doesn't happen a whole lot here, and she got this stern look on her face and she says 'Mr. MacLellan, you'd better start writing,' she says, 'that's what you're

CBC-TV Publicity

A 1984 CBC *studio shot of Gene MacLellan with*
Marty Reno (left) and Tom Kelly (right).

supposed to be doing.'" He laughed and added "I got my coffee and my bran muffin and I took off. Shortly after that I was starting to write again."

Gene MacLellan's attitude to writing differs from that of many other songwriters, in that he sees it as more of a vocation than an artistic pursuit or a mere job. Lyrics seem to be the hardest part of the writing, he says, adding "Melodies seem to be fairly easy.... I get a feel first, then a first line is usually what happens, then I usually sort of build on that.... If it doesn't look pretty to me, if it doesn't seem to be poetic, it doesn't last long." Of the song folio he's produced, each one is unique in design and melody. He rarely composes according to the set formulas (verse with so many lines, bridge to the chorus, modulation to a new key) that guide many writers. Each song is unique, with its own reason for being, a tradition more typical of classical art song than country music. MacLellan told Duerden, "I have a God-given talent, yeah. I believe that. I didn't always recognize it as such. I thought I'd lucked into things at times, that anybody could do this." Later in that interview he mused, "I try to touch people where I am touched myself. I'm touched by the lyrics of certain writers and I try to do the same thing myself, in whatever level I can do it at. And that's when the music industry is listening to you too."

The music industry has never lost track of Gene MacLellan as it did of Stompin' Tom. His disappearance from the scene was motivated more by personal reasons than political principle. He has kept in touch with Balmur, Anne Murray's management company, which still regards him as a possible source of hit songs. He says of those connections, "If you have any kind of a track record at all, those doors never really close for you. I'm in touch with her (Murray's) office maybe once a year, or whenever they need songs, they contact me and see if I have anything that is suitable." Some of his songs have expressed a gospel/inspirational mood, such as *The Reunion*, his contribution to the 1991 *Christmas on the Island* cassette from radio station Q-93. His quiet but strong spiritual beliefs manifest themselves with absolute sincerity in songs like *Put Your Hand in the Hand*. It is not at all a gospel treatment, but an expression of a simple faith. When Duerden asked Gene if he saw any of his future work taking that direction, he responded "No...I like to write songs about what's happening, I call it the real world [though] the spiritual world is quite real to me.... I like to write love songs. Probably my favorite songs are about love. I believe in man-woman relationships. I think that's where it starts. If you don't have that, your pursuits are pretty empty."

MacLellan has settled into a quietly productive life with his family. The move back to P.E.I. is a permanent one, he says, though he welcomes opportunities to travel occasionally. He has begun laying down tracks in a Hamilton studio for a new album, and hopes to record the rest of the songs when production money becomes available. The wistful sadness expressed in many of the early MacLellan songs has been replaced by a more positive feeling, possibly because MacLellan himself seems to have found both happiness in his private life, and a renewed focus in his creative work. As he told Charles Duerden, "For the first time in my life really, it feels proper. It's almost like, I don't want to go to heaven today. I'm not ready. It feels too nice sometimes." Other songwriters have felt that way about the tiny island that constitutes one of Canada's 10 provinces. As MacLellan talks so contentedly of his adopted home you are reminded of the title of a "Lonepine" Breau song called, simply, *Prince Edward Island is Heaven to Me*.

CBC-TV Publicity

CHAPTER 6

John Allan Cameron

For kilt and country

In all likelihood, John Allan Cameron was the first person to appear on the stage of the Grand Ole Opry in Nashville wearing a kilt. Part of Cameron's usual costume as a Cape Breton patriot, the kilt set him apart from the other guests on that day in May, 1970. Opry audiences are used to performers who wear striking and even outlandish outfits; cowboy hats and boots, fringed rawhide jackets, elaborate hairdos and sequined suits from Nudies of Hollywood are still favored by many country stars. Still, Cameron had been pacing about backstage before his solo spot, nervously wondering if maybe the kilt wasn't a bit too much, when he ran into fellow Opry guest Ernie Ashworth. Ashworth had just scored with a hit single called *Talk Back Trembling Lips.* He was wearing a cream-colored suit with a repeating design of big red lips, plus the title of his song patterned all over it. "His hit was written all over him," recalls John Allan. Cameron decided that if Ernie Ashworth could appear in that jacket, he, John Allan, was going to wear his kilt.

But if the audiences were at first puzzled by the sight of a young man wearing a kilt, there was no doubt about their reaction to his music. They loved it. He began his timespot with a traditional slow bagpipe air, played on his 12-string guitar, and then cut to a bouncy uptempo song called

Anne—the kind of rollicking tune that country music fans love. In the middle of his set, Cameron noticed that the host, Roy Acuff, had planted a chair close to him and was peering at the Scottish singer with deep interest. When the crowd exploded into applause at the end, Acuff stood and requested another song. At the end of that song, the host stood and did an impromptu radio interview with John Allan—seven minutes of unscheduled talk on a program where the guests know that a five-minute set should never go overtime, on pain of being yanked off the stage. The pleasure of that recognition lasted for a long time. Twenty years later, John Allan remembers that Hank Snow told him after the show, "Whatever you're doing, boy, keep it up because it works." Back home in Cape Breton later, disc jockey Freeman Roach told John Allan that the two biggest ovations at the Opry that season had been for singer Marty Robbins, and for John Allan Cameron.

There was a time when so-called ethnic acts would not have graced the Opry stage, but in the past 20 years the definition of country music has expanded to embrace (albeit uneasily) several new sub-headings, including Cajun country and roots music. John Allan Cameron and the other musicians who play Celtic traditional music don't fit neatly

93

into any of the customary categories such as gospel, bluegrass or honky-tonk. Instead, John Allan's music is a hybrid that shows all the influences that have touched him during all his years in the business. He's sung and played everything from contemporary folksongs by Stan Rogers to light country-rock by John Prine and Gordon Lightfoot, but his major interest has always been the heritage music of Cape Breton. It's a style that Cameron jokingly calls "old-wave music"; songs in Gaelic and English, and the tunes originally played by fiddlers in Scotland, and treasured since the earliest Highlanders came to Nova Scotia in the 18th century. In a way, that traditional music may have the same significance to Canadians that the mountain music of the Appalachians has to Americans; it's the music of immigrants, mainly from the British Isles, who were often isolated from mainstream culture and who have clung to the songs and stories of the old country for 200 years.

Listening to John Allan's voice is a curious experience at first. It's not a perfect instrument; a slightly reedy baritone, without the sweetly cultivated tones of other Celtic singers such as Irish soprano Mary O'Hara, or tenor Frank Patterson. Sometimes he seems on the verge of cracking the tone or even wandering off pitch. But after listening for a while, you realize that it's like hearing a fiddle or set of bagpipes transformed into a human sound. It's an intensely personal voice with emotional depths that he conveys through inflexion and tone color. He can croon a sweetly poignant Gaelic lovesong such as *Calin Mo' Ruinsa*, or briskly snap out a contemporary song such as Rogers' *Mary Ellen Carter*, but whatever he sings, his voice carries an uncanny quality of timelessness. Like his ancestors, Cameron's voice still retains a trace of the Gaelic lilt; when he sings the centuries-old tragic ballad *The Four Marys*, it's like hearing the distant, faintly melancholy sound of a lone piper at dusk.

Even before that appearance at the Opry in May of 1970, John Allan Cameron had begun to establish himself as a presence on the Canadian music scene. Dr. Neil Rosenberg had just moved to Canada in 1968 and can remember the early days of the folk revival. Of John Allan, Rosenberg says, "You have to tie his popularity, I think, to the fact that these were the early Trudeau years which were years of strong national pride and reaction against the American model. John Allan stressed the region, the religion and the ethnicity." Rosenberg believes that Cameron was one of the first folk/country performers from the Maritimes to emphasize heritage and origins, and to work with musical literature that was indigenous to the area rather than imitate Nashville.

Despite his fresh-faced appearance—today at 50, he doesn't look much older than he did in his "Singalong Jubilee" days—Cameron is one of the veterans of the Canadian music business. After 20-odd years on stage, his enthusiasm for playing music is undiminished. During a May, 1991 interview on CBC "Morningside," Peter Gzowski commented, "You've slugged it out for a long time…and you have the same energy." Cameron, ever the good-tempered guest, agreed and added that he could remember the good old days when people could go to a coffeehouse and pay $3 to hear Gordon Lightfoot. But the days of the $3 admission are long since gone, as Cameron knows. Not only are ticket prices and artists' fees much higher, but the emphasis for many performers has shifted away from live concerts. And while Cameron is seldom out of work, his chosen musical style is not necessarily a formula for success in terms of commercial radio's Top 40 hits. In the past 20 years, he has had perhaps four charted singles from seven albums. In an industry that has increasingly relied on massive record sales and radio exposure, John Allan is one of the few performers to sustain a career mostly through his live appearances.

He was part of the folk revival of the '60s, the wave of young performers who rediscovered folk and traditional songs, and brought them back to life in concerts, hootenannies and festivals. There had always been an audience for such music, of course, but that audience tended to be older and more conservative and preferred a style that owed more to the music-hall tradition and Tin Pan Alley composers than it did to authentic Irish or Scottish musicians. The diehard loyalists of such music favored singers such as Sir Harry Lauder and Dennis Day, the Irish singer who was a regular on Jack Benny's television show during the '50s. But during the folksong revival, young performers were interested in a more vigorous kind of music. Musicians, such as Tommy Makem and the Clancy Brothers, straight from the old country were prime figures in the movement to rediscover roots music, as John Allan Cameron sees it. "Tommy Makem and the Clancy Brothers gave us the raunchy, authentic stuff.... Together with Tommy Makem, they took us out of the Dennis Day type of Irish song and gave us the real stuff." They revived the use of traditional folk instruments—the fiddle, concertina, pennywhistle, bagpipes —and created a sound that was closer to that which emigrants had heard back home in the villages. And it caught on with the public; pubs that had previously hired only country bands began to find that their patrons enjoyed Celtic music and bands. Numerous groups sprang up; the Irish Rovers, formed in Calgary in 1964, parlayed a hit single called *The Unicorn* into a CBC television series that ran from 1971-75. And there was the Carlton Showband, which made a specialty of playing lively dance music such as reels, polkas, jigs and hornpipes. They were the house band for CTV's "Pig and Whistle" which ran from 1967-77. But aside from the popularity of rowdy music that served as background for beer drinkers, many musicians were interested in taking the Celtic literature out of the tavern and into the concert hall.

Cape Breton has always been one of the major outposts of the Celtic revival. Ever since the first Scottish emigrants arrived aboard the *Hector* in 1777, they had struggled to maintain the customs, language and music of the Scottish Highlands. The folksongs they sang and the tunes their fiddlers played dated back in some cases hundreds of years, and even when new ones were composed, they conformed to the various genres already existing—the ballads, airs and laments, and the instrumental forms of the strathspeys, jigs and reels. Because of their relative isolation from the mainland—the Canso Causeway linking the island to the main-

land was not built until 1955—some scholars have agreed with the commonly held belief of the musicians that the traditional tunes may have been more accurately preserved there than in Scotland, which was more susceptible to outside influences.

The communities were held together by their common language of Gaelic, and in most cases the Roman Catholic religion. It was a hard daily life, trying to scratch out a living from rough rocky soil, and the settlers consoled themselves with music and stories. Even in the poorest village, it was rare to find a household without an ancient and battered violin. Fathers taught their sons to play, and while there were always a few people who "played by note" as music reading was called, many more learned by ear, and picked up the stylistic points by watching and imitating other players. Fiddlers played with careful attention to intonation, and variety in "cuts" (the ornaments a good fiddler could improvise off the top of his head) were critically judged by his listeners. Unlike the Don Messer style of fiddle playing, fiddlers depended on a high degree of ornamentation to accentuate the rhythmic differences between the kinds of tunes; jigs were in rapid 6/8 time, reels in duple time, while the strathspeys had a characteristic pattern of dotted rhythms that set them apart from hornpipes. Though each fiddler had his or her own sound, Cape Breton players had a few things in common; they often grasped the bow slightly above the frog, they used more bow pressure for a richer sound, and the fiddle was sometimes supported against the chest rather than under the chin. As often as not, beginners learned to play first by "jigging" the tunes—singing the tunes with nonsense syllables in order to learn the correct notes and rhythms and pitches before they had acquired their fiddle technique. A fiddler often supplied his own rhythmic backup by beating his foot on the floor. Some of the best players worked out complicated heel-and-toe patterns, and if they played while sitting down, could alternate feet until they seemed to be dancing while they played. The man or woman who played the fiddle well was second in prestige only to the parish priest.

John Allan Cameron was born into this tightly-knit community in Inverness in 1938. He was the second of Daniel and Katie Ann Cameron's seven children. The family was not well off; years later, Cameron's sister Jessie told writer Silver Don Cameron (no relation) that they were probably the poorest people in the county. But if they were short on cash, they were long on pride, independence and a strong sense of their heritage which they passed on to their children. John Allan was a gifted student and like most youngsters in the community, was interested in music. In those days, he says, children on the playground didn't argue about hockey players or pop singers, they argued over who was the best fiddler in the community.

One of the first names to come up would likely have been John Allan's uncle Dan Rory MacDonald. He was regarded as one of the finest fiddlers in the traditional style that the island has ever produced, and was also a gifted composer who wrote more than 2500 original tunes. Later collected in published form called *The Heather Hill Collection* by John Allan's brother John Donald, they had titles such as *The Red Shoes*, *Glencoe March* and *The River Bend Jig*. A sort of Pied Piper of the fiddle, Dan R., as he was generally known, travelled from village to village carrying little more than his instrument, and played at dances, weddings and other gatherings. He also made several recordings for the Rodeo Company, which carried country music exclusively. (Rodeo, formed in Montreal in 1949 and later relocated to Halifax, was a parent company to several other labels, including Celtic, whose catalogue of Scottish music began in 1933. Its recording studio opened in Halifax in 1956). After his retirement, Dan R. frequently visited his sister Katie's family, where two of his young nephews, John Allan and John Donald, closely observed their uncle and his playing.

The boys had begun to play guitar and fiddle after a neighbor named Red Johnny Campbell taught them to read music. They practised endlessly, listened to other fiddlers and to the Sydney and Antigonish radio stations, which broadcast an eclectic mix of Cape Breton fiddle music interspersed with mainstream country music, news, and agricultural reports. While still in their teens, the Camerons began to get invitations to play at any community gathering that called for music—which in Cape Breton parlance, was anything from a birthday party to a wake. They were sometimes paid in cash and sometimes given a free meal; a generation earlier, at the "pound parties" (admission followed upon payment of a pound of tea, butter or cheese) the musicians might have been paid with bartered goods.

Some of the gatherings were rowdy dances in church or community halls, where the party never broke up before dawn, while others took place in kitchens or parlors where the inhabitants spoke better Gaelic than they did English, and were shy about having outsiders listen to what, among themselves, they called "kitchen music." At these parties, the Camerons would play and sing in a haze of pipe and cigarette smoke, and the dance floor was always full. Aside from soloists who tried to outlast each other at stepdancing marathons, there were the square sets and Scotch fours— folkdances in which the steps were as intricately patterned as an 18th-century minuet.

The Cameron brothers learned a varied repertoire, which reflected their audience's tastes. They did the instrumental pieces—the strathspeys, reels and jigs, with John Donald on fiddle accompanied by John Allan picking out the melody and occasionally chording on his 12-string guitar. (Though John Allan has arranged many songs, he has never written original material.) John Allan also sang wistful ballads, such as *Peggy Gordon* and more roguish songs, probably locally composed, such as *The Old Woman of Mabou*. ("There was an old woman from Mabou/In Mabou she did dwell/She loved her husband dearly/But another man twice as well.") And since most of their listeners also listened to popular country radio, they kept up with Nashville hits by Hank Snow and Hank Williams. Years later, John Allan still enjoys introducing a traditional song with a mock-solemn genealogy; he learned it from his grandfather, who learned it from his grandfather, who picked it up from an old sharecropper, who got it off an old Connie Francis album.

John Allan left this world behind when he entered the seminary in Ottawa to study for the priesthood. For six years he studied Latin and theology and played sports, but managed to keep up some of his musical interest. One night at a "Gaudeamus"—"sort of a ceilidh," he says—John Allan was asked to fill in with a musical number to kill time during some technical adjustments backstage. Wearing his robe and a cross around his neck, he went on with his guitar and sang the first number that came to mind. Unfortunately, it happened to be a song by Hank Williams called *Loveless Mansion on the Hill*. Since the seminarians' home, Holy Rosary Scholastic, was itself situated on a hill, his superiors made the obvious though unintended connection, and the next day, he was sent for and an explanation was demanded. Cameron protested his innocence saying "Hey, it's only a song, a Hank Williams song."

Before his final ordination, John Allan left the seminary in 1964 because he had begun to doubt his vocation for the priesthood. He was at a loose end; in those days, an ex-seminarian had a hard time justifying his decision to a disapproving world. He began attending concerts again and met Gus McKinnon, who hosted a morning radio show at station CJFX in Antigonish. They spent a summer travelling around to various musical events, and that fall, McKinnon got John Allan a job at the station to help pay his tuition at St. Francis Xavier University. Three mornings a week, he played records and talked about music. He also picked up the threads of his performing career, as people called the station to ask him to sing or to request favorite tunes. Cameron acknowledged his debt to Gus McKinnon when he dedicated his first Columbia record, *Get There by Dawn*, to him. On the liner notes he wrote: "Along with yourself, I'll dedicate it to all the people, cows, horses, sheep, hens and other animals who listen regularly to your early morning show at CJFX."

While in Halifax, earning an education degree at Dalhousie, John Allan auditioned for "Singalong Jubilee," the CBC-TV folk music show then being broadcast from Halifax. The host, Bill Langstroth, must have been amazed by the force of the music, and by the impact of John Allan's forthright personality. There were plenty of aspiring folk and country performers who won guest spots on television, but many of them were clones of other, better-known stars. If they sang folk music, they imitated the voice and delivery of Joan Baez, or they picked up the southern twang of Nashville in order to sing like Patsy Cline or Johnny Cash. John Allan Cameron didn't imitate anybody; he sang in a robust voice, belting out Gaelic and English songs, picking out marches and reels on his guitar, and telling jokes and stories about growing up in Mabou. It was fresh and original, and nobody else was doing it with John Allan's confidence and skill. "Bill Langstroth never saw a guy like me before," says John Allan now. He was hired and eventually became a featured soloist.

There had been other Celtic entertainers who had ventured outside the Maritimes before, either to appear at clubs or dances in Toronto and Boston, or to make occasional recordings for specialty labels such as Rodeo or Arc Records. Some, such as fiddler Winston "Scotty" Fitzgerald, appeared in front of national audiences on "Don Messer's Jubilee," but few had ever tried to establish a following outside of the familiar Atlantic territory. John Allan was different; he was energetic, charming and ambitious and his early reception encouraged him to forget his career as a schoolteacher and plunge into performing full time.

Kenzie McNeil, a Cape Breton singer-songwriter, can remember John Allan's initial impact. He says, "Nobody ever really connected like John Allan did. His first album, *Here Comes John Allan Cameron*, that was magical. John Allan himself was magical. You'd see him in a club and come out feeling great. He really put a signature on those Celtic and tribal tunes like *The Four Marys*." Cameron had a well-received first album, television success, and the next step was to get out on the road.

There were other young hopefuls doing the club circuit in those years, the late '60s and early '70s. Coffee houses,

A kilted John Allan gives Grand Ole Opry host Roy Acuff a thoughtful moment as he plays Scottish fiddle and pipe tunes on the guitar, supported by Allister MacGillivray (left) on rhythm guitar and Dave Isner (right) on bass guitar.

pubs, nightclubs and lounges hired entertainers each week to help fill up the room. Holiday Inn lounges, J.R.'s Prince Edward Lounge in Charlottetown, the Colonial Inn in Amherst and the Monterey Lounge in Halifax all hosted the likes of John Allan, Stompin' Tom Connors and Anne Murray. Later there were bands as well as solo acts; bands such as Ryan's Fancy, Old Blue, and the Garrison Brothers, who played rowdy, good-time music that patrons could clap and sing along with. For performers, it was experience that

counts as "paying your dues"; it wasn't always glamorous or well paid work, but it toughened you. There was nothing like a day of travelling, a quick sound check and rehearsal at the venue and then a four-hour gig to smarten you up and teach you about the practical side of performing. Most performers travelled long distances by car and tried to keep expenses down by using only one or two backup players. During those years, anybody who dropped in to the Starlight Lounge in Moncton's Brunswick Hotel could, for a modest cover charge and the price of a few brews, spend an evening listening to John Allan Cameron or Anne Murray.

Musicians learn many things on the club circuit, and one of the first lessons is that it's not enough to have good rapport with the fans and a tight musical act. You must also sell beer, as Cameron discovered during an early tour of Newfoundland. With his backup players David Isner and Allister MacGillivray, Cameron was booked into the Chignic Lodge which was located on an isolated stretch of highway in the Codroy Valley. Thirty-five miles from the nearest sizeable town, Port aux Basques, there seemed to be only a few houses nearby. But that night an audience materialized from somewhere. Over 400 people crammed themselves into the lounge for the show and John Allan recalls, "I did an extra hour that night, and I think it was one of the nights that the RCMP came in and closed us up." Like the Cape Bretoners Cameron knew best, Newfies love a riproaring party with a band playing tunes that everybody recognizes. It was the kind of response club owners dream about—a band that can play well, and sell drinks. One night the club owner happily showed John Allan the empties that told the story of a successful booking; the patrons had consumed 82 cases of beer and 14 cases of hard liquor.

Success in the regions usually is a step on the way to making it big in Toronto. Cracking the Upper Canadian market meant playing at the Horseshoe Tavern. It was, Cameron says, "the Mecca for all the country people"—crowded, noisy and the biggest honky-tonk in the country. Its owner, Jack Starr, liked John Allan and his act went over well—so well that he could have 500 people in the room, and more lined up outside waiting to get in. By comparison, Willie Nelson, when he played Toronto in those days, would draw maybe 25 people on a Saturday night. But as Cameron points out, Willie Nelson had a reputation for being unpredictable. Club managers liked acts who showed up on time, didn't take too many breaks, and stayed relatively sober on the job.

It was Jack Starr who got Cameron his guest spot at the Opry. Celtic acts at that time were a rarity, but Starr, a longtime country music booster who was highly respected by the Nashville establishment, had a hunch that John Allan's style would go over well. He guessed right; host Roy Acuff gave Cameron extra time on the air, and the applause and

ovations reinforced Cameron's conviction that he was doing the right things. But one successful Opry appearance doesn't make a career. Without a manager to plug the records, book the tours and take care of business, there was less chance of a career development strategy that would take care of the future. Not that he was idle; in the next five years, Cameron appeared at Expo 70, in Osaka and at folk festivals in Vancouver, Winnipeg and Mariposa, and continued to play club dates. His second album, *Get There by Dawn*, showed that he was branching out from his former identification as a purely Celtic entertainer; though there were the reliable pub-crowd songs like the wistful *Liverpool Lou* and a hearty rendition of the traditional song *Old Maid in the Garret*, he also recorded Bruce Cockburn's *Goin' Down the Road*, and his characteristic reedy voice was beginning to suggest the harder, more nasal edge of country-folk musicians like Bob Dylan.

As he diversified his repertoire, the opportunities for moving out of the tavern circuit and into the more serious concert venues grew. Cameron appeared at the Riverboat Coffeehouse, where serious musicians of various persuasions—folk, country and jazz—played to quietly attentive fans. Joni Mitchell, Bruce Cockburn and Murray McLauchlan all played the Riverboat, and John Allan found that he preferred the concert setting to the rowdier scene at the clubs. Of his decision to cut back on his club bookings he says now, "I could do the clubs every night of the week, but there's no future in that and it makes you musically sloppy. One of the troubles I did have in my club act at the end was that the owners figured that if you were entertaining their patrons a whole lot, they wouldn't drink until you took a break." Around that time, he hooked up again with another "Singalong" colleague, Anne Murray. Murray was also based in Toronto and had formed a management company which she named Balmur. John Allan signed a management deal with Balmur and spent the next five years opening shows for Anne Murray.

The period between 1970 and 1980 was a busy and productive time for many Celtic musicians, and for John

Two Nova Scotians in the big-time—John Allan Cameron and longtime friend Anne Murray.

Allan in particular. He and his wife, Angela, had settled with their son Stuart, in a Toronto suburb, and John Allan was on the road eight or nine months of the year. The Murray show travelled internationally, and John Allan opened shows all over Canada and the U.S., including the glitziest venue of all—Las Vegas. Often he wore his kilt, and played his Celtic tunes for the showroom audiences. Yet there were still many skeptics who couldn't believe that anything less than a Liberace-style show would suit Vegas audiences. "People asked, 'Do you play your kind of stuff in Las Vegas? Does it go over?' I said, 'Look, if I had your kind of attitude I probably wouldn't have gotten within a hundred miles, or three hundred or a thousand miles of a stage.' Because with that attitude, you get nowhere." Las Vegas, as Cameron likes to remind people, may be the place where the high rollers go, but the casinos and showrooms are also full of ordinary folks;

housewives, insurance salesmen and people on holiday who appreciate some down-to-earth entertainment.

Cameron's travels with the Murray troupe also meant mingling with more people in the country music industry. At concert receptions, hotels and recording studios, Cameron met many of the up and coming generation of country songwriters such as Kris Kristofferson, John Prine, and Steve Goodman, who wrote *City of New Orleans*. Unlike some of the older Nashville songwriters who specialized in cliché songs of rejection and heartbreak, these writers were younger, more introspective and interested in a wider variety of song topics. They wrote intelligent, ironic lyrics and tunes which intrigued not only John Allan Cameron, but other singers who wanted to synthesize different elements—jazz, folk and ethnic—into mainstream country music. John Allan began to add some of these songs to his repertoire. He claims to be the first Canadian performer to sing John Prine's songs, beginning with a 1973 performance of *Spanish Pipedream* at the Fredericton Playhouse. Cameron was especially fond of writer Steve Goodman, whose clever lyrics and strong melodic gift appealed to Cameron's taste. John Allan was a regular guest on the 1974-75 television show "Ceilidh," had his own show on CTV during 1975-76, and hosted the annual Juno Awards show of 1976. The television series gave him a chance to do one of the things he liked best—push new talent. The guests were diverse; they included Acadian singer Edith Butler, his Nashville buddy Steve Goodman, and John Allan had a chance to pay back a longstanding debt to his boyhood hero Scotty Fitzgerald, by inviting him to be a guest soloist.

Audiences, television executives and people in the record business had gradually noticed the revival that was taking place in their midst. Early in the '70s, filmmaker Ron MacInnis had sounded an alarm with his film *The Vanishing Cape Breton Fiddler*. MacInnis explored what he feared was a dying breed; the homegrown fiddler who played Celtic tunes in the distinctive Cape Breton style. Early in the film, many of the oldtimers MacInnis interviewed assured him that there were few left. "No young ones coming up now like there used to be," said one, while another added that in his opinion, they were watching too much television. MacInnis observed that at many of the events he attended, the audiences appeared to be middle-aged and older, and that many people had told him they feared that with so many young people moving to the big cities to find jobs, the Cape Breton style would die out from sheer neglect.

In his documentary, MacInnis showed the traditional ceilidh or house party to thousands of people who had never before seen one. In one scene, people are gathered in what is obviously a small private home with half a dozen fiddlers and a piano accompanist squeezed into a corner. As they play, there are dancers in the center of the floor marking out the complicated heel-and-toe patterns. And contrary to one of MacInnis assertions, this crowd consisted of all ages from toddlers falling asleep on their parents' laps to vigorous oldsters, still nimble enough at eightysomething to do a step. But despite the invasive presence of cameras and lights, there was sense of artlessness about their enjoyment. Though many of the performers were too shy to look directly at the camera, it didn't seem to cramp their style.

Ron MacInnis interviewed numerous fiddlers who talked about their music, including the legendary Dan R. But as a kind of counterbalance to some of the alarming statements about the impending death of the tradition, MacInnis also introduced one of the most promising younger fiddlers—a lad named John Morris Rankin. Rankin, then barely into his teens, was one of the up and coming musicians on whom the fans were pinning their hopes for the future, as he was developing into both a talented fiddler and skilled piano accompanist. Together with a constantly changing cast of siblings from the 12 members of his family, John Morris began to appear frequently with a traditional group that billed itself as the Rankin Family Band.

Ron MacInnis may have pushed the panic button at just the right time. His film, broadcast on the CBC network, jolted a motley group of worried parents, teachers, clergy-men and fiddle fans into efforts to reclaim the Scottish culture. All over Cape Breton, courses were organized in the Gaelic language, piping, fiddling and dancing, so that the young people might be reminded of their community history. The Cape Breton Fiddlers' Association was formed to encourage more people to take up playing the instrument, and at the first Glendale Fiddling Festival in 1973 more than 10,000 excited fans gathered to listen to as many as 130 fiddlers assembled onstage at once. The established generation of musicians—fiddlers such as Wilfrid Gillis, Donald Angus Beaton, Scotty Fitzgerald, Buddy MacMaster, and Lee Cremo—was being joined by a younger group, many of them in their early '20s. Players such as John Morris Rankin, Jerry Holland and Dave MacIsaac appeared with John Allan Cameron on his tours, television appearances and records.

A double album issued by Columbia in 1976 has some of Cameron's best recorded work on it. Titled *Weddings, Wakes and other Things*, it's a cross-sectional glance at all the music that interested him most. Three of the sides were recorded in a studio, and the fourth was taped live at a concert in Halifax. The album was produced by another longtime pal, songwriter Robbie MacNeill. Two sides have a mix of the country/folk repertoire that was becoming Cameron's trademark, ranging from the purely country song *Anne* which was his standard tribute to Anne Murray, to a contemporary folksong by Ewan McColl called *Dirty Old Town*. One entire side contains instrumental solos of Scottish material such as *Charles Sutherland Reel* and *Prince Charlie's Farewell to the Isle of Skye*, with John Allan as soloist on twelve-string guitar, backed up by piano and bass.

True to his habit of promoting work by new talent, Cameron included three songs by writer Allister MacGillivray; two of them slightly wistful, *Looking Back* and the now-famous *Song for the Mira* and the third one a bouncy tune with a strong country feel called *Tie Me Down*. Full of the yearning for home and a settled life, its wistful lyrics about wandering make it a tune that suits John Allan's voice perfectly. No whining, no regrets, just simple statements about the loneliness of the traveller, as he sings: "I've been wheels/and I've been rails/ I've been dusty roads and grassy wagon trails/ But I miss the friends that linger/In the streets of my hometown/ If you love me you'll believe me, tie me down." It's reminiscent of the old train and truck songs about getting away from it all, but with a twist; in this case, the singer wants to get off the road and go back home.

The final side, recorded at a live concert in the Cohn Auditorium in Halifax in 1976, may be the best representation of Cameron's musical personality and onstage manner. He connects easily with his audience in much the same manner as Rita MacNeil would, some years later. In between songs, he tells stories about his Cape Breton childhood; after a gently nostalgic version of *Song for the Mira* he talks about growing up in Glencoe Station and how, on his first trip to Antigonish, "the height of excitement was going into Woolco and trying on gloves." Obviously, he taps into the base of experience that most of the audience probably shares—growing up poor, strong family ties, and a willingness to laugh at himself. Later, leading up to the final cut of John Prine's *Please Don't Bury Me*, he cracks jokes about going into a Glace Bay funeral home "to watch the coffins warp." Then he swings into the song, whose mildly irreverent lyrics deal with the writer's request not to be buried, but to have his body parts dealt out-head north, feet south, ears to the deaf and so on. Just as in his days in the seminary, when he was able to put across a Hank Williams song to a crowd of disapproving religious superiors, Cameron is once again able to win over his audience through his personal warmth and charm. If at first they might have been mildly jolted by the saucy lyrics, by the end they react with a burst of laughter and loud applause.

In 1978, John Allan started his own record label called Glencoe which produced a solo record of his own called *Freeborn Man* and one called *Fiddle* by a group called the Cape Breton Symphony which he had helped form. The members were his brother John Donald, Scotty Fitzgerald, Wilfrid Gillis, Jerry Holland and pianist Bobby Brown. They appeared on his 1979 summer variety series for CBC television and did a tour to Ireland. The CBC show received good ratings—viewers were calculated at about 350,000 but the show was distributed through a network called Metronet, which reached only 13 major cities. Since the bulk of his fans lived in rural areas that didn't receive Metronet and therefore could not tune in the show and boost the ratings even higher, the show was cancelled. It may have been the best solution, since many people who saw the show felt that Cameron's magnetism was less apparent on the screen than it was in live concerts. In retrospect, Cameron believes that it might have worked out better if he had done a television show at the local Sydney television station first, in order to learn more about production techniques, planning and audience building. It also would have allowed him to use the large pool of talented local performers and writers—Allister MacGillivray, guitarist and fiddler Dave MacIsaac, and singer/songwriters Fred Lavery and Leon Dubinsky.

One of the musicians who most impressed Cameron in those years was singer/songwriter Stan Rogers. Sometime around 1972, record producer Paul Mills had mentioned a talented new writer to John Allan, and after hearing some of Stan's songs, John Allan became convinced that he was going to be the next big star. Cameron played backup guitar on Rogers' album *Fogarty's Cove*, gave him an early break by booking Rogers to play on his Montreal television show, and the two men became close friends. John Allan believes that he was the first person to hear Rogers' shanty *Barrett's Privateers*, and they often appeared together in concert.

Their personalities were different. John Allan was the soul of tact, while Stan Rogers' outspokenness occasionally caused his friends some difficulties. Cameron remembers one tour together in Alberta during which they appeared in a concert in High River, the home town of then Prime Minister Joe Clark. Rogers cracked a joke about Clark, saying to the audience, "Well, High River, you've given us a prime minister." Pause. "Better luck next time!" "Not everybody could understand Stan's sense of humor," says

Cameron wryly. He had to go on next, and the audience was more than a little upset—some people were getting up and walking out. John Allan, ever the diplomat, smoothed over the remark with a few personal reminiscences about meeting Joe Clark, and the crowd soon settled down. He says now of that show, "He didn't hand me the audience on a platter at all. They were pretty hostile, but I got them around."

Their Nova Scotia roots were a strong bond, for though Rogers had been born in Ontario, family connections and history gave him a kinship to the region. When the Nova Scotia government organized a troupe of performers to represent the province in Edinburgh at the International Gathering of the Clans in 1980, both Cameron and Stan Rogers were asked to go, along with a group of other performers including singer Jennifer Whalen and fiddler/guitarist Dave MacIsaac. The tour was plagued by numerous hitches; promotional posters that were accidentally left at the airport for three weeks, inadequate publicity for their concerts, and last-minute scrambling to find the musicians a place to stay in Edinburgh. The show went on, despite the many difficulties, but it was a triumph of determination over adversity, says John Allan. "It was a hell of a good show—two and a half hours of quite solid entertainment—and our biggest audience was 22 people and the smallest was six. We played in a sort of third class cabaret space. In Edinburgh the ceilings seemed to be coming down on us because there were punk rock people upstairs virtually every night. And we were trying to do quiet songs and all this stuff from Nova Scotia." But the critics loved the show anyway. Radio Clyde gave them a rave review and after the concerts ended, Cameron and Rogers rented a car and spent the next two weeks touring Scotland together—a trip John Allan still treasures in his memories. At a concert at the Argyle Folk Festival, someone recognized them and requested that they play a few numbers. The crowd wouldn't let them off the stage for an hour and a half, and after the show, they returned to the hotel with the rest of the performers, took over the bar and locked the doors to play music until seven the next morning.

Rogers and Cameron remained good friends up to the time of Rogers' tragic death in an airplane crash in June of 1982. At the funeral service held in Dundas, John Allan paid tribute to his friend by reciting the words of one of Stan Rogers' most moving songs, *The Mary Ellen Carter*.

John Allan's own career track was altered in the early '80s. In 1984, Balmur suggested that he might be better off with a new management company. Faced with the burgeoning success of Anne Murray's career, Balmur employees had their hands full and felt that another manager would be better able to concentrate on his plans. Cameron moved to Bruce Davidsen of Entertainment Management Corporation, who handled his business for the next five years. But it did not work out as well as expected. Cameron felt that the idea that he present himself as a children's entertainer was not expansive enough, though he did get bookings on the lucrative kiddies' concert circuit, as well as spots on shows such as the Canadian segments of "Sesame Street." But he hungered for the continuing contact with adult concert audiences, who would appreciate the variety and scope of his material.

Those concerts still existed, but it meant plenty of weeks away from home, touring courtesy of various Arts Councils to communities all over rural Saskatchewan or Ontario. Some big-name performers shunned such appearances, feeling that they were beneath their dignity, but John Allan, a country boy at heart, thrived on them. "I love the small towns I play in," he insists. "I can't wait to get onstage. I can't wait to find out what's happening in this little town I'm playing in." He did many gigs as a soloist and when he needed another guitarist to act as a backup player, often called on friends back home in Cape Breton or Halifax, though rising airfares often made this an expensive proposition. His rural fans were loyal, still remembering the kilted young man who appeared on "Don Messer's Jubilee." But the attitude towards the live concert was changing, at least among some performers he met while on the road. Cameron was beginning to dislike the phoniness of some musicians—

players or singers who told residents of the grubbiest industrial town about what a lovely city they had, and who then went on to shamelessly plug their albums, tours, and upcoming television specials. John Allan had no such pretensions; at one concert in a small prairie town he candidly told his listeners, "Ladies and gentlemen, trying to get hold of my albums is like trying to get a private audience with the Pope." But at that particular concert, he did have records and tapes with him and afterwards in the lobby, sold 125 units in an hour.

He was discovering one of the cardinal rules of the music industry in the 1980s: radio play was vitally connected to commercial success. There were more stations with a country format, but John Allan had concentrated on albums rather than releases of single songs suitable for the Top 40 programming which dominated most country stations.

In 1987, Cameron plunged into the mainstream country music format with an album produced in Nashville by Randy Scruggs and John Thompson. The production values were standard for that period; the steel guitar, heavy drums and wall of synthesized sound. Not surprisingly, that sound didn't always suit either the songs or the quality of John Allan's voice. He sounds ill at ease with the thick layers of sound, and the electronic instruments did not accompany his voice with the sympathy of the lighter, acoustic sound on his earlier albums. Several of the tunes are in country-rock style; *Burning the Daylight Hours* is contemporary country style, complete with steel guitars, and percussion and heavily harmonized voices backing him up. There's a version of Stan Rogers' song *Forty-five Years* which is scored more lightly with an acoustic setup and which he is able to deliver with more ease and eloquence. There's a John Prine song, *Be My Friend Tonight*; with a little rasp in his voice, Cameron adapts Prine's humorous lyrics imploring a girl to stay overnight. *Overnight Success* is the half-ironic tale of a musician in Nashville who finally makes it big after 15 years of hard work. Another pop-oriented song is *Shot in the Dark* with liner notes that mention a comment from his friend and fellow musician

Matt Minglewood saying, "John Allan, welcome to the world of rock and roll."

Some of the songs are undistinguished: the duet *Woodcarver* with singer Mary Joe Talley, *Harvest the Wind*, which can't be saved from mediocrity despite a splendid country fiddle intro by Graham Townsend, and one of Scruggs' own songs *There is a Comfort*.

Another friend from the Maritimes, Kevin Evans of the Evans and Doherty duo, wrote the lyrics for *Peter Behind the Wheel*. The best cut may be Mickey Newbury's *That was the Way it Was Then*; it has a more classic country sound, a muted and simpler backup that brings out John Allan's talent for nostalgic, unaffected singing. The title cut, another Kevin Evans ditty called *Good Times*, is a catalogue of the best things about being home in the Maritimes, right down to the feeds of lobster and the bottle of beer in his hand. Album sales were moderately successful—possibly the Nashville sound and style were not what Cameron's longtime fans expected from him—but it put him back in the record stores and in front of the record-buying public.

As an established name, John Allan rarely lacked for concert opportunities but they tended to be seasonal; jamborees and festivals, the main money-makers for country/folk performers, were often clustered in the months between June and September. Winter could be slack. John Allan's next musical venture was spread over a year between 1988 and 1989, during which he coordinated a large musical show for the Canadian Armed Forces, which toured the Middle East in June of 1989. With a cast of 23 performers plus technicians and a "MuchMusic" film crew who taped segments for broadcast, the preparation of the show entailed a lot of office time and paperwork, but it was a chance to learn more about talent management—something for which John Allan feels he has a flair. "One of the things I think I'm really good at is finding people who can perform and getting those people into a good, solid high-energy show that has reality to it. I'm not talking about Las Vegas shtick, I'm talking about being Canadian." He didn't clear a large profit personally, but the show was a success with the troops in the Middle East.

The effort to diversify his professional commitments has led Cameron into another area that has long intrigued him—theater. The idea had been with him since he was a young man watching the Clancy Brothers. Accomplished actors as well as musicians, they had the dramatic ability to work a crowd to the edge of tears, and then fits of laughter. John Allan had often wanted to try his luck on a stage. He got a chance, first appearing in the role of an alcoholic ex-hockey player in a CBC "Morningside" radio drama, and then onstage at the 1989 Stephenville Festival in Tom Gallant's play *Stepdance*. At Christmas of 1989, he won a starring role as Scrooge in Neptune Theatre's production of *A Christmas Carol*. He didn't seriously contemplate switching from music to the theater, but the the additional work as an actor helped to even out the seasonal fluctuations in income that tends to affect all performers. Cameron felt that it also helped his personal stage manner and presentation because of the discipline of teamwork and preparation with other cast members.

Around that time, Cameron signed a deal with Michael Ardenne of Brooks Diamond Productions, the management company that was at that time handling Rita MacNeil's career. The alliance proved to be temporary; though it got him more bookings in the Maritimes, the agreement lasted only a year.

Occasionally Cameron has toyed with the idea of moving back to the region, if only because many of the backup musicians he knows and prefers live there. His connections with home are strong; he appears frequently as a headlining act at various conventions, as a presenter at the annual East Coast Music Awards held in Halifax, and is a popular host at charitable events and fundraisers such as Old Timers' Hockey games.

After several years without a record release, Cameron broke through with a new record on the Margaree Sound label in the spring of 1991. Titled *Wind Willow*, with a title

cut by fellow Maritimer Tom Kelly, the album seems to indicate a return to the style of his earliest recording efforts. Gone are the heavy layers of electronic sound that characterized *Good Times*; the studio production by Russell Daigle and Larry Folk is immaculate, and the overall impression is of simplicity and dedication to the music rather than of flashy production effects. Some of the songs are re-releases of longtime Cameron standards; the first cut, *Ballad of St. Anne's Reel* by David Mallett is a quick, lighthearted rendition of the favorite song. The ballad's text tells the fanciful legend of the tune *St. Anne's Reel*, with fiddler Graham Townsend playing the reel tune in the breaks between verses. The title song *Wind Willow* is classic country-folk writing. The arrangement is simple, almost sparse with a bass line, electric piano and an accompaniment picked out on guitar, following the ebb and flow of the vocal part. The sweetness of the scoring allows Cameron's voice the chance to explore the melody with a liberty that the pop/country sound, with its heavy bass and drums, never did.

There's a new version of *The Four Marys*, one of the Cameron standards that songwriter Kenzie McNeil likes to call the "tribal tunes." It tells the story of Mary Hamilton, a maid to the ill-fated Mary Queen of Scots; the maid was charged with bearing a child out of wedlock and condemned to death. The song, written by an unknown balladeer of the time, describes Mary's thoughts shortly before her execution: "Last night the Queen had four Marys/Tonight there'll be but three/There was Mary Beaton and Mary Seton/And Mary Carmichael and me." (*Trad.*) With just voice and twelve-string guitar, the scoring is subtly affecting. After one unaccompanied refrain, a full chorus of voices swells, adding drum beats that create ominous images of Mary's long march to the scaffold.

There is only one Gaelic cut on the record, the lovesong *Calin Mo' Ruinsa* by Donald Ross. It begins with bagpipes sounding in the distance, gradually increasing in volume until a lilting piano introduction brings in Cameron's voice. The Gaelic title translates *Do You Remember*; each chorus is in Gaelic with verses in English. Despite the text, and the Celtic inflections in John Allan's voice, the song in its chord structure and lyric content could be mistaken for an old-fashioned country song. The first side finishes with a performance of Hamish Henderson's *Banks of Sicily*, the song that Cameron had previously recorded on *Weddings, Wakes and Other Things*. Henderson, a soldier in a World War II British regiment stationed in Sicily, wrote the song as an

All-round Celtic back-up player and soloist Dave MacIsaac in the backyard of his Halifax home in 1986 on the occasion of the release of his first solo recording of Scottish fiddle tunes on guitar. He plays all those instruments equally well.

ironic farewell to the island and though the tune is contemporary, it could be mistaken for one of the ancient ballads in its melancholy sense of loss and sorrow. John Allan's voice wraps itself around the mournful melody as though he wrote it himself; he sings sweetly on the first "Fare thee well" line of the chorus, then two lines later, energetically punches out Henderson's lyric about the weary "jocks," the common slang for Scottish troops.

On the second side, Cameron sings *Flower of Scotland*, an exhortation to patriotism written by Mrs. Norman McLeod. Following that is a revamped version of *Mary Ellen Carter*; after a fast, peppy intro on twelve-string guitar, John Allan comes in with a driving vocal line. Instrumental backing is modest; except for a chorus of voices which enters near the end, the production focuses on the lyrics, and Cameron crackles out Rogers' lines with gusto. Next is Gordon Lightfoot's song *Sit Down Young Stranger*. Stylistically, the backup combo of drums, piano, bass and guitar make the song sound more like the country-folk songs which John Allan first discovered 20 years ago. He deliberately modifies his voice, much as he did on his album *Get There by Dawn*, into a more typical country sonority, with a slight nasal edge. *Molly Bond* is next—the song of an immigrant in the distant west remembering his dead sweetheart. The lyric style has a faintly dated style— "an angel claimed her for his own"—that is more like the songs sung in the 1930s by a very young Hank Snow or Wilf Carter. The final cut, a daring selection for a Cameron album, is *Liberty*, written by Williamson and Weir. There's a lot more drive supplied in the instrumental arrangement from the bass and the offbeats of the drums; appropriate, since it's an anthem to freedom, a rousing call to liberty. But there is one oddly interpolated solo—a blazing electric guitar break between two verses that suggests a rock and roll band rather than a country/folk artist returning to his roots.

Was the solo added with a view to coaxing country stations into giving him more airplay? In an interview with editor Larry Delaney in the June, 1991 issue of *Country Music News*, Cameron talked about his experiences with station music directors who find it hard to fit his recordings into their format, saying, "The lack of radio airplay doesn't really bother me…. It's always been a situation where radio just doesn't know what to do with me—my music is enjoyable to most, but admittedly, it is different." In his review of the album in the August edition of *Country Music News*, Delaney described *Liberty* as being "a free-flowing and daringly produced (for a Cameron offering) tune that becomes infectious." Delaney tagged two tunes as being Cameron's best bets for radio exposure: *The Ballad of St. Anne's Reel* and the title cut *Wind Willow*. That same issue ran a photo of a smiling John Allan sporting a cowboy hat during his appearance at the Big Valley Jamboree in Craven, Saskatchewan.

One of the ideas that has long obsessed Cameron is the notion of organizing a troupe of Cape Breton performers—singers, dancers, pickers and fiddlers—to take to Nashville. Fiddler Dave MacIsaac recalls a 1978 trip to Nashville with John Allan, who was opening for the country group Asleep at the Wheel. Backstage at the concert, Cameron, fiddler Jerry Holland and Dave MacIsaac were doing a little playing to warm up for their show. After playing a string of fiddle tunes, they were surrounded by a group of Nashville musicians who blurted out, in tones of mixed appreciation and puzzlement "Where y'all from, Mars?"

Later, Cameron went to visit a friend at a publishing company and MacIsaac and Jerry Holland waited for him outside in a van. "He didn't come back, and he didn't come back," says MacIsaac, adding that finally he and Holland decided to make the best use of the time by playing a little music. Since they were crammed into an uncomfortably small space, MacIsaac held his guitar with the neck pointed upwards to the roof while Holland fiddled with his bow going in and out of the window. Completely absorbed in their music, they were unaware of the crowd that was gathering outside the vehicle; MacIsaac says that when he finally looked up, he saw 35 people dancing on the sidewalk to their music.

Shortly afterwards, a car pulled to a stop beside them and the driver rushed over to them shouting, "You're Jerry Holland! You're my favorite fiddler!" The enthusiastic fan turned out to be musician and songwriter John Hartford. Though he had never met Jerry Holland before, he recognized his playing from tapes he had heard. John Hartford was already a friend of John Allan; once, during a casual conversation, Hartford mentioned that he had recently heard a cassette tape of music recorded at a fiddler's funeral. In honor of the occasion several dozen other fiddlers had gathered to pay final respects to one of their own. The story sounded familiar and after John Allan asked a few questions, he discovered that the funeral was that of his own uncle Dan R. MacDonald. Hartford, best known for his song *Gentle on my Mind*, remains a friend of John Allan, and travels widely over North America studying various types of fiddling that are indigenous to the regions. "When he reached Cape Breton," says Cameron, "he stayed for two months."

Aside from taking care of his own personal business and appearances, John Allan remains a godfather to some of the emerging musical groups in the region. A family group that is achieving recognition is the Barra MacNeils, an attractive young ensemble of three brothers and one sister from North Sydney, Cape Breton. Lucy MacNeil sings and plays fiddle and bodhran, Kyle plays fiddle, Stewart sings and plays whistle and accordion, and Sheumas sings and plays keyboards. The MacNeils' musical style is also Celtic traditional, augmented as required by electronic keyboard or synthesizer. Their use of percussion is more sparing than some of the electric Celtic groups such as Rawlin's Cross. A preference for the bodhran, or Irish drum, and their use of the accordion and penny whistle often add a distinctive touch to their arrangements of dance and original tunes. On their three albums, the most recent being *Timeframe*, the MacNeils play a blend of Celtic traditional tunes plus their own original topical songs such as *Didn't Hear the Train*.

Another increasingly popular Celtic group is the Rankin Family Band. In a sense, they owe John Allan a debt of thanks for their debut; the 12 Rankin children made their earliest appearance on a stage with John Allan at a concert

Rising Cape Breton family band, The Barra MacNeils, in 1990. Left to right are Kyle, Sheumas, Lucy and Stewart MacNeil.

in Whycocomagh, Cape Breton, sometime in the late '60s. Since then, the group, now a mere five siblings—John Morris, Jimmy, Raylene, Heather and Cookie—are regarded as one of the brightest hopes of the folk/country business. Like John Allan, they got their start playing at country dances and parties and as a result, their music is often hybrid. They play and sing Gaelic traditional songs and instrumental tunes, but they also got to know a lot of old Hank Williams songs. Raylene Rankin, unofficial spokesman for the group, says, "We've been doing country songs as long as we've been singing Gaelic songs, maybe longer." And as is inevitable with musicians under 30, there's a hint of the rock and roll influence in their use of a drum set.

Since their sound is a quirky blend of tradition and innovation, a concert with the Rankins is somewhere between a kitchen racket, complete with duelling fiddlers and spirited stepdancing by the Rankin sisters, and a hootenanny where somebody smuggled in a synthesizer. Though many country and folk purists still frown on the use of electronic instruments, the Rankins say that they have discovered through touring that the variation in the condition of pianos in halls makes an electronic keyboard a necessity.

They have gradually moved closer to the mainstream of the music industry. Since their earliest days of playing at dances in the church hall at home in Mabou, the Rankins have found that what was once a pleasant weekend occupation has turned into a full time job. Appearances at folk festivals in Mariposa and Winnipeg exposed the Rankins to a large and eager audience, as did a half-hour CBC television special aired in the fall of 1990. And aside from their rollicking renditions of traditional songs such as *Tell My Ma* and *Mairi's Wedding*, the Rankins have an asset in that they write strong original material. Jimmy Rankin, a singer, percussionist and guitarist, writes gutsy songs about social issues close to home: *The Tramp Miners* deals with the lives of Cape Breton miners who travel the world as tramps looking for work, while *You Left a Flower* is a pure country song ornamented with dobro solos, and with a sweetly reproachful lyric.

John Morris Rankin has produced original fiddle tunes with titles such as *Jack Daniel's Reel* and *Molly Rankin's Reel* (named for his small daughter). The Rankin sisters sing in both Gaelic and English, their trademark being their high, sweet voices and close three-part harmony. Amazingly, none of the three read music; of the ear arrangements they work out, Cookie Rankin says "I think we come up with some inventive harmonies that way." The Rankins managed their own bookings until 1992 when they signed on with Brooks Diamond. They released two independently financed and produced albums which sold more than 50,000 copies, before signing a record deal, also in 1992, with Capitol-EMI. Compared to the mega-sales of country stars such as Anne Murray, the Rankins' sales may seem trifling, but for an independent group, the numbers are unusually high. The

Halifax Chronicle Herald/Bob Smith

Cape Breton's The Rankin Family accepting awards at the
1991 East Coast Music Awards for best recording band, best
roots-traditional artist and best live artist. From left, Heather,
Cookie, John Morris, Raylene and Jimmy.

Rankins have been winners of multiple awards at the annual
East Coast Music Awards show held in Halifax every February, and were nominated for three 1992 Juno awards, including best country group. The Rankins have also been helped
by their exposure on radio programs including Max Ferguson's
Saturday morning show on CBC Stereo, and Eric MacEwen's
weekly radio show, broadcast from P.E.I.

If only there were a national, or even international
showcase for all the talent, says John Allan. "The best thing
about a lot of these musicians is that they're so versatile. A
lot of them can stepdance and some of them can sing and
they can play piano or fiddle and they can mix it up…. Let's
face it, if we get on American television in Nashville, if we
get on TNN, we'll be appreciated by that many more people
in this country. It works like that."

Ten years ago, the idea of Celtic fiddlers appearing on the
same stage as Loretta Lynn would have been ludicrous; now,
it is not just possible, but probable. A St. Patrick's Day show
at the Opry in 1991 featured a troupe of Irish dancers straight
off the plane from Ireland, and Irish singer Maura O'Connell
guests on TNN shows such as "American Music Shop." The
Chieftains, Ireland's best-known traditional music group,
released an album called *The Greening of Nashville* in the spring
of 1992, featuring big-league Nashville personalities such as
Emmylou Harris, Chet Atkins and Ricky Skaggs. Wearying
perhaps of the whine and twang of traditional country, and
the relentless hard drive of contemporary country, Nashville
may finally be ready for the sweet melancholy of the Celtic
sound. As one Nashville veteran told fiddler Dave MacIsaac
after hearing him play, "I don't know what kind of music that
is, but I know it's my kind of music."

CHAPTER 7

Anne Murray

The lady with a plan

Is she country, or is she pop? When fans ask her, Anne Murray likes to answer with a resounding "YES!" And she's not just being cute or evasive. Anne Murray is one of the top-selling female vocalists in the history of recording, and she's achieved it by scoring high in two categories. Her album *Greatest Hits, Volume I* ranks second only to one by the late Patsy Cline in the ranking of Top 25 country albums. Yet that same album also appears on the listings of the Top 50 Pop hits, putting Murray in 22nd place ahead of pop stars Billy Joel, Chicago and U2.

Aside from the sheer thrill of selling so many records, Murray has enough awards to fill a small house: more than 20 Junos, gold records, silver records, platinum records, and Grammys. Her other accomplishments are diverse too; she's been inducted as a companion of the Order of Canada, and she's hosted an episode of the "Muppet Show." If she wanted to, she could probably retire triumphantly from the business, but she's a hardworking girl. As Murray told CBC "Morningside" host Peter Gzowski in a 1989 interview, "I don't have to prove anything.... I can play where I like."

Anne Murray has one of the most distinctive voices in the music industry. Other country music divas may wail, whine, twang or belt out the lyrics over a strident rock beat, but Murray's contralto voice is a refined instrument with the clear, articulated quality that most people expect only from a classical singer. In a business where many singers ruin their voices through bad habits, or strain to sing songs that are outside their range or ability level, Anne Murray stands out. The voice that pours out of her throat is luscious, melting, and flexible over a surprisingly large range. Some might argue that the gift of such a natural voice means that Murray has a jump start on other singers, but the fact is that she's spent a lifetime honing not only her voice, but her musical and interpretive skills. In the same radio interview, Murray told Gzowski, "I work very hard singing, I work as hard as Barbra Streisand.... She's more theatrical." It's an interesting comparison, since in English-speaking countries, Barbra Streisand may be Murray's only serious rival as bestselling female singer of all time. Streisand's theatricality, her knack for sweeping the listener off his feet with the sheer intensity of her emotion is undeniably powerful, but not to everybody's taste. Murray's emotional impact on her listeners is more subtle; she caresses the lyrics, relying on the richness and intimacy of her delivery to put across the song.

Anne Murray is one of the handful of megastars who can write her own ticket. Her life is compartmentalized; two weeks on the road, two weeks at home, two months off in the summer for vacation at her Nova Scotia home. With a crack management company at Balmur, the company she established in 1971, Murray can relax and concentrate on the matters dearest to her own heart; putting on the best possible show each night, and then getting back to her husband and children in Toronto. Unlike other country or pop stars who prattle about the art form and the serious impact of their music, Murray takes a professional attitude to her singing. She told Gzowski, "I treat it as just another job...no different from any other job except I share it with a lot of people."

If that sounds like the down-to-earth outlook of a smalltown girl, it's not surprising. Many of the women who sing country music seek to capitalize on their rural backgrounds with plenty of references to hard times down on the farm and all the heartbreak and difficulties they've suffered on the way to the top. By comparison, it's hard to picture Anne Murray yodelling or dressed in cowgirl fringes, hat and boots like the Girls of the Golden West. Murray knocks down many of those ideas about the female country singer; she doesn't sob or sing plaintive ditties about her man walking out on her. Instead, she picks songs that suit her personality and which she can sing convincingly, using her intelligence and interpretive skill as well as her lush voice. In *Billboard* magazine of April 27,1991, Edward Morris, reporting on the Nashville scene, called Murray "...glamorous, sassy, and open-minded." He praised her for remaining within the country format since 1970 without ever submerging her personal convictions and identity within the larger stereotype of the female country singer.

Anne Murray is not a coal miner's daughter, but she's from a coal miner's town—Springhill, Nova Scotia. Springhill has been a one-industry town since coal was discovered there in 1828. The population hasn't changed much since Morna

Anne Murray was born there in 1945; it's about 5,000, give or take a few. It's a hardscrabble town, the kind of place where most of the action takes place on the main street, and Saturday night at the Legion is about as wild as the social life gets. Visitors to town notice the usual number of stores and small businesses, but the largest local employer is still the nearby prison, the Springhill Institution. Since the Anne Murray Centre opened its doors in 1989, the local tourist industry has been given a boost by fans who travel from all over North America to have a look inside the small brick building which houses the collection of Murray memorabilia.

Anne's father, Dr. Carson Murray, was the only surgeon in town and as such provided a comfortable living for his wife and six children. Anne grew up as a tomboy and the Murray Centre displays some of her sports equipment—the baseball mitt, skates and skis that belonged to a young girl who, as she later told Gzowski, felt uncomfortable in dresses. But the athletic talent was accompanied by an unusual voice and an aptitude for music. She took piano lessons and made a weekly bus trip to nearby Tatamagouche to take voice lessons. She had the natural gift of a richly resonant voice with a large range, but she also worked to acquire technique. She studied repertoire, interpretation and learned to breathe correctly and sing harmony. At home, she was surrounded by different musical styles. Her parents liked crooner Perry Como and her brothers and friends followed the pop hit parade. And there was talk about folk music too; her aunt Elizabeth Murray was a music teacher who had worked with folklorist Dr. Helen Creighton. In fact, about the only music Anne Murray didn't like was country music, as she told a writer for *Country Music Beat* in 1975. As a young girl, she was mostly interested in the quality of the voice and intensely disliked most of the country singers she heard on the radio.

She spent a single year studying at Mount Saint Vincent University in Halifax, and during that time participated in a talent show in which a nun reproved her for sounding "too black" in her rendition of George Gershwin's *Summertime*.

Though wrong in her judgement and racist in her choice of words, the sister may have put her finger on the exact vocal quality that was to figure in Murray's eventual success; the rich, sensual intimacy that makes a lot of listeners feel that she's singing to them personally. Bill Langstroth certainly thought so when Murray auditioned in 1964 for a spot as a singer on "Singalong Jubilee." Langstroth later told writer Elspeth Cameron in a 1988 *Chatelaine* magazine profile, "The voice went right through me and had me pinned like a specimen to the wall. Voompf!" Murray didn't get the job that time, but when there was another opening two years later, Langstroth called her at the University of New Brunswick in Fredericton where Murray was working on a degree in physical education, and offered her the job. She was interested, but after a year teaching physical education at a Prince Edward Island high school in Summerside, Murray had to decide whether she should commit herself to the featured spot as a soloist she'd been offered, or continue with her teaching career. At least two of her new colleagues encouraged Murray to take the chance on herself as a singer: Brian Ahern, the musical director who would produce 10 of her albums, and Bill Langstroth, who would become her first manager and eventually her husband.

Anyone who watched Anne Murray during those years on "Singalong Jubilee" remembers her as the smiling, radiantly blond girl dressed in contemporary chic clothes such as miniskirts and pants suits. A blurb in a November 1967 issue of the CBC *Times* mentioned that Murray's voice was in such a low register that some of the men in the "Singalong" cast joked that they wanted her moved to the tenor section. "Singalong Jubilee" was the perfect place for a budding singer to learn her craft; the atmosphere on the show was relaxed, but the cast members worked on solos as well as ensemble numbers, and they had to be versatile. Bill Langstroth as host projected an easygoing charm, whether

Anne Murray in 1968 as she appeared on CBC-TV's "Singalong Jubilee," her first important break in show business.

CBC-TV Publicity

Halifax Chronicle Herald

he was leading them in a chorus of *Farewell to Nova Scotia* or doing the limbo.

It was during this time that Anne Murray met several of the people who would shape her career for many years. Aside from Langstroth and Ahern, there was Fred McKenna, the blind singer/guitarist whom Anne would later credit on her 1980 album, *A Country Collection*, with having introduced her to country music. And there was Gene MacLellan, who wrote several of her earliest hit songs. She was getting enough work to keep her and a number of other aspiring musicians steadily employed, what with "Singalong Jubilee" and another CBC half-hour show named "Music Hop" that was broadcast every afternoon, five days a week. Each show came from a different city—Montreal, Toronto, Winnipeg and Halifax—and featured live bands playing Top 40 rock and roll. The Halifax segment, "Frank's Bandstand," was hosted by popular, wise-cracking deejay Frank Cameron, and live bands travelled from all over the Maritimes to be on the show. Murray was busy learning, and formulating her own standards and tastes. In a profile in *Maclean's* magazine in 1972, she told writer Bill Howell, "I learned pretty well everything I needed to know before I left Halifax."

Her first solo album in 1968 was a cheapie by today's standards. It was cut in Toronto on the Arc label for about $3000. Bill Langstroth wrote the liner notes, and Brian Ahern produced the album, which was called *What About Me*. The record content showed the strong influence of the folk and contemporary pop songs that at that time comprised her repertoire. There's Joni Mitchell's *Both Sides Now*, Bob Dylan's *Last Thing on my Mind*, and a single venture into country music, *There Goes My Everything*. Back in Nova Scotia, Anne picked up a few friends to play in a backup band and started on the touring trail of clubs, coffeehouses and gyms.

During a summer booking at Confederation Centre in

Anne Murray in a 1970 concert. Note her bare feet, her trade mark at the time, a sign of her easy-going informality.

Charlottetown, a jazz bass player named Skip Beckwith heard Murray sing. Beckwith was appearing locally with Bryan Brown's jazz trio, and already knew Brian Ahern through their mutual interest in jazz. Both originally from Halifax, they had often met during student days to do a little playing together at the fraternity house to which they both belonged. Beckwith went on to study jazz at Berklee College in Boston, and subsequently worked in Toronto as a jazz bass player for some years. As a seasoned professional, Beckwith was impressed by Murray's vocal ability and the calibre of her musical presentation. He recently recalled, "The quality of her singing was incredible. She was dead in tune and she had this very interesting voice which nobody had ever heard anything about. Really, nobody had ever heard anything like that before." When Beckwith was back in Toronto, he got a call from Brian Ahern asking him to round up musicians for an Anne Murray recording.

Murray had been approached by executives at Capitol Records-EMI of Canada. Since Capitol's parent company was American, Murray stood a better chance of having her records released internationally instead of merely to the Canadian market. She signed a deal to make a record for $18,000, again with Brian Ahern as producer. Compared to today's expensive and elaborate production techniques and studio setups, *This Way is My Way* was modest. Beckwith remembers an eight-track studio in the north end of Toronto where Ahern usually worked. Many of the arrangements were head arrangements, improvised from a melody sheet with chord symbols, and Ahern would add overdubbed tracks of steel guitar or piano as required. Rick Wilkins, a prominent Toronto musician and arranger, did the string arrangement for *Snowbird*.

Several other songs by Gene MacLellan made it to the record; *Bidin' my Time* and *Hard As I Try*, along with a tune named *No One is to Blame* by another "Singalong Jubilee" buddy Steve Rhymer. However good the other songs were, *Snowbird*, the song released as a single, was in a class by itself. Skip Beckwith says, "I know that Brian Ahern felt that the

string arrangement that Rick Wilkins came up with put the icing on that tune.… It satisfied the country people, it satisfied the pop people." With its soaring string parts, light country beat, and a set of lyrics that were a bittersweet blend of memory and regret, the song meant a lot of things to a lot of people. It captured the subtle melancholy of MacLellan's musical style, and the image of the snowbird flying away to freedom touched an entire audience who had previously dismissed country music. It was the beginning of the crossover hit—songs that were aimed at listeners who had no interest in acid rock, but who were not yet ready for hardcore western and country music.

It took a little pushing from the parent company, but *Snowbird* became a hit after stations such as CHUM-FM in Toronto began playing it. Murray's career, and that of many other Canadian artists of that time, was assisted by the new CRTC regulations that mandated a percentage of Canadian content on radio stations. Having a hit song on the radio paid off in two ways: royalties on the record itself, plus the public interest in a hit performer, which translated into a demand for live concert appearances. After selling a quick million records, Anne Murray decided that for the sake of her career she needed to be based in Toronto. A generation earlier, the goal would have been New York or Nashville, but moving to Toronto was a reasonable compromise. It would allow her to keep in touch with important people in the music industry, it was a central point in terms of airline connections, and yet it would guarantee her some kind of normalcy in her private life. When she bought her first house in Forest Hills with a whopping royalty check of $90,000, Murray invited her brother Bruce, her trusted advisor Leonard Rambeau, and several others to move in with her.

A hit record such as *Snowbird* virtually guaranteed a major tour, which would work in turn to boost record sales even higher. Murray was already receiving inquiries from the producers of Glen Campbell's television show in Los Angeles. Campbell, also a Capitol artist, took a shine to Murray's voice and invited her to be on the "Glen Campbell Goodtime

Anne Murray in 1969, radiating country girl charm and good looks.

Halifax Chronicle Herald

Hour," which gave her a high-profile introduction to the large American television audience. Her first gold record was awarded during an appearance on the Merv Griffin show, and Murray flew back home to Toronto where Skip Beckwith was putting together a band for the upcoming tour.

Beckwith was to be Murray's man-on-the-spot for several years; a combination road manager, band leader, and fixit person for problems during the tours. After a decade of work, "beating my brains against the wall, playing jazz music," as he describes it, Beckwith was ready for a change. The solid support from Capitol Records made the invitation from Murray an enticing one. He says, "I was interested in the quality of the music, it was very high—and the idea of learning production techniques, studio techniques." The Canadian segment of the tour opened with a well-publicized gig at the Royal York Hotel's Imperial Room. "Bare feet and all," laughs Beckwith, of Anne's casual style at that time. The Canadian tour went off with only a few hitches, but the American tour had a rocky start. Though they were treated in high style—limousine service from the airport, first class airfare and the best hotels—their initial booking at a Chicago club was a rude shock. They arrived to find that the club was recovering from a flood a few days before, and the place was still full of water. After a sound check that afternoon, the band members left their instruments locked in the dressing room, assuming they were secure there. A few hours before showtime, they returned to find everything gone. Beckwith's bass was stolen, and sideman Lenny Breau's two guitars were gone. The record company took care of rentals and replacements, but as Beckwith recalls, it was an unpleasant reminder that they were in a big, tough business.

Murray's backup band was an outstanding one in those years, according to Skip Beckwith. On her solo concerts it included two guitarists, a keyboard player, two horns, drums and a bass. For major concerts or in Las Vegas, the act was augmented by extra musicians hired to play strings, wind instruments and even harp. At various times the backup band opened the Anne Murray show by billing themselves

as Richard, and then playing a fast-paced opening set before introducing the star of the show. A number of prominent jazz and country players passed through the ranks; sax player Don Thompson and jazz guitar virtuoso Lenny Breau, to name only two. If Murray ever worked as an opening act, it was for hot acts such as Loggins and Messina or Seals and Croft. Of those concerts in the early to middle '70s, Beckwith reminisces, "We'd be playing for ten or twelve thousand people. The Yale Bowl or something—pretty marvellous experience." Murray had by this time an enthusiastic and extremely vocal contingent of fans almost anywhere she appeared, who would greet her outside the concert venue and follow her to her hotel, begging for autographs and photos.

Though she was working with country musicians such as Glen Campbell, Murray did not define herself exclusively as a country singer. A look at the contents of her albums in the early '70s shows that her taste was as much a reflection of current rock music as of the country music of that time. Sometimes they appeared cheek by jowl, as on her 1971 album *Talk It Over in the Morning*. Murray did a soulful version of Carole King's hit *You've Got a Friend* alongside a country-rock song by Gordon Lightfoot called *Cotton Jenny*. It's also worth noting that the songs that usually caught on with the public and got the most radio play, such as *Cotton Jenny* and Shirley Eikhard's *It Takes Time*, were often indistinguishable from contemporary pop songs, except, perhaps, for the presence of a pedal steel guitar in her arrangements.

Another record released in 1971, this time a duet record with Glen Campbell, is again more typical of the sound being aimed at the country market. Some people in the industry would later label the style as countrypolitan, a citified version of country. It had a country sound, but without the fiddles and mandolins often associated with hard country, honky-tonk, bluegrass or hillbilly music.

Anne Murray was only one of the artists who would prosper under the countrypolitan definition. So did singers Olivia Newton-John, Kenny Rogers, and John Denver. Their vocal style was a far cry from the nasal, pleading tones

Songwriter Shirley Eikhard, whose song, Something To Talk About, *became a big hit for Bonnie Raitt.*

of country singers in the '40s and '50s. Usually the country-politan musicians sang with a sweeter, more articulated vocal quality. And the topic matter was different; instead of songs about little cabins in the hills, or about Mom, trains and prison, these singers sang about disappointed love affairs, and the unfairness of life. Often the backup instrumentation was hard to distinguish from a middle-of-the-road rock band, though often including a pedal steel guitar as a

nod to tradition. Electric guitars, basses, keyboards, and later synthesizers formed the nucleus of the new country sound.

Some of the finest work on Murray's early albums has been with country material. *Country*, produced by Brian Ahern in 1974, is a good example. It was a compilation of previously released songs, and from the patchwork quilt depicted on the jacket to the mournful whine of the steel guitar solo on *He Thinks I Still Care*, the album showed Murray's flair for country phrasing and tunes.

On the same album there was also a version of Gene MacLellan's gospel rocker *Put Your Hand in the Hand*. Ahern's punchy, energetic arrangement recalled the pop/rock style of singer Elton John. Murray belted the lyrics out over a hard-edged scoring that included saxes, lots of percussion and a rocking piano accompaniment, a feat which proved that she had the talent and drive to sing more than middle-of-the-road music. Skip Beckwith, along with other Murray colleagues, has always maintained that with Anne Murray's vocal equipment, she could, if she wanted, sing anything from hard rock to light jazz. He, for one, regrets that she chose not to do so.

In later years Murray would joke with her audiences, claiming that with those first albums she believed in her naiveté that the way you made a record was to pick songs you liked, arrange them, and record them. The problem is, as she says, that the record stores have to know into what bin to file her tape or record. Country? Folk? Pop? Her albums' contents ranged from contemporary folk such as James Taylor's *Fire and Rain*, to what was for her a hard rocker, *You Can't Have a Hand on Me*. The sheer variety in style and treatment of songs must have left disc jockeys shaking their heads in bewilderment.

Murray often asked Skip Beckwith to scout out new songs for her while they were on the road, particularly while in Nashville. She has never written a song herself, and was extremely choosy about the songs she picked to interpret. She didn't care for the saccharin style of many country songs; possibly, her early interest in folk music gave her a preference

ANNE MURRAY

In 1973, backstage at the Troubador Club in Los Angeles, Canada's newest singing star hobnobs with, from left to right, John Lennon, Harry Nilsson, Alice Cooper and ex-Monkee Mickey Dolenz.

MUSIC GREATS

for intelligent story-songs rather than weepy ballads. Beckwith during his travels encountered Rodney Crowell, at that time one of the crop of new songwriter/poets who were re-inventing and re-invigorating country music with their highly personal, soul-searching songs. The Murray troupe also encountered singer Emmylou Harris, a protégé of the late Gram Parsons and the Flying Burrito Brothers. Harris was working on her solo career and struck up an acquaintance with Beck-with, and a more important relationship with Brian Ahern, whom she later married. Their marriage ended in 1983 but Ahern was to produce some of Harris's most significant albums, including *Quarter Moon in a Ten Cent Town*.

While they were collecting and then choosing material for any new Murray album, Beckwith can remember that there were marathon sessions of wading, almost literally, through piles of demo tapes. Hundreds of aspiring songwriters with varying degrees of talent mailed their material to Balmur. Says Beckwith, "We'd go through boxes and boxes and boxes of tapes. Brian had a house on Maple Street in Rosedale, and he had a pool table in the front room along with the stereo stuff. When we were working on an Anne Murray project that pool table would become full of cassettes and demos. The whole pool table would be stacked three or four feet high." But it took a while to create a followup to *Snowbird*. Of the songs that finally made it to the recording stage, it wasn't until 1973 that Murray scored another bona fide hit in *Danny's Song*. Later, another Murray hit song, *Send a Little Love My Way*, became the theme of the movie *Oklahoma Crude*.

Murray's management company Balmur, formed in 1971, was named for several of the most critical people in the operation; 'B' stood for Brian Ahern and Bill Langstroth, 'A' and 'Mur' were for Anne herself, and the 'L' was for Leonard Rambeau, a member of her organization from the beginning, who rose to become her manager and Balmur's president in 1976. There were several others involved in Anne Murray's business operations too, such as accountant Lyman McInnis

and lawyer David Matheson. They formed a group of people who, together with a talent pool that included John Allan Cameron, Gene MacLellan, Steve Rhymer and Robbie MacNeill, were fondly known in Toronto as the Maritime Mafia.

Still, in the early '70s some things were not working out quite as Murray and company had expected. Her personal life was on hold, since, until Bill Langstroth got his divorce, the couple could not marry. Her tours were extensive, but they didn't always make money. Murray has said that she sometimes went home to Toronto close to broke. Speaking of those days to writer Elspeth Cameron in 1988, she recalled, "I'd go on the road for three months and come home deeper in debt. I finally came home broke and I bawled my eyes out as I told the whole thing to Bill."

She tried a new strategy. In 1973, she hired Shep Gordon, best known as manager of the outrageous rocker Alice Cooper. The plan was to break Anne out of the wholesome, barefoot country-girl image. Her first gig under Gordon's management, booked for the American Thanksgiving Day in November of 1973, had Anne Murray climbing out of a wooden turkey onstage at the Troubadour Club in Los Angeles. A photo taken on the occasion shows Anne Murray with John Lennon on her right, Harry Nilsson resting his chin on her left shoulder, Alice Cooper (minus his trademark heavy black eye makeup) and ex-Monkee Mickey Dolenz grinning widely. The idea had been to associate Anne Murray with a funky group of musicians, but in retrospect, Murray dismissed the idea. She told writer Perry Stern in a 1988 *Canadian Musician* interview, "...it goes against my very grain to do that kind of thing. It's surprising what that can do for a publicity person, and I realize that, but it bugs my ass that by being in a picture like that, all of a sudden you're hip."

Reviews were mixed. The rock-and-roll industry began to notice her. Writing in *Rolling Stone*, critic Lester Bangs called her, in his inimitable gonzo style, "...a hypnotically compelling interpretrix with a voice like molten high school

Anne poses in 1975 with Canadian Prime Minister Pierre Trudeau and his wife Margaret at Government House in Ottawa where she had just received the Order of Canada from the Queen.

*Anne receives a Joseph Howe commemorative
dollar from Blair Beed during the 1977 Joseph
Howe Festival in Halifax-Dartmouth.*

driving young rocker from New Jersey named Bruce Springsteen.

And still, through no fault of her own, all the hard work she and her company put in failed to produce the kind of results she was looking for. Of that time, Murray told *Canadian Musician* in 1988, "I had four bona fide hit records and the career was going nowhere.... It wasn't well thought out. It was just fill in the dates. A touring strategy is very important. Built around the release of an album, a television special or whatever, everything has to be carefully planned."

By 1975, Murray was ready for a break. When Bill Langstroth's divorce finally came through, Murray and Langstroth married in June of that year. Murray was ready to retire from performing, if not permanently, then at least while she got a start on the private life and family she'd wanted for so long. Her production team underwent a shakeup; Brian Ahern left Toronto for Los Angeles to start his own production company, though he would connect again with Balmur in the late '80s to produce an album for their new client George Fox. Another change on the Murray team was that bassist Skip Beckwith, now married and with a small child, was tired of touring and tired of Toronto. He parted company with Anne on the best of terms and when he returned to Halifax, the termination of his contract gave him title to a piece of land outside the city. It was part of a deal they'd made in which Beckwith had foregone financial bonuses or extra pay as music director. He built a house on the property located in Indian Harbour, and began playing jazz again. Beckwith eventually moved to Antigonish where he now teaches in the jazz program at Saint Francis Xavier University.

Of the time he spent in the Murray backup band, Beckwith has only high praise for the singer. He says now, "I stayed with her for six years and I never heard her sing one note out of tune. Ever, on any of those shows. Monitors or no monitors, she has the voice." Beckwith's favorite Murray recording is still her 1974 album *Highly Prized Possession*. On this album, Murray began one side with a version of the early

rings and a heavy erotic vibe." Yet around the same time, music critic William Littler, writing in the *Toronto Star* in March of 1974, expressed some reservations about Murray's emotional range. But Littler was quick to add: "And yet she obviously does have something. Call it Doris Dayism if you will, but there is an appealing naturalness about the musical Maritimer, reinforced by the kind of sexuality that manages to be both provocative and clean." Murray changed her hairstyle from a modified long shag cut to a mop of tight, frizzy curls. Sometimes she shocked her audience by saying saucy things such as "You bet your ass," that were hardly consistent with a Doris Day image, and at one concert in New York's Central Park, Murray's opening act was a hard-

ANNE MURRAY

'60s hit *Dream Lover*, began the flip side with the Beatles tune *Day Tripper*, and ended with what was virtually a protest song, *Please Don't Sell Nova Scotia*. Critic Jon Landau praised it in *Rolling Stone* saying, "In the past she's been classified as middle-of-the-road but the drumming (by Pintii Glan) is too hard, the arrangements too intimate for her to qualify for membership in that dreary genre."

Back in Toronto, Murray's next step was a controversial one. After the birth of her children (William in 1976 and Dawn in 1979) she wanted to spend the maximum amount of time with them, yet keep herself in the public's mind. Murray cut a children's record, *There's a Hippo in My Tub* in 1977, for which she received a liner credit as associate producer. But there were much bigger opportunities waiting for her. When she agreed to become commercial spokesperson for the Canadian Imperial Bank of Commerce some critics scoffed that she'd gone Establishment, but Murray had her own reasons. She'd spent years working on a career, and she felt she had earned the right to concentrate on her marriage. Eventually her whole schedule would be oriented to that domestic life and she would never apologize for it. Murray told writer Lee Anne Nicholson of *TV Guide* in September 1989, "As much as I sometimes might want to try other things, my children are more important to me than everything."

At the same time, Murray was planning a second phase to her performing career. Now with Leonard Rambeau as her manager, she set out her priorities: quality time at home with her kids, and touring with a designated plan, rather than just random dates. And there was her desire to be a Top 40 star as well as an acknowledged country star. That finally happened in 1978, when she was nominated for a Grammy in the pop category for *You Needed Me*. The competition was stiff; she was up against Carly Simon, disco queen Donna Summer, Olivia Newton-John and Barbra Streisand. But *You Needed Me*, written by Randy Goodrum, had the makings of a surefire hit. It suited her silky low range and had the kind of tender, positive lyrics that the new Anne Murray—a

contented wife and mother—could deliver with heartfelt conviction. In the Murray Centre in Springhill, a quote from the singer herself says that she regards *You Needed Me* as the best song she's ever recorded, and also her personal favorite. She won the Grammy for best female pop vocal and was able to launch, if not exactly a comeback, another shot at superstardom.

Ironically, the album *Let's Keep it That Way*, which contained the hit single, had been intended for the country rather than the pop market. The collection has some subtle and varied work; the arrangements sound as though they're custom-tailored to her singing style, focusing on Murray's voice rather than on a lush background. The title cut, *Let's Keep It That Way*, is as close as Murray ever gets to singing an actual cheatin' song; the lyrics depict a woman who is tempted by a new love but at the last moment finds herself unable to contemplate lying. *Hold Me Tight* is a sampler of the hip, occasionally outrageous side of Anne Murray with a funkier, almost reggae backup plus a melodic line that stretches her voice into the extremes of its range. And there are a couple of straightforward country ballads. One of them was the suggestive *We Don't Make Love Anymore*, another a cover version of *Tennessee Waltz* that could pass as the last waltz played at a barndance, complete with steel guitar and Floyd Cramer-style country piano.

But on the second time around, and with a smash hit song, Anne Murray was not going to be playing any barndances, hoedowns or outdoor jamborees. Her venues were strictly uptown; a sold-out week at the Royal Alexandra Theatre in Toronto, sold-out shows at Radio City Music Hall and Carnegie Hall in New York, and appearances on the talk-show circuit: the "Today Show," "Phil Donahue," "Dinah Shore." And when they went back on the road with a hand-picked new band, the rules were clear-cut; no drinking the day of a show, and strict adherence to decisions about rehearsals and schedules. Unlike the old days when shows might start late or there might be problems with the sound system or lights, Murray, always known as a perfectionist, was now able to insist that when she walked onstage, she didn't want to be concerned about anything except how she sang.

There were other revisions to the act. When Murray first began appearing in Las Vegas, she occasionally went barefoot and wore hot pants, which were at the time the trendiest apparel for stylish young women. In the early '80s, Murray's visual image was overhauled, and it wasn't just a change in hairdo. She appeared onstage in heels, her statuesque figure sheathed in beaded and sequined gowns. Unlike the early days in which she sometimes seemed to be ill at ease with the patter between songs, Murray joked with the audience, told anecdotes as though they had just occurred to her, and even added a soft-shoe dance routine to her act. She became relaxed enough to poke fun at herself, even at her reputation for being an ardent sports fan. Deborah Cowley, writing in the August 1985 *Reader's Digest*, told of a San Francisco concert at which Murray told her fans at intermission, "I've gotta phone to check on the hockey scores!" Like Barbara Mandrell, another country-pop singer who appealed to an audience far beyond the traditional country music fan, Murray was creating a musical show that seemed more aimed at Las Vegas or Broadway than the Grand Ole Opry.

Back at home in Canada, a controversy was brewing. Anne Murray had been performing on the Juno Awards for some years, but had long been exasperated by what she considered the technical sloppiness of the show. The final straw, she told Peter Gzowski, came when Ed Schreyer was trying to make a dedication to the late pianist Glenn Gould but could not be heard over the noise of the crowd. Murray vowed she'd never appear on the Junos again until people showed some respect. Aside from the noise, there were technical glitches that bothered her. Murray told organizers that when they cleaned up the show and found somebody who could light and shoot her properly, she'd be back.

It made a minor tempest in a teapot. One of the sillier suggestions made at the time was that Murray, a perennial Juno winner, should gracefully withdraw from the Best Female Vocalist category and give somebody else a chance. Murray refused, and that, coupled with her expressed opinions about the award show's shortcomings, caused a few people to react angrily. Bruce Allen, at the time the manager of rock singer Bryan Adams, lobbied Murray to return, hinting that Canadian entertainers had the duty to show up at the biggest award ceremony the Canadian music industry offers. Eventually the show was redesigned. It now takes place in a more subdued theater setting with no eating or drinking during the awards. Murray admitted to Gzowski that upon her return to the fold she was mildly nervous about what kind of reception she'd get. But she was greeted with a standing ovation.

Standing ovations were becoming the norm. Anne Murray was now one of the biggest draws on the international concert circuit, travelling to Europe, Australia, Japan, and all over the continental United States. She appeared regularly at the Las Vegas Hilton, where her show is one of the few remaining acts that can guarantee a jammed showroom.

Yet Murray has an ambiguous attitude to the glitzy world of high show business. As she told Peter Gzowski, "I don't like Las Vegas.... I like it for a weekend." She has called it a "wonderful school" for learning about all aspects of the business, but also offered the opinion, "...Vegas is tough because they aren't a cohesive group. They're from all over." Unlike some performers who play in Las Vegas, Anne Murray will only do one show a night. There have been a few changes since the glory days of the early '80s, when a performer such as Dolly Parton could demand and often receive weekly fees rumored to be as high as $350,000. Under that financial pressure, many Vegas showrooms, unable or unwilling to meet those prices, have closed or else have switched from big name headliners to revues or talent that isn't as "hot" (read "expensive").

Luckily there are other venues. Murray's longtime company president and close personal friend, Leonard Rambeau, is regarded by his peers as being one of the most alert businessmen in the industry. Brooks Diamond, formerly Rita MacNeil's manager, says of him, "Leonard is a pretty hands-on guy. He knows the world market, he knows the Canadian market, he's particularly familiar with the American market." Yet the Murray-Rambeau association is somewhat unorthodox. Addressing a seminar sponsored by the Music Industry of Nova Scotia in 1990, Rambeau told the audience that in more than 20 years he and Anne had never signed a contract. A simple handshake was all these Maritimers needed to guarantee their contractual relationship. It's an unusual situation in the music industry. Even with legal contracts, managers, agents and producers are hired and fired, sometimes with nasty public repercussions. Bitter squabbles and lawsuits are unfortunately as much a part of the business as big egos. But Rambeau, a native Maritimer from Smelt's Cove in Cape Breton, told writer David Livingston that he would never ask Murray to do anything that would make her uncomfortable. By all accounts, he is content to manage business for Anne and leave the artistic details to her, her musical director and her current record producer.

The apparently smooth progress of her career was jarred with her 1985 album *Something to Talk About*. It was a venture into the new field of electronic pop and the single release *Now and Forever*, produced by whiz kid David Foster, was an even bigger jolt to the Murray fan club than rock critic Lester Bangs' endorsement had been a decade earlier. In the song video a sleek Anne Murray—miniskirted, with bleached and spiked blonde hair—was seen chatting up and eventually kissing a strange man in an elevator. For fans whose idea of Anne Murray was either the barefoot girl strumming *Snowbird* on the guitar, or the conservatively coiffed matron plugging the Bank of Commerce, *Now and Forever* was a shock. Some critics called the album a calculated effort to score on the pop charts; but *Now and Forever* ended up at the top of the country charts instead. The album may have been a mistake as a concept, but as Leonard Rambeau commented to writer Perry Stern, "How

many other people's mistakes sell 750,000 units?"

Using David Foster to produce might have been perceived by some as cynical, but the odds were that Foster was more than amenable to the chance to work with a such a major talent. During the taping of *Tears Are Not Enough* that Foster produced, he had been impressed by Murray's professionalism, and the fact that her segment of the ballad was perfect on the first take. But despite its position at the top of the country charts, the *Something to Talk About* album had a plush, over-produced sound that for country purists put it well outside even the extended boundaries of country music.

Although radio play is acknowledged as the bottom line for both country and pop artists, there is still the need to get out in front of the public on the concert stage. Murray travels often through the U.S., but her appearances in Canada have been less frequent in the past decade. The problem, common to all touring acts, is logistical. Since Murray's days of playing high school gyms are long gone, the challenge is to find a suitable venue in a location where the costs of mounting the show will not exceed ticket revenues. Distance is another problem; in the midwest U.S., for example, several major cities with a large enough population base to guarantee good attendance often lie within reasonable travelling distance of each other. Canadian cities are so spread out that the time and effort required to transport the Murray show—musicians, technical crew, makeup and wardrobe assistant and the star herself—from city to city can be daunting.

Murray undertook a major Canadian tour in 1987 with the Ford Motor Company as a corporate sponsor. There was some sniping at her from several quarters, despite the fact that many major artists nowadays have their tours underwritten by a variety of corporate sponsors, from Coca-Cola to utility companies. Anne Murray discussed the tour in her 1988 *Canadian Musician* interview with Perry Stern, saying: "That was a big, big tour for me.... Canada's a difficult place to tour. The cities are so far apart.... In New York, every time I play there, I play in a city I've never heard of and they say, 'Oh yeah, there's 150,000 people here!'" Of the admittedly snarky comments about the corporate sponsorship, Murray dismissed them by telling Stern, "I don't think a person out in the audience gives a shit whether I'm being sponsored by Ford."

Rising costs were affecting all aspects of the music business, and corporate production of tours was the only solution. Soloists who had once carried large bands and backup singers on tour were having to cut back, partly because they couldn't manage the expenses associated with hotels, transportation and salaries. And with the advent of electronic keyboards, programming and synthesizers, it was possible to reduce bands even farther since one musician could cover several instrumental parts by duplicating the sounds on a keyboard. Audiences didn't always like so much electronic edge to the sound. They complained that it was often too loud and that unlike the good old days of players who could show off by improvising a new solo each night, drum machines and dense electric sounds made every band sound alike. But it was often much easier for the music arranger and director. A synthesizer, some argued, is utterly reliable, costs less to transport, and never takes an extended coffee break or asks for more money.

Yet Murray still seemed unwilling to make up her mind whether she was more interested in pursuing the country or the pop market. The solution appeared to be to stay in the middle of the road, and to follow trends rather than create them. Her 1988 album *As I Am*, recorded in Nashville, had another new producer, Kyle Lehning. It featured Murray's cover version of Rita MacNeil's *Flying on Your Own*. The song was already a proven hit and Murray had high hopes for her single, as she told Stern: " I'll be really upset if *Flying On Your Own* isn't a hit because I really believe in that song." The Murray version did get airplay, but wasn't a smash hit. In a profile of Rita MacNeil published in *Maclean's* in 1988, Murray was quoted as telling writer Ann Finlayson: " That song, which I loved the first time I heard it, got terrific response from live audiences.… It died for one reason: it is written from a woman's point of view—and all the radio

programmers are men. I don't have much time for people like that, but that's the way it is in this business."

Until her 1990 release *You Will*, Murray had not had a major hit on the U.S. charts in nearly 5 years, as she reported to *Country Music News* in February, 1991. She admitted that the album meant a comeback of sorts—not that she'd gone anywhere, or in any way dropped out of the business. Murray can still pack them in at the Las Vegas Hilton and the Trump Plaza in Atlantic City, or anywhere in between, but she has always regarded recording albums as the most satisfying and creative part of her work. She told *Country Music News*,"I get totally caught up in my recordings and feel I'm most creative there. It also allows me to be myself—I can forget what I look like, no hairdos, no wardrobe—just concentrate on singing."

Working with producer Jerry Crutchfield, Murray had created an album that was more reminiscent of her work in the middle to late '70s. The electronic edge was muted, and the single release, *Feed This Fire* was a more acoustic setting featuring guitars and mandolin. Another single release, *Bluebird*, had a simplicity and directness of style that harked back to her first hit, *Snowbird*. In *Country Music News*, Murray gave credit to Crutchfield when the interviewer asked whether the choice of a more country feel was intentional: "You can thank Jerry Crutchfield, producer of the album for that!… Jerry, right off, set it straight…he told me that we were going to keep within the confines of what we set out to do, and not go expanding those boundaries with a whole lot of musical styles." Country audiences, apparently relieved by the unmistakable twang of a real, straight-ahead country tune, made *Feed This Fire* her 25th Top 10 record on the U.S. country charts in 20 years. The critical reception was favorable as well; one Music Row publication described her as "…a woman who has shown exquisite, almost flawless musical taste for years."

Murray's pickiness about the songs she will and won't sing is legendary. Since she doesn't write her own material, she depends on other people to produce songs that fit her voice and personality, and after years of constant use, her

Anne in Toronto, dresses in chic punk to film her 1986 video of the song Now and Forever.

Anne surrounded by friends and dignitaries at the 1989 opening of the Anne Murray Centre in her home town of Springhill, Nova Scotia.

Anne Murray and Nova Scotia Premier John Buchanan sing along with the Men of the Deeps miners' choir at the opening of the Anne Murray Centre in the mining town of Springhill.

intuition is razor-sharp. She told *Country Music News*, "…I feel I have a knack for picking the right song. Lord knows I spend enough time listening to demos and material that is submitted to us." She has a reputation for making up her mind quickly; if the song doesn't strike her fancy, it's off the list. Sometimes there are exceptions; Murray told writer Perry Stern in 1988 that one song on *As I Am* (she wouldn't say which one) had been submitted three times, each time by a different source, before it was accepted for recording.

Murray rarely sings topical material, but she made an exception for her recording of *A Little Good News*. With its references to war, politics, robberies and other contemporary issues, some might have regarded the song as being too left of center for Anne Murray's style. But perhaps she chose it because the lyrics expressed a positive, upbeat attitude with

which Murray wished to be associated, and which she felt her fans could appreciate. By the fall of 1990, U.S. President Bush, no left-winger but a self-proclaimed country music fan, was referring to *A Little Good News* as one of his favorite songs.

Aside from her concert appearances, Murray has filmed many television specials since the days when CBC, sensing a star on the rise, signed her to an exclusive two-year contract in 1970-72. Her Christmas show, "Anne Murray's Family Christmas," has drawn top ratings since its initial broadcast and on subsequent reruns—as many as 4.3 million viewers. Yet Murray has deliberately chosen not to commit herself to the rigorous schedule of a regular television show, perhaps remembering the fates of other singers whose overexposure on television killed requests for live appearances. Besides that, Murray told *Country Music News*, the restrictions of filming a weekly television series would not allow her enough time with her children.

The Balmur organization has to do more than protect Murray's valuable time; they screen telephone calls, mail, and routinely deflect many media inquiries for interviews, quotes and stories. The main reason for Balmur's vigilance, aside from saving her from time-consuming nuisances, is the persistent attention of Robert Kieling, the Saskatchewan farmer who has been harrassing Anne Murray for years. Pursuing Murray by phoning the Balmur office, Keiling apparently believes that she returns his ardor, a form of mental delusion which some psychiatrists refer to as erotomania. Kieling has been warned, dragged into court, and has even spent time in jail for his apparent inability to control his fixation.

Anne Murray's private life as Mrs. Bill Langstroth remains shielded from all but her oldest friends. She described herself to Peter Gzowski as, "a real Gemini—one person on stage and another in private life." She protects her children from the spotlight that can overwhelm the families of celebrities. At a Halifax music recital in which her son Will played, Murray slipped in anonymously, listened to him play, and left as unobtrusively as possible. She maintains strong family connections. Summers at her quiet Nova Scotia home usually mean that she entertains relatives and old friends, and she sometimes drops in unannounced at the Anne Murray Centre in Springhill.

Murray works hard to stay in shape, caring both for her physique and her voice. In her middle '40s, she is still trim and athletic from regular workouts at tennis, golf and swimming. The brashness of her image in the middle '80s has given way to a more conservative elegance. Her onstage costumes have become a little more daring, with designs that show off her sleek figure. She's acutely aware that her voice is her fortune. Once a smoker, she's now a militant non. Rarely does she party till dawn. As she told Gzowski, "I'm very aware of my voice. I pamper it. I lost my voice a few times—my crew was using a smoke onstage and it would diffuse the lights. I was allergic to it. Never used smoke since." Surprisingly, Anne Murray told Elspeth Cameron in 1988 that it was only in the last three years that she'd felt at ease on the stage. But occasional mishaps don't faze her any more. During her "Morningside" interview, Murray told Gzowski that only a week earlier in Grand Rapids, her pants had fallen down onstage. Murray hiked them up gamely, then kidded her audience that she'd never played Grand Rapids before and was trying to make a good impression.

Although she has settled into a comfortable stage presentation, Murray's music is still sending her audience a mixed message. Since she is a highly intelligent woman with a keen sense of changing trends in the musical marketplace, she sometimes decides to touch all the bases—country, pop, rock and inspirational—for good measure, as shown in her first television special of 1991. It was another family-oriented show called *Anne Murray in Disney World*. Filmed in Florida, it was a predictable commercial effort aimed at families, small children and the stay-at-home audience. Murray appeared more relaxed in it than she has in some of her other television specials as she was shown kidding around with comedienne Andrea Martin, eating ice cream cones and wandering through Disney World with a group of children. If the script was a little stilted—one segment starring Andrea Martin and the Teenage Mutant Ninja Turtles was something only a very small child could love—the musical menu was wildly varied. Murray sang a soulful duet with crooner Julio Iglesias, but also belted out a raucous version of a rock song *Lady Marmalade* together with guest Patti Labelle, much to the delight of the live audience. What was even more of a surprise was that Murray's final tune with her assembled guests was a gospel song written by another guest, Paul Janz, in which Murray and company were backed by a full gospel choir.

This choice of material sparked rumors that Murray was considering veering a little more to the right of the country music spectrum, to do some gospel. In his January, 1991 column for *Country Music News*, disc jockey Paul Kennedy

Halifax Chronicle Herald/Dave Grandy

Anne Murray sings in Halifax in 1991.

reported the industry rumor that Murray would begin work on an album of gospel music later that year. Nothing happened to substantiate the rumors. Instead, the big news was the announcement of her first Atlantic tour in several years. With corporate sponsorship, this time from IGA, the troupe was booked into venues in Halifax, Sydney, Saint John, Charlottetown and Moncton.

The Halifax concert in early June turned out to be more than two hours of tight, high-energy entertainment. Both musically and technically, there was never a glitch, a miscue or even a hesitation. Murray's eight-member band filed quietly onstage first; two keyboards, a drummer, two guitarists, a bass player and a backup singer. Dressed discreetly in black, they looked casual yet polished. The first tune was the golden oldie *What About Me*, but with a considerably zippier instrumental arrangement than it had on Murray's 1968 debut album. The band members appeared to be singing backup harmonies, and even had some choreography—they did a side-to-side shuffle in time to the beat. Though the 8,000 seat Metro Centre did not appear to be sold out, the mostly middle-aged crowd applauded loudly when the star herself emerged into the spotlight. Anne Murray strode out dressed in a knee-length peach outfit and spike heels which displayed a great pair of legs. Between songs, she joked, told the audience how glad she was to be home in Nova Scotia, and talked about the times in American hotel rooms when she turns on the TV to hear the weather. If a forecaster mentioned "a cold front moving in from Canada," she always felt personally responsible. The patter was doubtless scripted, since there are few things left to chance in the performance of a major star, but Murray delivered it with a sense of timing that had the audience laughing as though she were ad-libbing.

Quick to put down any pretensions about her own grandeur, Murray cracked, "If there are any songs you don't recognize, they're from my latest album." She was quick to notice any lull in the applause, and to cut smoothly from patter back to singing. Hit song followed hit song; *I Just Fall In Love Again*, then *I Still Wish the Very Best for You*. Since she was back in her home province, Murray traded on the background and history she shared with the audience, telling them how naive she was as a girl fresh from Nova Scotia, thinking she only had to record the songs she liked, and failing to take account of the difficulty record stores had in classifying her style. To prove how confusing categories can be, Murray introduced a medley of songs, some of which she had recorded as pop songs and some as middle of the road, but all of which showed up at the top of the country charts. Murray did only a verse or two plus a chorus of each song: *Lovesong, Another Sleepless Night, Walk Right Back, He Thinks I Still Care, Just Another Woman In Love* and *Daydream Believer*. There are probably only a handful of artists besides Murray who could program an entire concert with nothing but number-one hits.

Introducing her current hit *Bluebird*, Murray teased her audience, saying, "Do you realize it's twenty-one years and seven months since I had a hit with a bird song?" Like *Snowbird*, the new bird song was sparkling and buoyant but unlike the earlier song with its high, sweet string sonorities, *Bluebird* had almost a calypso feel. After the next song, *Time Don't Run Out on Me*, Murray accepted the warm applause with mock self-praise, saying, "I *am* singing great tonight." That bit of stage chat led her into a brief catalogue of some of the humbling experiences she'd undergone in her career. There was the fan who enclosed a sketch he'd made, asking for her autograph…the sketch was of singer Helen Reddy. Then there was the appearance some years ago at a fair, at which her hosts told her, "We tried to get Lassie." Her sallies worked; the audience gradually loosened up and was laughing more easily and after *Feed This Fire* and *A Little Good News*, Murray dared to ask how many people had never seen her perform live before. Surprisingly, quite a number of people hadn't. Murray responded that in that case, they don't know about her amazing talents for dancing. Donning a top hat and cane, Murray went into an entertaining, and completely professional dance routine to the tune of *Everything Old is New Again*, and finished the first half by singing *Snowbird*.

After intermission, Murray appeared in a different outfit—half pink, half purple, sequined, and again wearing high heels. After such a long first set, one would expect a shorter second set but Murray showed no signs of fatigue. She sang the title song from her 1990 album *You Will*, and then, in honor of being at home and back among friends, she sang Allister MacGillivray's *Out on the Mira*. All around the Metro Centre, people quietly hummed or sang under their breaths to the gently lilting acoustic guitar accompaniment. After that quiet, almost lullaby mood, Murray picked up the pace again with *Shadows in the Moonlight*. While she sang, a light show of flickering, starlike patterns played across the backdrop of the set. Then, Murray introduced keyboard player Brian Gatto, who sang a duet with her on *If I Ever Fall in Love Again*, which she originally recorded with Kenny Rogers. Then another crowd pleaser; Murray introduced *You Needed Me*, murmuring softly, "Still my favorite," before she began the first verse. After a rocking version of *You Won't See Me*, Murray left the stage briefly, only to be called back by the applause. And for an encore, the band cut into the familiar strains of a real, honest-to-goodness country waltz—the song *Could I Have This Dance*. Murray, after singing a few verses, asked the audience to sing a chorus alone. She held the mike towards them encouragingly, and some did try a line or two. Finishing up the final chorus, Murray waved and headed towards the wings, this time for good.

Just before her tour, in a interview with reporter Tim Arsenault of the Halifax *Chronicle Herald*, Murray talked about another proposed recording project: the possibility of doing an album of standards. Just what standards aren't clear—jazz? broadway? country? show tunes?—but Murray did mention the album made by another crossover singer, Linda Ronstadt. Presumably she meant Ronstadt's album *What's New*, made with band leader Nelson Riddle. Murray

was aware of the pitfalls inherent in tackling any material outside her usual territory, as she told Arsenault. "I was really disappointed in Linda Ronstadt's [album]. She tried too hard to sound like the people that sang it before her and she doesn't have the chops for that. I would have to be very careful in my approach to it."

Careful in what way, one might ask. Murray has never been an innovator, and stepping outside the comfortable niche of middle-of-the-road music means taking certain risks. What about her target audience, the over-30 crowd who prefer adult contemporary stations? Would they buy an album of Anne Murray singing jazz or Broadway standards? Though that audience is an extremely stable and faithful one, an album of so-called standards is not what they expect from Anne Murray. But tastes change. Harry Connick Jr. has made an impact with his repertoire of '40s and '50s swing. And if Murray wants to maintain her position in the industry, she has to keep coming up with the hits. And a singer's career lasts only so long. Murray is still in remarkably good voice and excellent health but on her Disney special and some of her recent recordings, there is a distinctly raspy edge creeping into her upper notes, the odd one of which she sings on the low side of the pitch, as though she were no longer comfortable with the range.

Even if Anne Murray decides to stay within the category she's more or less marked out for herself, she faces an ever-increasing group of contenders. In Canada, a wave of dynamic female singers—Michelle Wright, k.d.lang, Rita MacNeil, Joan Kennedy—are making their presence felt. At the 1991 Canadian Country Music Awards held in Hamilton in September, Murray was a headliner of the show, but watched as the sultry Michelle Wright walked off with several awards including one as Female Vocalist of the Year.

South of the border and in Nashville, where new girl singers are as changeable as the flavor of the month, Murray seems to be re-asserting her claim to country star status. She sang as a guest star on a 1990 television tribute to Nashville Now's host Ralph Emery, took her show to the Grand Ole Opry in the late spring of 1991, and appeared on the "Christmas in Washington" show in December.

Later that same year, Murray surprised many industry people by announcing that after several dozen records and a 20 year relationship, she planned to leave Capitol Records. With one of the longest-lasting and most financially successful careers in popular music, Murray could probably pick and choose among the record company giants. And there is little doubt that country artists mean big bucks for record companies; early in 1992, both *Entertainment* and *Forbes* magazine published lengthy features about the raging popularity of country music, which is now estimated to be an industry worth some $3 billion a year.

Anne Murray has never seemed comfortable with being labelled a country artist. But country music, established by the record companies in the '20s, has been put through so many changes of instrumentation, subject matter, and styles of musical treatment in its pursuit of bigger and bigger audiences, that the borderline between country and pop barely exists anymore. One need look no further, for example, than American singer Garth Brooks, a strong leader for weeks at the top of both pop and country hit charts. It is that borderline audience, an audience that doesn't really care about such distinctions anyway, seeking only a fine voice, an easy-going treatment, and a way with a song—that has been buying Anne Murray's recordings for two decades.

Canadian superstars Anne Murray and k.d. lang performed together on CBC-TV's three-hour, two-part "Country Gold" special in February 1992.

CHAPTER 8

Carroll Baker

Sweet and sultry

Anne Murray was not the only prominent country singer in Canada during the '70s and '80s. There was Carroll Baker too, also a Nova Scotian by birth, but, unlike Anne, unambiguous about her musical identity. She stands out as one of the few widely popular Canadian singers to wear the country label proudly during those two decades. She told Halifax *Chronicle Herald* reporter Gretchen Pierce in 1976: "I want to be branded a country singer, that's what I am. Some people try to cover several markets, the pop and folk, with a crossover song but that isn't right."

While she was growing up in Port Medway, however, Baker dreamed of a career in acting rather than music. Marilyn Monroe, the Beatles and rhythm and blues counted for more than a wailing steel guitar and uncool broken-hearted lyrics. "I hated [country music] when I was a child because I thought people always sang it through their noses and I thought the songs were for people who were illiterate," she told writer Dick Brown in a 1980 *Atlantic Insight* profile. She was nearly out of her teens and living in Toronto before she found out she could identify with the emotions of country music. Later on, when she was well-launched into

her career as a popular country singer, she co-wrote a song called *I'm an Old Rock and Roller* about her earlier preference for rock.

Though many of her colleagues protest that they want to be known as all-round singers of pop, folk and adult contemporary material, Baker has stuck to country since her first song *Mem'ries of Home* was released in the late '60s. She has also gained a reputation for singing songs with suggestive titles and lyrics, such as *I've Never Been This Far Before and Hungry Fire of Love*. Many articles about her manage to mention sex, smut, and honesty either in their titles or in the content of the interview, but she's far from being a northern version of torchy personalities such as Tanya Tucker or Madonna. She's a middle-class wife and mother who admits to interviewers that she likes to watch soap operas, go bowling and eat Big Macs. Associates have described her as a perfect lady, yet she's a spontaneous and lively performer who has been known to kick off her shoes onstage, sass the audience, and give television cameramen and producers an adrenalin rush whenever she makes an unrehearsed foray into a studio audience during a live show. It's a quality that

endears her to fans, who want to see a real person up there rather than a stage personality. Unlike Anne Murray, she doesn't fit the image of the girl next door. She is more like your big sister or cousin who lights up a room with the liveliness of her personality whenever she comes home. Yet she is like Murray in that her life as a performer has always been directed by her greater need to be with her husband and daughter, with resulting limitations on the amount of touring and recording she is willing to do.

Born in Bridgewater in 1949, Baker grew up in Port Medway on the south shore of Nova Scotia. As in many rural Maritime families, there was always music at home. Her father, Gordon Baker, was a popular country fiddler, her brother Fordon played guitar and several aunts played piano or organ. Religion and gospel music constituted a vital part of their lives. The family often went to church twice on Sundays and sang hymns and gospel music at home in the evenings while Carroll's Aunt Irene played piano. Carroll sang in the church choir but her powerful voice, an asset to any singing group, had to be carefully handled by choir directors. Baker later told a Canadian Press writer, "The closest I ever got to singing was in the church choir where they'd stick me at the back because they said my voice was so distinctive I used to drown everybody out."

The family was not wealthy, but they got by. For a while Gordon Baker worked for a company that did contracting on breakwaters and scrap metals but the company eventually went out of business. When Carroll was 15, the Bakers had to move from Port Medway to Ontario. The adjustment was not easy; back home in Nova Scotia, Carroll had been busy and popular, playing guitar at school and performing songs and musical acts with friends. In Ontario, she was regarded as provincial and the other students at her high school teased her about her downeast accent. Carroll left school early to take up a series of jobs as a waitress, a clerk, a factory worker and a Canadian Tire cashier. Her working class background

Carroll Baker singing in 1982.

stands in strong contrast to Anne Murray's patrician up-bringing in a doctor's family, and no doubt accounts for much of the earthiness that Baker's fans love her for.

She met her husband-to-be in 1968. Double-dating with a friend, Carroll didn't much care for the fellow she'd been fixed up with, but she did like her girlfriend's date, so the couples switched. Her partner was John Beaulieu, originally from Edmundston, New Brunswick. Carroll married Beaulieu when she was 19. She has sometimes said that she didn't truly appreciate country music until she heard it on her honey-moon while travelling in Pennsylvania. She was particularly struck by a country song she heard on the radio called, appropriately, *Almost Persuaded*; it's one of the "almost cheated, but just in time I found out he was married" variety. From her new perspective as a married woman, and for the first time, a country lyric meant something real to her. Back home in Ontario, she began singing for friends at parties. One night at a local bar, her companions urged her to get up and sing with the band. She impressed the band leader enough to offer her a steady job at $15 a night. She did not quit her day job as a cashier, however, which made it difficult to learn new songs fast enough for the rest of the band. After only a few weeks, she lost the band gig, but soon got another one singing on a country show in Markham called "Jamboree."

Baker's recording career came about after an appearance on station CHOO, a small suburban radio station. A listener asked her to record a song of his called *Mem'ries of Home*. It was recorded as a single on the Gaiety label, owned by Don Grashey, a record producer and songwriter who had worked closely with singer Myrna Lorrie. He later became Carroll's manager. *Mem'ries of Home* was only modestly successful, but Baker refused to be discouraged and continued to sing at clubs and concert halls across Ontario with occasional forays into the United States. A Canadian performer who tries to establish a concert career in the States without the proper promotion to gain extensive play on American radio faces an enormous challenge. Carroll confided some of her experiences to writer Dick Brown: "I did a tour of Michigan in 1974 with David Houston and we played auditoriums that hold seven and eight thousand people and we'd get, like, 300 people. I felt terrible about it. I wouldn't take my pay." The poor audiences were hardly Baker's fault. She had simply tackled the U.S. market too soon, and not in the right way. Since the birth of her daughter Candace in 1974, it became impossible to focus exclusively on her career. Her time was divided between the needs of her husband and small child, and her desire to sing.

In 1975, Carroll won a Big Country Award as best female vocalist and the same year, she recorded a cover version of Conway Twitty's *I've Never Been This Far Before*. Since *Mem'ries of Home*, Baker had been plodding away, recording singles that usually made their way onto the Cancountry charts, but none of them had ever touched off the sales reaction or the popular success of her cover of Twitty's song. The single zoomed up on the Canadian country charts and she was soon booked to sing at the 1976 Juno Awards.

Her performance stole the show. Carroll began in the song in a subdued mood and built it up to an emotional climax that knocked out not only the Juno audience, but the 4,000,000 or so viewers who were watching at home. As usually happens when a performer makes a surprise impact, the term "overnight sensation" was bandied about, but Baker was hardly a newcomer on the country music scene. Still her explosive performance on the Juno show gave her career a powerful boost. (Baker would win Junos in 1976, 1977 and 1978 as best country female vocalist.) Partly as a result of her Juno appearance, Baker was given a sheaf of new offers to consider. By the fall of 1976, she was taping a one-hour special for CBC television as part of the "Sounds Good" mini-series, recorded for broadcast after only one day's rehearsal. Baker and her guests, including a country band with the unlikely name of Prairie Oyster (a top country group in their own right by the beginning of the '90s), taped the show in only two and a half hours in front of a live audience.

That summer, Carroll also had a homecoming. She made her first professional appearance in Nova Scotia since leaving for Oakville, Ontario 12 years earlier. She told writer Barbara MacAndrew in the *Atlantic Advocate*, "I was so nervous my knees shook. For the first time I was singing before all my old friends and relatives. I really wanted them to accept me and was scared they wouldn't like me." She need not have feared; at her concert at the South Shore Exhibition, 10,000 fans turned out to welcome their native daughter. Shortly afterward, RCA Canada offered Don Grashey, then her manager, a favorable deal to distribute her records through their system. RCA executives promptly nicknamed her "Miss Dynamic" in tribute to her extroverted style.

Shy, she is not. Baker soon developed a reputation for unusual frankness with her fans. Don Grashey told Dick Brown in 1980 about an episode in which Baker nearly lost a tooth while eating some fried chicken. According to Grashey, "She was appearing at a fair, and it was about 15 minutes before she was supposed to go onstage. She bit into a piece of chicken and a tooth came out of her bridge. Somebody found some glue or something and Carroll got the tooth stuck back in. Now anybody else would have kept quiet about it but Carroll got out there onstage and she told everybody." Unabashedly emotional and direct, Baker has been known to choke up at the mention of her adored daughter Candace. Sometimes she openly weeps in public; at a ceremony making her an honorary daughter of Thunder Bay, Baker's torrent of tears caused her to lose a false eyelash. Needless to say, all of these qualities and their evident sincerity endear her to her fans even more.

That same honesty showed up in her songwriting. Baker had started writing by composing the music for *Mem'ries of Home* and she soon began to write original lyrics and music about her own feelings and experiences. Many of those songs were at first considered explicit, since they dealt honestly with sensuality and a woman's feelings about sex and love.

Carroll Baker in 1982 received her second platinum record for her RCA LP Carroll Baker, *from Conway Twitty.*

Carroll Baker entertaining fans of all ages at the South Shore Exhibition in Bridgewater, N.S., 1988. Her 14-year-old daughter Candace sings backup.

One of her RCA singles, a song called *Hungry Fire of Love*, dealt with her wedding night. Not that suggestive songs were new to the literature; country songwriters have been producing songs about "slippin' around" for several decades. Loretta Lynn's earthy personality had made itself known through such songs as *Don't Come Home a-Drinkin' with Lovin' On Your Mind* and *The Pill*. But Canadian singers, especially women, had formerly been more modest, even a little prudish in their choice of song topics. Baker has always insisted

that, first of all, her husband does not mind her writing such material, and second, that the songs aren't dirty, they're love songs. At a Halifax concert in 1978, Baker jokingly told her audience, "...if that guy thinks they're dirty, well, here's another one."

Baker may be able to get away with the frankly sensual nature of many of her songs because of her obvious sincerity, and a kind of sweetness and innocence. Guitarist George Brothers, now living in P.E.I., was a member of the group, Old Blue, which toured Nova Scotia with Baker in 1978. Baker seemed to arouse the protective instincts of her audience, says Brothers. "She had the same combination of vulnerability and naiveté that Rita MacNeil has. When people saw her, there was something they cherished. She would say things that somebody else would have said as a double entendre, and nobody would take it the wrong way. She's a really nice, genuine person in the same way Rita is."

Brothers also observes that as with Rita MacNeil, Carroll Baker live in concert could deliver an emotion-packed performance that rarely failed to captivate the audiences. Of the short Maritime tour on which Old Blue accompanied Carroll Baker, Brothers says, "We did Truro, North Sydney and Bridgewater, and I was converted. In North Sydney she could have asked the audience to walk off the end of the pier, and they would have. She had them." Of her vocal delivery and stage presence, Brothers says, "Carroll Baker live was as good as anybody I've seen. Johnny Cash, the Gatlins, Rita— she was as magnetic live as Rita is.... She's a hell of a singer live. She had a range and she could nail you to your seat. When she showed her emotions, she really had that much. That was the only way she knew how to deliver the song."

However, Baker's exuberant style was not as easily reproduced on records or television. As with many other performers, the excitement of a concert situation seems to ignite a spark in Carroll Baker that makes each show a best effort. Recordings, no matter how polished and professional,

Carroll Baker in a 1981 publicity photo.

CBC-TV Publicity

Carroll Baker and backup singers in a 1983 concert.

do not always capture that spark, but her debut album for RCA titled simply *Carroll Baker* won her a 1976 Big Country Award as album of the year. She made a number of hit singles between 1976-78 for RCA, including *One Night of Cheatin' ain't Worth the Reapin'*, *Tonight With Love*, *Little Boy Blue*, *Ten Little Fingers*, *Portrait in the Window* and *I'm Getting High Remembering*.

By the end of the '70s Baker was gradually moving closer to the status of a major star. Her appearances in 1977 and 1978 at the Wembley Country Music Festival in England won her considerable acclaim. Surprisingly enough, the United Kingdom has a large and knowledgeable community of country music fans, and they tend to be extremely picky about what they like and don't like. In her autobiography *Get To the Heart*, singer Barbara Mandrell related her experience at Wembley, in which she appeared to a hostile audience. It may have been Mandrell's glossy, Las Vegas style of presentation that put them off. The warmth accorded Baker recognized her as more of country traditionalist, both in her vocal mannerisms and in musical arrangements and material. In 1980, she became the first Canadian country performer to headline a Canadian television special from the Grand Ole Opry stage, and in 1982, Baker made a well-advertised tour of Nova Scotia during the Old Home Summer promotion with another country music expatriate, the venerable Hank Snow.

She was gaining a reputation as a hard-working performer willing to tour the sticks and play the small towns, as well as the larger centers. Growing up in a small Nova Scotia town taught Baker that live entertainment is a precious commodity. Unlike some stars who minimize contact with their fans, she has always been willing to appear at country fairs, exhibitions, and shopping centers to sign autographs and pose for photos. She told *Halifax Herald* reporter Gretchen Pierce as early as 1976,"I feel country singers will outlast any rock singers—their longevity is assured because their fans grow with them, and don't drop them for a more glamorous face."

Baker hosted her own television series, the "Carroll Baker Jamboree," in 1983. It was an exception to the unofficial rule she'd established, that she preferred to spend the winters at home managing her household and caring for her family. She made occasional guest appearances on the "Tommy Hunter Show" and other variety specials but otherwise she chose to limit her amount of television exposure. The "Jamboree" was a six-part series of half-hour shows with production split between CBC Halifax and Vancouver. The concept, courtesy of producer Jack Budgell, was that of a town hall entertainment, with musical guests who would complement Baker's easygoing style. Baker told reporter Barbara Senchuk of the *Chronicle Herald*: "I didn't want to be just a standup host to the average country music show that you see—I'd been offered that before and I turned it down. I wanted something that will have a little warmth to it, something that will communicate with an audience."

Skip Beckwith, ex-bass player for Anne Murray, was living in Halifax at the time and worked on the show. Beckwith says of Carroll Baker's band, Baker Street, "It was a real tight, professional operation. And she was also quite funny—great sense of humor. She used to kid around with the audience—good rapport—she would go sit in some guy's lap and muss his hair while singing a song." Beckwith remembers one situation they set up carefully; Beckwith's neighbor was known to be attending a taping, and the musicians planned that Baker would take him by surprise when she plunked herself into his lap. The video clip of the incident was spontaneous and funny enough for CBC to run it as a promo for the shows. Baker's duties as hostess included introducing her crew of musical guests, mainly country-oriented players, many of whom were Maritimers by birth. They included singer Bruce Murray (Anne Murray's younger brother), singer/songwriter Shirley Eikhard, Paul Eisan, Eddie Eastman, the Minglewood Band, and the Bluegrass Four. Working in front of a live audience, they taped six shows in two or three days.

Baker also confided to Barbara Senchuk some of the headaches associated with trying to get her records released and distributed in the States. After leaving RCA, Baker had signed with an American label called Excelsior. Her first release had made some progress on the country charts, but the company went out of business and for two years her progress had been blocked. Baker told Senchuk that if she managed to arrange an American tour, it would probably mean cutting back on her travel in Canada, so as not to spend too much time on the road away from home. Eventually,

Baker ended up taking a sabbatical through part of 1983 and 1984. She completely stopped touring in order to stay at home, rest, and work on her songwriting. Discussing her year off, she told one reporter, "In this country, you have to tour a lot and it's a big country. There's a lot of travel and you can't keep going back to the same places. I thought it would be better for my career if I took the year off, and it was." Carroll came out of the self-imposed rest with a collection of songs, and a new determination to record.

By 1986, Baker's new gospel album *Hymns of Gold* had sold 200,000 copies and was named top-selling album in Canada at that year's Country Music Awards. Her competition included top acts in American country music—Alabama, Kenny Rogers, and the Judds. Baker has an authentic interest in gospel music dating back to her childhood. In a Canadian Press interview later that year, Baker said that in her earliest days of singing in clubs, she would often end her final set of the evening by singing *How Great Thou Art*, sometimes to the dismay of the club owners. In the same article, Baker still fretted about her continuing struggle to make a dent in the American country market.

Nobody knows why some acts grab the imagination of the American public and others don't, try as they may. Baker has all the ingredients for a big success—a distinctive voice, songwriting talent, lots of experience, and a dynamic stage act. But one thing that may count against her, unfair as it may be, is the fact that most female singers are still expected to conform to certain conventions of physical appearance. Carroll Baker, while she is an attractive and vivacious performer by nearly any other standard, would be considered matronly by rules modelled on the glamorous appearance of the Mandrell sisters. Talent and onstage magnetism count for much, of course, are even indispensable. But, in the showbiz atmosphere of Nashville, whether or not the public expects its singers, models and actresses to be bone-skinny and elegant, producers do.

In Canada, however, it's an off year when Carroll Baker

Carroll had scored another hit that fall at the 1989 Canadian Country Music Awards; coincidentally, it was with another remake of a Conway Twitty song. Baker's gutsy rendition of *It's Only Make Believe* nearly stopped the show, and in 1990, Tembo Records released a new Carroll Baker album called *Today and Yesterday*. Tembo also released *It's Only Make Believe* as a single and by December of 1990, the cut had climbed to fifth place on the Cancountry charts.

Her position, at least in the Canadian industry, seems solid. She is frequently referred to as "the queen of Canadian country" and is a regular presenter at awards ceremonies. She also hosted the 1990 Big Country Awards. Late in 1990, Tembo Records released a compilation album called *Her Finest Collection* which included three new songs in addition to the previously recorded material. Nine of the 12 songs were recorded in Toronto, eight of them produced by Mike "Pepe" Francis, and one, a duet with Roger Whittaker, produced by Eric Robertson and Hayward Parrott. Don Grashey and Les Ladd produced the three songs taped in Nashville. Liner notes were sparse except for the production credits; no text and no musician credits are given.

Though some critics maintain that Carroll Baker sings everything the same way, whether it's gospel, ballads or up-tempo songs, this collection proves the contrary; she shows off her big vocal range, and demonstrates a considerable amount of musical sensitivity in adapting her voice to each song. The lead song, written by Baker and Terry Frewer, is *I'm An Old Rock and Roller*. It is kicked off by a pounding piano part reminiscent of the two-fisted style of Jerry Lee Lewis. The lyrics sound like the story of Carroll Baker's life; she used to dance to rock, but now she melts at the sound of the fiddle, steel guitar and banjo. Against a hard rock beat in the rhythm section, Baker's voice takes on a driving urgency and while the instrumental scoring would suit any country radio station, the solos on banjo, fiddle and steel guitar are spiced up with a sax solo—not exactly a standard instrument in a country band, but not unheard of either. The next cut is one that would probably qualify as one of Baker's famous

Hockey star Wayne Gretzky and Carroll Baker following CBC-TV's "National Hockey League Awards Show," and just before she hosted the 1984 Canadian Country Music Awards in Moncton, New Brunswick.

CBC-TV Publicity

doesn't list a couple of singles on the Cancountry charts. Awards such as the Martin Guitar Lifetime Achievement Award she received in 1989 continue to come her way, as well as albums like her first Christmas recording, also in 1989. Along with the holiday favorites and classic carols, a new song written especially for the album—a duet called *Christmas Carroll, Christmas Candi*—featured Carroll singing with her daughter Candace. It was the highlight of the album contributing greatly to its successful marketing through television ads by Quality Records.

smutty songs, titled *It's How You Make Love Good*. Co-written with Bryan Way, it's an easy-going ballad about an adult love affair—the kind of song Baker does best. The arrangement is subdued and tasteful, never overbalancing her crooning delivery of the lyrics. It's followed by *I Should Have Put a Hold On Love*, another Baker/Frewer collaboration. A basso voice enters first, followed by a kind of doo-wop harmony from the backup singers and finally Carroll herself. Perky and up-tempo, *I Should Have Put a Hold On Love* proved to be one of the most popular songs on the record, eventually climbing to the top position of the Cancountry charts by June of 1991.

The fourth cut, *It's Only Make Believe*, follows a sure-fire traditional formula: Carroll starts the song quietly, picks up a little speed in the middle and by the the high notes at the end of the verse, she's built up an intensely emotional crescendo of sound. The next cut is *Too Hot to Sleep Tonight*, a duet with Newfoundland country singer Eddie Eastman. The story line is vaguely suggestive: a woman and a man listening to the sound of crickets while tossing and turning, unable to sleep because of the heat. The two singers alternate lines on the verses and team up on the chorus with Eastman singing harmony. Baker, as always, sings the sexy text with her own unique combination of sultriness and innocence. *I'm Taking Care of Myself*, a slow ballad, is not her own composition but it could have been written with her in mind. The lyrics describe a spunky, assertive woman deciding that she won't torture herself by hanging around her man's door waiting for him. The instrumental treatment of this track, first recorded in 1985, is light and brittle, with electronic effects and drum machines instead of acoustic piano and guitars.

The second side begins with *Cheater's Moon*—a beautifully muted introduction on fiddle leads into the vocal part. The story is somewhat abstract for Baker. Most of the songs she sings concern specific individuals and situations, but this

Carroll struts her stuff in a 1984 publicity photo.

one, written by Bernie Nelson and Lee Satterfield, deals with the idea of the "cheater's moon" and its effect upon all the fools who live under its influence. *Right or Wrong* was recorded in Nashville, with a band arrangement reminiscent of the early '60s Nashville sound favored by Patsy Cline, rather deliberately underlined by the shimmering string sound, and the chorus of voices in the the background. Baker's voice seems to be full of tears each time she begins

Carroll sings a duet with Bruce Murray.

the descending melody line; unless you read the liner notes, you might think Connie Francis was singing. When Baker sings "I'll do what you ask me to," she drops her voice to a shuddering whisper on the word "ask," hinting that underneath the peppy personality of Carroll Baker, there lurks an old-fashioned woman who stands by her man.

Death & Taxes & Me Lovin' You is Carroll Baker's shot at western-style country music. The lyrics with references to bumper crops, farmers and farm life from the midwest to Carolina do not live up to the promise of the catchy title.

CBC-TV Publicity

Baker does her best to energize the cliché-ridden lines penned by Charley Black, Austin Roberts and Bobby Fischer. *One Night With You* was originally recorded in 1988 with Roger Whittaker. The song, written by Whittaker himself, is an easy-going waltz but the production has a grandiose quality that is ill-matched to the voices. Whittaker, the king of easy listening, sings with his usual pleasantly light if unvarying baritone, but Baker's fervent performance makes him appear to be sleep-walking through his part.

A Star in Momma's Eyes is another song which Baker did not write herself, but which seems tailor-made for her emotionalism. The story deals with a self-sacrificing mother who promotes her child's ambition to sing. No matter how great the adulation of the crowd, says the singer-storyteller, the child will always shine most brightly in he mother's eyes. It's a sentimental idea, but Carroll no doubt had in mind her own daughter, and her sincerity, as always, is unquestionable. The final cut, *Jesus It's Me Again*, is a country-gospel ballad written by Dick Damron. The instrumental backup is unremarkable, except for several harmonica solos in the breaks. Baker sings it with a childlike sense of pleading.

Today, Carroll Baker continues a rewarding career as one of the busiest headliners in Canadian country music. She is guaranteed to draw large crowds almost anywhere she plays. In his column in the November, 1991 *Country Music News*, Bill Oja commented on the opening of a new 800-seat nightspot in the Niagara Peninsula by saying, "Tembo Records artist Carroll Baker, who opens more new country rooms than anybody I know, was again chosen as the first headliner for this new venture." If there is a secret to her success, it's that Baker knows how much she owes to her faithful public and is always ready to acknowledge the fact. Other singers have come and gone over the past 20 years; they drop in and out of the business, buffeted about by managers, agents, bad deals and fickle audiences. But Baker seems to be driven less by pride, ego and financial need than she is by the simple desire to entertain. Although she has sometimes spoken of retiring early, it's not likely that her fans will allow it. In the CBC special "Country Gold," Baker told the interviewer, "The loyalty of the fans is such that I can never, never forget it. I think to myself, if I had to thank any one part of the industry for what I am today, I would have to thank the fans." The thing is, she really means it.

CHAPTER 9

Rita MacNeil

One foot in the heather

There was a time when Rita MacNeil was so fearful about performing that she sometimes hid backstage before it was time to go on. Her friends and colleagues, aware of her nerves, knew that when they found her in the dressing room, Rita would need a few words of encouragement to give her confidence a boost. But once onstage, she is another person and the audience knows it. When she kicks her shoes off and steps in front of her band to sing, they forget her awkwardness and her matronly figure and hear only her voice—that sweet, penetrating voice that comes straight from the heart of her experiences.

Rita's songs are like pages from a diary—all the pain and confusion of life, together with flashes of illumination, love, and exultation. She may be 40-something, an established entertainer and the mother of two grown children, but inside Rita MacNeil there's still a young girl who feels things with the acuteness that most of us leave behind in adolescence. Kenzie MacNeil, a singer/songwriter from Rita's days as a cast member of the *Rise and Follies of Cape Breton*, believes that all the events in Rita's life are contained in her consciousness, and that singing is like a physical release. Says Kenzie, "All this is bottled up and jammed inside her over

the years. That's why she's so intense. It all comes out in front of a microphone and that's why she's so good. La Pasiónara.... That's the magic in Rita."

Like Anne Murray, Rita doesn't care to be bracketed as a country artist. She will politely but firmly correct people, telling them that she prefers to think of herself as a singer/songwriter without the country prefix. One admiring critic, discerning what he felt was a strong Celtic inspiration, once described her as still having one foot in the heather. But there's little doubt that her records have had the most play on country and adult contemporary radio stations rather than on those with a rock format. She appeals to a large, if mixed, audience: folkies, fans of easy listening, aging baby boomers, and all the people who were left behind when pop music turned nasty and electric. Ever since she switched over to a peppier sound—more synthesizer and keyboards, more focus on percussion—many of Rita's songs fit into the country format, though many people grumble that sometimes you can't tell country radio from rock radio any more.

With Rita, the appeal has always been in her lyrics. They tell stories that are drawn from her life or from things people have told her about themselves. Some of her most successful songs, such as *Leave Her Memory* and *I'll Accept the Rose* carry all the weight of her own history, and the messages are the ones that country music fans have always looked for: the sentiments of home, lost love, regrets and wistful memories. Yet there's a subtlety in her music that is often missing from the performances of many female country singers. The earlier, more passive generation of singers believed in wearing their hearts on their sleeves, and sobbed their way through countless songs about cheatin', heartless, good-for-nothing men. Rita's music is closer to the confessional spirit of Joni Mitchell, whose songs are a Michelin guide to her life. Rita manages to be honest, but at the same time artful. In *When the Lovin is Through*, for example, she traces the gradual breakup of love—the silences, the regrets and finally the sense of resignation, when she sings, "How long can we stay/ Livin' this way/When the lovin' is through." Her voice, with its characteristic quick vibrato, bends and becomes part of the melody she's singing—so much so that it's difficult for anybody but Rita MacNeil to successfully sing a Rita MacNeil song. She takes chances with a lyric; sometimes you wonder if she can negotiate the melodic leaps or make it through to the end of the line, but she's always there.

Rita's success in the music business represents a kind of repatriation. She has carved out her own career without making the compromises and choices that many, perhaps most Maritime musicians have had to make. Not so long ago, most of them felt that if they didn't move to the big cities, where the jobs, the management agencies and industry hotshots were, they didn't have a chance. Rita stayed at home in Cape Breton, and Brooks Diamond Productions, which for six years plotted her success, was based not in Vancouver or Toronto, but in Halifax.

Female singers are often judged as much by appearance as by singing ability, but while other singers dyed their hair, dieted and crammed themselves into miniskirts or spandex pants, Rita steadfastly refused to appear as anything but her natural self. She has evolved her own style of dressing, with her trademark fedora, dangly earrings, and sweeping dresses. Former *Country Music News* columnist from Prince Edward Island George Brothers says, "I felt Rita's success gave great hope to Maritimers and also [to] people who didn't fit into the standard market.... Her success was actually a rejection of that plastic system. She proved that someone who wasn't moulded and imaged and coiffed could make it on talent and uniqueness."

In another lifetime, another situation, Rita MacNeil's emotional intensity and the quality of her voice might have made her a classical singer of lieder or opera. But the necessary training and education wasn't there for a little girl growing up in Big Pond, Cape Breton. Rita was one of eight children in the MacNeil family. In 1952, they moved to Sydney so that her father, a carpenter, would find more work. There was a postwar boom in many industries but Sydney was, and still is, a tough place to earn a living. The MacNeils were no different from plenty of other Maritime families; Rita's father worked hard and her mother kept house but it was often hard to feed and clothe eight growing children.

Rita was a shy, sensitive girl with the added problem of a harelip. After several operations to repair it, she missed time at school and had to struggle to keep up. She told writer Myrna Kostash in an interview in the early '70s, "...It was a hell of a job later to get me back into a grade that would suit my age and height. I was real backward. And so emotionally stricken because I was so different. I struggled through somehow. God, I was so dumb. But I really tried. And by grade nine I led the class in History and Science." Music was one of her comforts. She would leaf through a songbook by Stephen Foster and tried to pick out some of the tunes on the piano. She listened to the radio—folksongs, country, gospel, blues. Later she would admit to being a big Elvis Presley fan.

Even in those earliest years, hampered as she was by paralyzing shyness around strangers, Rita had an unusually good voice. Her parents sent her to a teacher for singing lessons, but she was too shy to open her mouth. Several times, Rita entered the local Kiwanis Music Festival but again, her shyness about singing in front of a group made her freeze up. She was happier singing at home.

Rita observed the people around her with a maturity far beyond her age—her hardworking father, whom she later remembered in her song *Old Man*, and above all, her mother. Renee MacNeil must have treasured her young daughter's talents, hoping that somehow Rita could, through hard work and good luck, break out of working-class Sydney into something much better. The title song on Rita's 1988 album, *Reason to Believe*, is a loving tribute to the mother who hoped for so much, and who transferred that attitude, sometimes wordlessly, to her child. Country music is full of sentimental paeans to mothers, but *Reason to Believe* is unique. The emotions are fresh, tender, and free of clichés. MacNeil never mentions her mother by name, but the references in the lyrics are unmistakable. "And I know you walk beside me/On the earth beneath my feet/And though you're only a memory/You still give to me/A reason to remember/And a reason to believe." Rita credits her mother with giving her strength and determination that carried her through many difficult times.

After finishing eleventh grade, Rita, as so many Cape Bretoners before her, left Sydney for Toronto and a succession of mediocre jobs. She clerked for CNR, worked in an office at Eaton's, and thought about singing. After a brief sojourn at home, working as a domestic helper, Rita went back to Toronto, saved money, and got up her nerve to take serious singing lessons. Under the guidance of a teacher, she developed a better vocal range and a repertoire that included everything from showtunes and pop songs to blues, gospel, and country songs. The teacher was encouraging and a career singing in nightclubs was a distinct possibility. Rita was a pretty, dark-haired girl with a wardrobe of nice clothes. Her friends supported her ambitions. Recalling that time, MacNeil told Myrna Kostash about one night at the Colonial Tavern when friends urged her to sing. She stood up and did

Ramblin' Rose and *The Wild Colonial Boy*. MacNeil told Kostash, "They all near went crazy for me. They all stood up and started shouting and screaming. Getting that kind of a reaction from an audience is a real high."

But it was to be some time before any of her ambitions became real. She was sidetracked by her personal life. Rita rarely talks about her period in Toronto now, except to say that she's had some hard times. Marriage and the birth of two children took a physical toll on her; she was depressed, overweight, and underemployed. Her husband, David Langham, worked as a draughtsman but Rita often worked at part-time jobs just to get out of the house. She hadn't given up her dreams of being a singer, but there was a yawning gulf between her ambitions and the daily life she was living.

Rita began attending feminist meetings with a friend. In Toronto in the early '70s many women were questioning what they'd been told about themselves, about marriage and about their place in society. Still too shy to speak out in a large group, Rita went home from a meeting and wrote her first song, *Need For Restoration*, which expressed the feelings that were surging through her. And just as some people who stutter can sing flawlessly, the Rita MacNeil who was bashful almost to tears around strangers finally found her own voice and the courage to use it. Words and music came together, and the result altered Rita MacNeil's life. After a concert at the University of Toronto in 1972 at which Rita sang, Kostash wrote, "She had done for me, for one, what nothing and no one else had done, not even the Chicago Women's Liberation Rock Band: bridged the chasm between the rhetoric and sensation of sisterhood." Rita became a regular invited guest at rallies and other gatherings around Toronto. As word of her singing spread, there were more contacts— a booking at the Riverboat Tavern, a gig at the Mariposa Folk Festival. Then came her first record, *Born A Woman*, produced by Jim Pirie for Boot Records in 1975.

The album reflects the standard studio production values of the time. The instrumental backup consists of acoustic and rhythm guitars, drums and steel guitar on the country numbers, and a little background sweetening from a string section on several cuts. Judged solely on the backup, the record would be merely competent studio work, but Rita's voice lifts it up beyond that mundane level. Even in this very early period of her career, the voice is unmistakable with its fast vibrato and cutting purity. Her range is not as big, nor is her intonation as secure as it would become in time, but the depth of emotion is pure Rita.

Many of the lyrics express the strongly feminist perspective that Rita espoused during that time. The title song, *Born A Woman*, depicts some of the frustrations that she felt with the images of women in advertising. Don't offend men, lose five pounds, wear Cover Girl makeup to mask your imperfections—it's a catalogue of the messages she had received, but was beginning to reject. The songs of that time also reflect the political and social upheaval of that time. In *Angus Anthony's Store*, Rita sings about war, toys, and the warlike games which boys and girls sometimes played during her childhood. The anger and confusion in Rita's own personal life comes through clearly in *Sometimes I Feel like Giving Up*, an up-tempo country ballad in which the last line of each chorus is a sly reference to country singer Tammy Wynette's hit song *Stand By Your Man*.

The song with the most significant emotional content is the one Rita wrote for her mother, who had died of cancer in 1972. Titled simply *Renee*, it tells with painful honesty of Renee MacNeil's quiet life. The instrumental background is unobtrusive and gentle, the melody haunting. The lyrics convey images of Rita watching her mother, trying to understand her life and her dreams, describing her as a woman who sacrificed herself for other people. Though the album's production is clean and professional, it does not have the polish of Rita's later work. But the record, and a book which contained the lyrics of the songs, were widely distributed among the growing feminist network and netted her more invitations to sing. *Born A Woman* became a cult classic.

But it didn't solve the turmoil in her private life. Rita split from her husband and they eventually divorced in 1978, but remained friendly. Rita wrote tenderly about her marriage and its dissolution in *Southeast Wind*. There's little bitterness, and more than a hint of regret as she writes about the life they shared—collecting old furniture, living on their farm—and the unpredictable southeast wind that eventually came and blew them apart. Another bleak period, one Rita dislikes dwelling on, came after the divorce. She moved to Ottawa where she worked cleaning houses and occasionally subsisted on welfare payments to feed her children. Little things kept her going such as an occasional concert date, or something as small as a royalty check for $29 that would give her morale a boost. She thought for years about moving back to Cape Breton, and finally did so in 1979.

Back home, Rita came into contact with a thriving group of singers, songwriters, and musicians who were all trying to make their way in the music industry, but didn't want to leave home. Songwriters such as Kenzie MacNeil, Leon Dubinsky, and Allister MacGillivray were only a few of the talented people who stayed in Cape Breton to scratch out a living. They travelled when they had to, to the Atlantic Folk Festival or to Halifax for radio or CBC studio recordings, but a lot of the creative life began to center itself around a pub on George Street in Sydney.

Kenzie MacNeil (no relation to Rita) was one of the patrons who found the pub an exciting place to be. MacNeil already had respectable credits as a songwriter. In the early '70s, a tune he wrote called *Johnstown Boogie* was picked up by Peter Gzowski on his show "This Country in the Morning," and was played on the CBC network every day for a year. But Kenzie, then barely 20, turned down offers to be a contracted songwriter with a record company and went back to school. After graduating from St. Francis Xavier University, he spent time at Neptune Theatre and acquired ideas about musical theater and technical production. Back in Cape Breton a few years later, Kenzie recalls that there was a lot of creative talent around, but not many outlets for it.

He remembers those years when the pub flourished, in

Rita sings at the opening of the 55th Apple Blossom Festival in Kentville's Memorial Park in 1987.

Halifax Chronicle Herald/James Latter

the late '70s and early '80s as a heady time. He says of the pub where they gathered, "It was our base…the academic community plus the arts community plus the community. It was a great spot. You could go in there and you were guaranteed an argument no matter what time of day." Kenzie laughs when he recalls the mixture of intellectual and musical material that was generated as a result of what he calls "our salon." Rita was a part of it; always more relaxed in the company of friends, she could be coaxed into singing for the group. Her anxiety, Kenzie says, was lessened by the fact that the makeshift stage at the pub was so low that stepping up on it to sing was less terrifying.

Kenzie took an interest in Rita's songwriting. He was concerned that her involvement with feminist causes would make her too exclusively identified with a specific audience. Together with other friends, he encouraged Rita to branch out from feminist material and diversify into songs such as *Working Man*. Kenzie coaxed Rita into appearing on a national CBC radio broadcast in 1981 called *Cape Breton Night at the Cohn*. Rita had assembled a band by then, after years of singing unaccompanied, and one of the members was keyboard player Ralph Dillon, who was to be for a long time her piano man, all-purpose co-worker and friend. The concert was like an evening at home in the kitchen with friends: plenty of jokes about unemployment, and fiddle music from the Cape Breton Symphony. Rita was both a cast member and a featured soloist. A year later the record made of the event demonstrated the impact Rita had already made on the Maritime region. It was her first recording of *Working Man*. Beginning with a muted introduction on acoustic guitar, the accompaniment is an intimate setting for her voice. Compared to her vocal quality on her first record, the voice is fuller, more mature and expressive and the urgency of her delivery sweeps the audience along with her. It's also worth noting that the 1981 tempo has more movement than the later version, which had slowed down to the steady march of an anthem. As Rita builds to the final chorus, she doesn't slow down or get louder, but the last chords are

followed by shouts, whistles, and thundering applause. One participant close to the microphone shouts across the clapping, "I wish the people across the country could see the standing ovation that's happening here."

Working Man is the song that first defined Rita Mac-Neil's musical personality. She wrote it after a coal miner took her underground to show her the dark regions where miners spent their working lives. The experience affected her deeply. The song, as she wrote it, was a triumphant salute to ordinary men who do the hard, dirty labor and often go unrecognized. Cowboys and truck drivers are glamorous characters, frequently celebrated in country songs. But, except for a few songs about the Springhill mine disaster, no mining song had captured the nobility of such unrewarding work with such simplicity and force. *Working Man* sent a tremendous message not only to the miners, but to everybody constrained by necessity to spend their lives in unremitting toil. When Rita sang "In the dark recess of the mine/ Where you age before your time/And the coal dust lies heavy on your lungs," she was shining a light upon the lives of men who risked danger every day but are largely unrecognized by society. Broadcaster Eric MacEwen heard Rita sing her song early on, an event he's never forgotten, as he told writer Barbara MacAndrew: "I first heard her song *Working Man* at a Glace Bay show full of miners. They were a burly bunch of men and all were reduced to tears."

Eric MacEwen was one of MacNeil's earliest supporters. He worked at an office job in Sydney, but had a strong interest in music and musicians of the Maritime region. Working at station CJCB on a show that played traditional music, MacEwen came into contact with musicians such as Gene MacLellan, Ryan's Fancy and later Kenzie MacNeil. Rita's voice and original songs captivated him instantly. He travelled to Big Pond to meet her in person and listen to *Born A Woman*. He recalled that meeting when he spoke to writer Marian Bruce in a 1990 profile published in the Halifax *Daily News*: "She had her first album, but all she had to listen to it on was an Eaton's mail-order record player—one of those compressed-cardboard players. It was hard times for her then. I remember saying to her then that I would play her songs till the cows came home—just to give her that support, let her know that someone out there who could help was helping." MacEwen kept his promise; after he moved to Prince Edward Island and started his own syndicated radio show in 1981, he played Rita's music on the first show, and on each show for years after that.

In 1982, Rita released her third album, *I'm Not What I Seem*. (There had been an intermediate album called *Part of the Mystery*.) The new project was the brainchild of CBC radio producer Markandrew Cardiff. Since the first time he heard Rita sing, Cardiff had been strongly supportive of her talent and believed that she had the potential to have a major career. But Rita didn't read music or play an instrument, aside from a few chords on the piano, and she needed assistance in developing background and settings for her songs. When she was writing a song, she usually collaborated with her pianist Ralph Dillon, singing brief phrases of melody and lyrics which Dillon would then help her frame up into verses. Before meeting Dillon and working with a band, Rita had sung *a cappella* (without accompaniment) and many of her musical phrases had been long, with few breaks except when she paused to take a breath. Dillon helped her change that and develop more varied musical structures. Kenzie McNeil says, "Ralph would go to the house and Rita would have half an idea, a couple of lines, usually a lyric, and she'd sing out a couple of lines. There'd be a problem or a gap and Ralph, in his nice, accommodating way would say, 'Well, what about this?'" Rita herself always acknowledged the contribution her band members made to the process. She told Catherine MacArthur in a 1988 interview in *Music Scene*, "I don't work with pen and paper. I work in my head. And I sing to the band and they play. I love music and it's definitely inside of me. The fact that I can't read or write music down has not inhibited me from writing lyrics and melody."

But for a major recording venture, Rita's songs needed something better than "head" arrangements—the arrangements made on the spot by the band musicians playing from lead sheets which are little more than sketches. Cardiff contacted Scott Macmillan, a local composer and arranger, to create instrumental parts for the proposed recording session. Macmillan had many of the skills Rita needed at that point. He had studied jazz, composition and arranging at Humber College in Toronto, and was a professional guitarist. Cardiff asked Macmillan to come up with instrumental scorings for the 10 songs on the album, to give Rita's voice the best possible setting.

Macmillan hadn't known Rita until then. From Cardiff, he received a tape of a performance with Rita and Ralph. He also worked closely with Ralph to get a better idea of the backup Rita's music usually needed. Working with her vocals on tape, Macmillan scored the songs for a large and varied group—strings, wind and brass sections, percussion and backup singers—a total cast of 20 people. Rita was nervous at the prospect of recording at Solar Audio in Dartmouth. She was used to doing shows in front of an audience, but the stark atmosphere of the studio intimidated her. Macmillan says that once the tape tracks were laid down for the various accompaniments, he and Cardiff would dim the lights so Rita would be more comfortable in the booth, while she recorded her vocal tracks.

The songs reflected the events and the changes in Rita's life so far. *Southeast Wind* told the story of her marriage and its breakup, while in *Stephen Foster Song*, the adult Rita remembered herself as a child, looking over songbooks and trying to pick out *Oh Susannah* on the piano. *Here's to the People* showed a more lighthearted Rita, making ironic references to all the people who snipe, criticize, put you down and generally fail to help you along. Writing these songs was Rita's way of dealing with her troubles and internal conflicts, and to hear her sing them was almost like hearing her think out loud. But there was also Rita the pop vocalist, who had done enough pub gigs to know that you had to be able to rev up the crowd. In *90% Stoned, 10% Blue*, a wailing, bluesy electric guitar intro sets up the listener for a different Rita MacNeil—one who can belt out rhythm and blues.

At least two of the songs on *I'm Not What I Seem* are pure country music, both in the instrumental arrangement and in the lyric content. *Strung Out and Crazy* is a country waltz, a real hurtin' song complete with steel guitar licks in the breaks. And the title song, *I'm Not What I Seem* is a more quiet and reflective Rita. The song is short and sweet and shows that her songwriting was becoming more self-revealing, as she tapped into her deep and often complex feelings about her life.

Shortly afterwards, Scott Macmillan joined her band. In the summer of 1982, Rita and the band toured Nova Scotia as one of the musical acts on the Old Home Summer tour, promoted and arranged by the Nova Scotia Department of Culture, Recreation and Fitness. Besides Scott, there was Dillon on keyboard, Dave MacIsaac on guitar, and Joella Foulds, who sang backup and did some guitar work. The band had already travelled with Rita to the Winnipeg and Mariposa Folk Festivals, and for the provincial tour they added drummer John Alphonse. With Dillon as unofficial manager, the MacNeil band crisscrossed Nova Scotia. Macmillan remembers it as a no-frills tour: "We toured around Nova Scotia. Whatever halls were available, we played them. All of us, stuffed in a van. But we didn't have the gear with us anyway, so that was a luxury…. As the band and the accompaniment got more in tune with her, we got the woollies out and really started to simplify and play our arrangements nicely. We had a nice little package together." They played at small theaters: the deCoste Centre in Pictou, the Savoy in Glace Bay and the Kings Theatre in Annapolis Royal.

For Scott Macmillan, playing in Rita's band was only one of many pickup jobs. Macmillan lived the life of a typical free-lance musician in Halifax, taking on a variety of musical tasks as a commercial arranger and composer, always ready to respond to a call from Rita. They played a lot of pub dates at taverns and clubs such as the former Ginger's Tavern and the Lord Nelson Tavern in Halifax. It was during a date at the Lord Nelson Tavern that the incident occurred which has since become a favorite anecdote of any MacNeil concert. Rita had gone back to her room after the last set and gotten ready for bed, wearing what she describes as her "bug-ugly nightie" when a fire alarm sounded. People often wonder what they'd take if they ever had to rush out of a burning building. Rita tells audiences simply, "I took my teeth." In the crowded lobby and on the street outside, an embarrassed Rita, self-conscious in her shabby nightie, tried to remain inconspicuous in the midst of a crowd of firemen, police officers, and hotel guests who all recognized her.

Pub dates are usually more fun for the audiences than the performers. Many musicians find them exhausting because of the long sets, the late hours, the smoky air, and the noise of a crowd for whom the music serves mostly as a background for drinking beer. Occasionally there were more prestigious gigs—a CBC recording here, a television spot there. Rita by now had developed a devout following across the Maritime region. She lived in Big Pond, driving rundown old cars and living on a tight budget in order to make the rent. Whenever a booking came along she had to scramble for sitters for her kids, borrow a dress, and set out on the road to wherever the job was. Money was always tight; more than once, a For Sale sign went up outside her Big Pond home and then, after the next paying gig, the sign would come down again. Rita was probably earning more from concert dates than from her recording royalties at that point, for although the records sold perhaps 10,000 individual copies, the amount of radio play was limited. And radio play as the greatest source of public exposure eventually pays off too.

Within the band, Scott and Rita were developing a musical bond. Scott says, "Rita and I became very close musically because I was the only other line-instrument in the band. When it came to anything other than Rita singing, I was singing too on the guitar, so there was always a real dynamic between the two of us, musically." Both Macmillan and Ralph Dillon worked with Rita on her tunes, to transpose the lyrics and melodies she heard so clearly in her head

Nova Scotia Tourism & Culture

Under the spotlights at Big Pond, Rita's hometown on Cape Breton Island.

into something the band could play—song intros, turna-rounds between the verses and chorus, harmonies and rhythm ideas for the bass and drums.

In those days, Scott was often the first to hear a new song. "We'd get together, with Rita and I and an acoustic guitar, and she'd sing the song and I'd figure out the chords. Then Rita and I would go to the band and we'd play them and the band would pick up on it. Ralph would have suggestions and often he would take it home to his studio and work some-thing, so he had a lot of creative input—there was input as a group."

Macmillan says that he was constantly amazed by Rita's musical ideas. "I remember sometimes she'd be possessed. A song would take over. Sometimes she wouldn't even want to deal with it, but there it was, she had to resolve it and get it written down." As for the actual creative process Rita went through, Scott says he isn't sure how the ideas came to her. "My impression is, just a stream of consciousness…and then the whole thing would blow right out of her." MacNeil herself has verified that, as when she told *Music Scene* in 1988 that lyrics and melody tended to come to her simulta-neously, saying, "No matter where I'm at, if there's a need to express myself through song that's when a song will come. Sometimes I'll write seven songs all at once within a week and then maybe there'll be nothing for another few months." She also has a tremendous backlog of material, as she has said. Scott Macmillan agrees, estimating that there may be as many as 30 children's songs which Rita has composed but has not yet recorded.

On a more personal basis, Macmillan says that Rita's shyness sometimes made it difficult for people to get to know her well. They often made casual conversation; Macmillan talking about his two small sons, Rita talking about her son and daughter, then in their teens. Scott sometimes asked her about her songs: how did you write that one? Who is this about? When did that story happen? Rita would tell him about her memories, about things that had happened, and

would occasionally point out someone, saying, "I wrote that for him." He noticed that she was improving musically as her sense of tuning and time grew more acute, and she was always writing new songs. "That's the thing about her," Macmillan says. "She's very talented…. She has a lot to say and she knows how to say it. It still comes down to her being able to put down a verse and a chorus that no one else can do—say something in two words where it takes someone else twenty."

Aside from constant help and encouragement from her band members, Markandrew Cardiff in Halifax was a tireless booster of Rita and her music, as was Eric MacEwen. A lifelong fan of oldtime, traditional and Celtic music, MacEwen launched his radio show from North Rustico in 1981. Partly a kitchen ceilidh and partly a return to the tradition of *Outports*, MacEwen's show was, and still is, a jumble of fiddle tunes, stories, original poetry, reports on recent concerts and church socials, and ads for local dairies and other businesses, which MacEwen himself writes. He is renowned for his offhand manner: he likes to chat about concerts he's been to, the people he's met, the songs that have become his favorites. He often tells the audience where he's going for coconut cream pie and coffee after the show. He's unabashedly fond of certain artists whose records he plays regularly—folksinger Lennie Gallant, the Barra MacNeils, the Rankin Family Band, and of course Rita MacNeil. But even though MacEwen played her records faithfully, his show at that time only reached the Maritime regional audience. If she wanted to break further into commercial radio, bigger record sales and a national presence, she had to find the way to do it.

Rita found that way when she signed a management deal with Brooks Diamond Productions in 1985. Diamond, work-ing out of Halifax, had earned a reputation as a shrewd negotiator with good connections and plenty of smarts about the business. He had worked with Ryan's Fancy and had booked musical acts for a variety of local clubs and staged for several years the highly successful but now defunct Atlantic Folk Festival at Moxson Farm some 30 miles north of

Halifax. Diamond says that he was almost overwhelmed the first time he heard Rita sing. Early in their association he asked her what she wanted to do with her music. Her answer was, "I want to take the music as far as it will go."

The first step, as far as Diamond was concerned, was to try to increase the amount of exposure she received on radio. He says of her career until that time: "You can have a very strong, what they call a cult or underground following. Basically what that means is, you're an enormously talented artist who has a very strong following but you've never had a hit on the radio and therefore don't have a very large following." Diamond was confident that with a talent the magnitude of Rita's, all they had to do was make the right connections with the people who could do the right things for her.

There had already been a few lucky breaks. Rita had appeared at the Canadian pavilion at Expo 85 in Japan, where filmmaker Lulu Keating made a short film about her for Red Snapper Films of Halifax, which was aired on television. The concerts and travel in Japan acted as a creative stimulus to Rita, resulting in her catchy up-tempo song *Fast Train To Tokyo*. When she later recorded it for the album *Flying on Your Own*, Toronto producer Declan O'Doherty would give it a hard-edged electronic arrangement that highlighted the Oriental genesis of the tune.

But the real leap forward came during Rita's six-week summer run at Expo 86 in Vancouver. She had appeared in Vancouver before, but this time the crowds were bigger, and the public was more receptive than they had ever been. Scott Macmillan and the other band members realized that they were witnessing a major evolution in Rita's life, and possibly in their own lives as well. Macmillan says that he'd always known that Rita would break through because in their most recent performances leading up to Expo, crowd response had begun to reach a pitch of enthusiasm they'd never seen before. He says, "The response to Rita was unbelievable. I knew it was coming because I'd been on the stage with her

all the time. Standing ovations were the norm—midshow standing ovations. And finally in Vancouver, you'd have thousands of strangers and every time, a standing ovation. Every time. Lineups waiting for her. I knew she was going to be a world star." Rave reviews poured in. *Vancouver Sun* columnist Denny Boyd wrote in August: "It's more than singing, really; she opens her chest and her heart and her life spill out…. But for God's sake, you must hear Rita MacNeil. See her at Expo this month so you can talk knowledgeably when she becomes a star."

Thousands took Boyd's advice and as Scott Macmillan watched the eager crowds thronging into the Folklife Theatre for every show, he knew that Rita's career was about to accelerate into high gear. If things went the way he expected, Macmillan figured that he would either have to commit himself to an extensive touring schedule, which meant leaving his young family alone for long stretches, or he would have to leave the group. It was a tough decision, but Scott told Rita he would have to leave. He stayed around for the upcoming recording session for the new album *Flying On Your Own*, and he completed a dozen orchestral arrangements for Rita's first orchestral pops concert booked with Symphony Nova Scotia in February of 1987. Rita was reluctant to see him go, but Macmillan says that she understood his reasons for the split. He wanted to spend more time with his two young sons. He also hoped to resume his independent life as a composer and arranger doing commercials, studio work and larger commissioned pieces. The rest of the band stayed on—bassist Al Bennett, pianist Ralph Dillon, drummer Dave Burton and guitarist Clarence Deveau who replaced Macmillan.

Flying On Your Own was to be Rita's major break into commercial radio play. It was altogether more sophisticated than any of her three previous albums, with an obvious emphasis on producing individual cuts that would play well on either country or adult/contemporary radio stations. The backup musicians on all but two cuts included local players who had known Rita for some time—her regular band, plus a few additional singers and instrumentalists including Max MacDonald, John Alphonse, and Denis Ryan. Ralph Dillon produced nine of the 11 cuts, and those nine all used the Maritime crowd and were recorded at Solar Audio in Dartmouth. But the two tracks which received the most airplay, the title cut and *Fast Train to Tokyo*, were produced with Nashville-style opulence with synthesizer tracks enriching and filling the sound, by one of Toronto's fastest-rising young producers—Declan O'Doherty.

Flying On Your Own was the song that best expressed the newly positive attitudes that Rita was feeling, fresh from her triumph in Vancouver. Ten years earlier, the song might have appealed only to feminist audiences as a liberation anthem, but in 1986 Rita was a different person. She sang of the doubts and anxieties, saying: "You were never more together/You were never more apart/Once pieces of you were all that you knew/You're flying on your own." If *Working Man* was an anthem of affirmation for miners, *Flying On Your Own* was an anthem of affirmation for all those people, women and men, who were resolutely facing a new life on their own after having gone through a separation of one kind or another from those they had loved. It summed up her life until that point—the shakiness, the fears, and then the sense of exhilaration that she communicated each time she rounded into the chorus.

The album had plenty of variation in mood and instrumental textures; the bright tempo of *Neon City* was driven by extra percussion (drums and congas), and was one of the songs Rita had written out of her mixed memories of Toronto, and a remembered love affair. *Baby Baby* had a playful calypso arrangement and lighthearted lyrics begging an ex-lover to become a friend again. Several songs were arranged with a strong country feeling, both in lyrics and music.

In *Leave Her Memory*, a beautiful country classic with its characteristic rising melody, Rita built her lyric towards the highest note and then trailed off on the last word of the line, almost like a sigh. The message was gently reproachful, but not whiny—the plea of a lover begging someone to forget the "used to be," and concentrate on the "now." Then there was *Loser When It Comes To Love*—a scorcher with a strong '60s feel. Rita had always confessed to an interest in rhythm and blues music and in this song, she let herself go and belted out the words. Ralph Dillon's gutsy organ solo, and an answering snarl on Scott Macmillan's electric guitar neatly underlined Rita's lyrics—a denunciation of an incompetent lover.

Several songs demonstrated two of the strongest underlying themes in Rita's writing: memory, and homesickness. While performing at Expo 86 in Vancouver, Rita was stricken by one of her recurring bouts of homesickness. She worked out her feelings in a sentimental love song for her home province: *She's Called Nova Scotia*. She told journalist Denny Boyd of *The Sun* that she wrote it in one night, adding, "But it took me the whole night." With an introductory solo on pennywhistle played by Denis Ryan (formerly of Ryan's Fancy), the song arrangement returned to the simple, folk style that had been natural to Rita in the years before she worked with a band. And the other song which gave a look at Rita's inner life was *Realized Your Dreams* which she sang accompanied only by Ralph Dillon on piano. Just who the song was about was not clear. It could have been a relative, a friend or a stay-at-home neighbor who was always the one to prepare the welcome for visitors, yet was content to stay put. The notion of returning home, of missing home and familiar things, has always been present in MacNeil's writing, often expressed with a melancholy edge, but *Realized Your Dreams* conveyed warmth and a sense of fulfillment. It suggested that Rita herself had, maybe for the first time in her life, a sense of certainty not only about where she was from, but about where she was going.

The album was released on her own label, Lupins. (It is not uncommon for artists to establish their own independent record labels, which may later be picked up for national distribution by one of the larger companies.) *Flying On Your*

Own was the first sign, for MacNeil, of the newest trends in production, an album which was created in several different cities. Dillon's nine cuts were recorded in Halifax while O'Doherty's two cuts had their bedtracks (rhythm and bass) laid down in a Nashville studio, with overdubs and mixing done at Inception Sound in Toronto with all of the other selections. The quality had to be topnotch to attract radio play. Radio programmers listen to a lot of tapes each day from a variety of different sources ranging from major companies such as Capitol-EMI to independent labels and to homemade demos that frequently aren't even usable broadcast quality. Getting your song on the radio is complicated, as Brooks Diamond says. "You have to have somebody pounding on the radio stations to get them. There are lots of good songs out there. There's only a very few great songs, but there are loads of good radio-playable songs."

If her market was country or adult contemporary radio, Rita was competing with established artists ranging from Canadians such as Anne Murray to the latest releases from Nashville by megastars Kenny Rogers and Ricky Skaggs. Once an artist has an established following, he or she is a known quantity to the radio programmers, and getting a song into rotation—that magic format that means the record will be played a certain number of times each day—becomes easier. *Flying On Your Own* was nearly perfect for several formats; it had plenty of percussion, a prerequisite for pop or country stations, and it had a soaring vocal line and an inspirational message, which meant that it would appeal to the over-30 listeners who tuned in to adult contemporary stations.

This time it worked. Whatever the secret was, *Flying On Your Own* put Rita in front of the general public, who heard her as if for the first time. As Brooks Diamond put it, "The bottom line with any artist is radio play…any time you hear an artist singing on the radio it's a three-minute free ad. The fact of the matter is, that despite the magnitude of Rita's talent, and that magnitude not having changed once she

started working with management…she never really started to draw large crowds anywhere including her hometown or Halifax or anywhere else, until she had a song on the hit parade on the radio."

Flying On Your Own made Rita someone to be reckoned with inside the industry. It won her an 1987 Juno award as most promising vocalist— surely an understatement for a woman who had been working steadily at the job for more than a decade—but sweet praise nonetheless. The Canadian Country Music Awards named her a rising star and by the end of the year, *Flying on Your Own* had sold over 100,000 copies.

As many other managers and agents in the music industry will tell you, Diamond is right about the importance of making it onto the hit parade. Radio builds a desire in its listeners to see and hear in person the performers who have the hits. Television doesn't have the same impact, Diamond says, because of the possibility for too much exposure, adding, "on the radio, they don't get to see them. They only get to hear the song, and it builds up a kind of mystique."

Rita's 1987 tours capitalized on the roaring success of the album. She sold out regularly, including five consecutive sold-out concerts at the Vancouver East Cultural Centre alone. And if recognition from the fans wasn't enough, there was plenty of praise from the critics too. At a concert in Convocation Hall in Toronto that November, *Globe and Mail* reviewer Chris Dafoe noted that MacNeil was more relaxed and was developing a flair for off-the-cuff jokes, as when she introduced her song *Loser When It Comes to Love* by saying, "This song meant nothing to me when I wrote it…and it means less all the time." He also generously praised MacNeil's modest stage presence and good rapport with her audience, though in the process he inadvertently stole one of Rita's own favorite jokes about herself when he wrote, "If her concert demonstrated anything, it was that she deserves to be even bigger."

Her programs now consisted solely of her own material, but she was not averse occasionally to doing cover tunes of other performers' songs as encores. Dafoe noted that she did renditions of two old rhythm and blues classics, *Bring It On Home To Me* by Sam Cooke, and *Midnight Hour*, originally sung by Wilson (Wicked) Pickett. *Ottawa Citizen* reviewer Susan Beyer called Rita's version "…a rocking and totally transforming version of Wilson Pickett's *Midnight Hour*." Like most of the journalists, radio hosts and reviewers who were now writing about Rita, Beyer was won over by MacNeil's lack of pretension. At the end of 1987, in her regular country music column in the *Citizen*, she called Rita MacNeil the story of the year.

Brooks Diamond was building Rita's career slowly and carefully. His business partner Michael Ardenne handled deals for other clients, such as singer Joan Kennedy, but Diamond devoted himself exclusively to Rita MacNeil. In addition to personal artistic management, his agency provided Rita with many of the services that with other performers, in other agencies, would be in other hands. Breaking down the various aspects of the job, Diamond says: "There's concert promotion and production. There's album production, manufacture, distribution and promotion…. We tend to be an all-service management company, where we do take care of virtually all parts of it." Many managers, Diamond says, work with an agency for concert bookings, while concert promotion and often production is put into the hands of a concert promoter.

As Scott Macmillan had foreseen, Rita's time on the concert circuit away from home was to increase. In 1988, she appeared at Expo 88 in Brisbane, Australia (where she was a roaring success), though she would not undertake a full Australian tour until two years later. There was also a major national tour of Canada to assure her that the days of playing smoky, noisy pubs in small towns were definitely gone. One show at Roy Thomson Hall in Toronto sold out within several days, and when a second show was booked, tickets were gone in one day. This kind of public response put Rita in the league of folk idols like Gordon Lightfoot. At the

Queen Elizabeth Auditorium in Vancouver, MacNeil sold out for three nights and at nearly all of her western venues the rule was standing room only. That spring, Rita received an honorary Doctor of Letters degree from the University of New Brunswick, and the next year a similar award from Saint Mary's University in Halifax. In July, her fifth album, *Reason to Believe*, was released.

Reason to Believe marked another transitional point in Rita MacNeil's career. On *Flying on Your Own*, nine cuts were produced by Ralph Dillon and featured her regular band. The two cuts produced by Declan O'Doherty featured studio musicians from Toronto. *Reason to Believe* was almost the reverse; of the 11 cuts, only one was produced by Dillon with the MacNeil road band. The other 10 were produced by O'Doherty with studio musicians. Among them were some fairly heavy hitters such as backup vocalist Shirley Eikhard and guitarist Michael "Pepe" Francis. The sound mix was fundamentally different. Against the thick, over-produced cushion of electronic sound, Rita's unusually distinctive voice was reduced to sounding like that of just another good pop singer.

The amount of good fortune she'd been having—large record sales, awards, sold-out concert halls—was bound to be reflected in her work, and the result was that the attitude expressed in the songwriting was that of a writer who was feeling strong in herself. In topic matter, there was some eclecticism: inward-looking songs such as *Good Friends*, and the heartsore country ballad *Two Steps from Broken*. The mix was spiced up a little more by the presence of the song *Doors of the Cemetery* in which the arrangement skirted the disco-pop style of the late '70s, the lyrics sounded ominous, and her voice had none of the sweetness usually associated with Rita MacNeil. Though Rita's social commentaries, such as they were, tended to be based around home, friends and neighbors, this song was similar to the spirit of earlier songs such as *Angry People in the Streets* or *Angus Anthony's Store*. It signalled a songwriter who looked not only at her own history for ideas, but who turned outward to news events of the outside world.

Certain reflective words and key phrases occur often in Rita's lyrics—"memory" and "I remember" are two examples—and they have often been tinged with sadness. In *Walk On Through*, she wrote about small town events, the jealousy and the gossiping she undoubtedly remembered from the earliest time of her life, but the chorus and the jauntiness of the arrangement, complete with a saxophone solo, suggested a Rita MacNeil who has begun to conquer the pain of the past.

In *City Child*, written for her daughter Laura, the lyrics implied that MacNeil remembered her own life alone in a large city and wished her daughter strength and good luck, just as her own mother Renee had. *Causing the Fall*, the only cut produced by Ralph Dillon, had an intimacy that was often lacking in many of the other songs; the instrumentation was sparser and lighter and allowed her voice some interplay with the melodic lines of the guitar. And finally, in *The Music's Going 'Round Again*, there were hints that MacNeil had begun to work out her ambivalent relationship with Toronto. Memory mixed her past and present together, and rather than dwell on whatever unhappiness or trouble still colored those memories, the tone of the lyrics was of reconciliation.

The other notable cut was a reworked version of her classic *Working Man*, this time with a beefed-up production that included a backup chorus in the form of the Men of the Deeps choir from Glace Bay in Cape Breton. (To belong to this rough and ready men's chorus of 27 miners, formed in 1966 as a Canadian Centennial Year project, a man must have worked in a mine.) The cut was recorded on location at the Miners' Museum in Glace Bay. The keyboard introduction set up Rita's entry, and as the miners joined the chorus, the sound swelled. The tempo slowed as each repetition of the verse built to a peak of emotion by the end of the last chorus. *Working Man* was not the final cut on the album.

One more song, the subdued *Good Friends*, came as something of an anticlimax after the cascades of sentiment unleashed in *Working Man*.

Reason to Believe was picked up for distribution by the Toronto branch of one of the most innovative young record companies in the business, British-owned Virgin Records. With Virgin's extensive national and international connections Diamond Productions could be assured that Rita's product was reaching the largest possible buying audience. Rita was one of the artists Virgin picked up by listening to a tape sent "over the transom." Not all labels and artist representatives—those of Sony and RCA-BMG, for example—will listen to unsolicited material, partly because of the sheer volume of demo tapes they receive, but also partly because of the ever-present threat of lawsuits for plagiarism on the part of company songwriters, producers or executives. But Virgin was always on the lookout for new talent as artist and repertoire man Doug Chappell told Nancy Lanthier of *Canadian Composer* magazine. In an article printed in the fall of 1991 issue, Chappell said, "I listen to everything that comes in through the door," When asked whether he had signed any of the acts that had sent in a demo in a plain brown wrapper, Chappell responded, "…Yeah, everything I've dealt with—Northern Pikes, World on Edge, Rita MacNeil." Not that MacNeil was an unknown quantity. She had all the things an A&R man looks for: strong songwriting talent, a distinctive voice, and solid performing credits. Above all, her sales success on the independent release of *Flying On Your Own* made *Reason to Believe* a good bet for a second smash album.

In a profile of MacNeil published in *Maclean's* magazine that November, writer Ann Finlayson mentioned that some record reviewers had reservations about the lush production of *Reason to Believe*, and questioned whether it was a too-obvious aim at the middle-of-the-road radio market. Rita responded: "I am very nervous of labels—and any changes in my music are changes I make myself. There is no kind of music

Rita charms the audience.

I don't like and I see every song as a chance to grow. People forget that I got my start here at home singing in clubs where all they wanted was rock'n'roll. The fact is, I love it." Rita's former guitarist/arranger Scott Macmillan believes that in terms of gaining increased radio play through more sophisticated production quality on records, the best thing that could have happened to Rita was the connection she made with producer Declan O'Doherty. Macmillan says, "My impression of Declan is that he was a person who was very aware of what needed to be done to get Rita on AM radio play. He's a very good producer. Listen to his productions—they're crystal clear and they're impeccably played. They really struck it big because he did the right thing at the right time."

Audiences certainly thought so. *Reason to Believe* had gone platinum (sales of 100,000) by November of 1988, and when Rita released her Christmas album *Now the Bells Ring* it went platinum the same month it was released. A regional sales manager for the A&A record store chain told reporter Greg Guy of the Halifax *Chronicle Herald*: "Rita's Christmas album is outselling every artist in our stores.... It's not just outselling the Canadian artists, it's outselling everyone, from Dire Straits to Def Leppard and U2." Brooks Diamond, quoted in the same article, predicted that the sales of Rita MacNeil's last three albums were expected to top 400,000 by the end of 1988.

The stage was being set for an approach to the American market. In March of 1989, Rita MacNeil was a guest performer on the annual Juno Awards show, broadcast nationally on CBC television from the O'Keefe Centre in Toronto. The show had the usual number of miscues, flubs and mispronunciations, but Rita's spot was regarded by many as the peak of the evening. She was again joined in her performance of *Working Man* by the Men of the Deeps. While Rita and her band appeared onstage, the miners filed into the darkened auditorium dressed in working clothes and guided to the stage by the miner's lights built in to their hardhats. The audience responded with a lengthy standing ovation. Writer Greg Quill in his *Toronto Star* column the next day called it "...a brave and epic stunt, simple in its humanity and emotionally overpowering..." With plans already made to play in Boston early in the spring, such lavish praise couldn't have come at a better time.

MacNeil and her band appeared at the Berklee Performance Center in Boston in mid-April. Canadian performers often have a hard time receiving publicity in the States, especially in a city with a cultural community as enormous and diverse as that of Boston. But as reviewer Daniel Gewertz of the Boston *Herald* noted wryly, "Canadians form the largest ethnic group in the greater Boston area and they are deeply loyal to their own stars." They flocked to the concert, drawn by newspaper ads plus and the advance play of Rita's records on local radio stations such as the easy-listening station WJIB. Gewertz noted that the concert came close to selling out the Center, and praised what he labelled her "heart-tugging appeal." He rhapsodized over her voice, calling it a marvel: "It's a voice that could lull a squalling infant and inspire a forlorn adult to believe in life again." However, Gewertz had some reservations about the musical presentation. While he appreciated the quality of the songs such as *Working Man*, he nonetheless found some of the musical arrangements of those tunes to be less than exciting. He commented: "...numerous other songs seemed more like tepid American pop and adult-contemporary schmaltz. And her band, a slick faceless quintet with two synthesizers, seemed closer to Las Vegas than Halifax."

Reviewer Paul Robicheau, writing in the Boston *Globe*, agreed. He described her voice as rich, stately and captivating, but again, found fault with the backup: "There was a melodic, dynamic sameness to the songs, instilled by the precise cushioning of her five-piece band, including two keyboardists." Opinions from critics are recognized as subjective; brickbats from a reviewer or commentator will not stop the public from buying records or tickets, and critical plaudits do not always translate into sales or radio play. But a little praise never hurts, and the Berklee appearance was a good first crack at the massive American entertainment market.

At home in the summers, Rita achieved a long-standing dream. She opened a small tearoom in Big Pond. It was partly as the result of a joke she'd been making for years; during each concert, she would invite the audience to come visit her and have a cup of tea. "I didn't think they'd all show up," she said later, when the sheer volume of visitors drove her to amend the invitation (they could still come, but they should bring their own teabags). Rita is not the first musical performer to have a small business spin off the main one, as singer Murray McLauchlan would later point out. To McLauchlan, it was a comment on Rita's modesty: Dolly Parton has a theme park named Dollywood, Conway Twitty has Twitty City, and Rita MacNeil has a tearoom. Even while selling thousands of records, MacNeil could often be found working at the cash register or serving tea and biscuits like the proprietor of any small country restaurant—except that many of the patrons wanted her autograph.

She still found time to write. The mystic hills and inland seas of Cape Breton, and particularly the area around her beloved Big Pond, stimulate Rita's imagination. Her record label, Lupins, bears the name of one of the loveliest and most abundant wildflowers of early summer. MacNeil has often said that she'll never leave to live somewhere else again, and it does appear that the sense of continuity and security she feels in the familiar surroundings of Sydney or Big Pond nourish her creativity. Long stretches of travelling and giving concerts are balanced by time at home, where she can draw on support from her children and her friends.

The 1989 album, *Rita*, marked another transitional point in her recording career. If lyric content and vocal delivery provide any clue to a writer's mood and personality, Rita at this time was hitting her stride. She sounded confident and strong, and unlike *Reason to Believe*, in which the vocals sometimes were subordinated by the arrangements, the sound mix on *Rita* was better balanced. It was completely arranged and produced by Declan O'Doherty again, except for two songs arranged by new band member Lisa Evans. Production credits were lengthy: the album was recorded in three different studios in Vancouver, the sound mixed in Los Angeles and Toronto. Rita had come a long way from the modest sound booth of Solar Audio in Dartmouth.

With the perspective of her new life, MacNeil, in *Rita*, was continuing to grow both with respect to the quality of the songs she was writing, and in the way she sang them. There was more variation of mood in her love songs. Rather than evoke the usual emotions of loss, abandonment and hurt, the lyrics instead created images of resilience. In *You've Known Love* and *Why Do I Think of You Today*, the words expressed less of the pain of failed love affairs, and more of the remembered joys of those experiences. But there was nothing self-deluding or passive about her relationships. *The Other One*, a song about an unfaithful lover, had a brisk tempo, feisty lyrics and a gutsy delivery. Another song about love gone wrong, *Crazy Love*, featured a pop-reggae instrumental setting that gave it a sauciness not often found in Rita's other lovesongs.

But her song *Midnight and Clover* was a throwback to an earlier musical style. Only a girl who had herself either been a wallflower or been very close to one could have written this sentimental country waltz about a lonely girl who was never asked to dance at the hall. Even the instrumentation recalled the simple sound of an old-time band: just piano, bass, and a drum set played with brushes for a soft percussive sound. *Anna I.O.U.* was another song in which MacNeil reflected on her previous life in Toronto. It was like a snapshot of a very young Rita MacNeil with her friend, the Polish woman from whom she rented a room. As she did in *The Music's Going Round Again*, Rita seemed again to be examining her earlier life for significant events, but her memories had undergone subtle revisions. Now she remembered a friend, Anna the landlady, and the feeling of love and acceptance. The backup was limited to a few discreetly chosen instruments, such as piano and mandolin.

Black Rock was recorded live at a concert in Saint John, with Rita singing against solo acoustic guitar accompaniment by Al Bennett. It was one of Rita's spirit-of-place songs

*Rita singing her heart out for more than 7,000 fans
at the Halifax Metro Centre in the fall of 1991.*

about Cape Breton, in which the concrete details—sea, sky, waves, and the black rock—remind the listener of how much Rita relied on the unchanging strength of her surroundings to foster her sense of herself. The final cut on the second side, *We'll Reach the Sky Tonight*, had a bouncy rock sound like that of *Fast Train to Tokyo*. Backed by a rhythm section driven by drum offbeats, Rita's vocal took on a soaring, positive quality that ended the album on a triumphant note.

One of the lovesongs, *I'll Accept the Rose Tonight*, was released as a single and spent a long time on the country charts. The arrangement, one of two by keyboardist Lisa Evans, signalled its mainstream country sound with a piano intro in the by now almost obligatory slip-note style of Floyd Cramer. By the end of 1990, *I'll Accept the Rose Tonight* had reached sixth place on the yearly Cancountry hit list published in the January issue of *Country Music News*. Rita's song finished ahead of singles from George Fox, Anne Murray and Ian Tyson.

That year, 1990, was an eventful one. As always, extensive touring continued and Rita began building a new house near Sydney. But the accelerated pace of travelling, tours, songwriting for a new album and taping a television special early in 1990 took their toll on Rita's health. Rita spent time in a local hospital for minor surgery that summer and during her convalescence at home, wrote several songs and recorded vocal parts that would eventually wind up on the album she released later that year. By July, she had recovered enough that she was able to participate in the Big Pond summer music festival. Her concert, an open-air event, attracted more than 4,000 fans to the annual two-day festival. But the verdict on that concert was mixed. Outdoor concerts are notoriously tricky to stage because of the vagaries of weather, sound systems and sometimes rowdy crowds. Later that fall, the news broke that two longtime band members, bassist Al Bennett and pianist Ralph Dillon, would be leaving. (Dillon showed up in the band again in Rita's 1991 Halifax Metro Centre concert.) Changes in a band's personnel are by no means unusual, but both Bennett's

and Dillon's connections with Rita went back the better part of a decade. There were rumblings of discontent within the band, but that fall the MacNeil entourage left for a western Canadian tour, another Australia tour, and a London concert in which Rita appeared at a celebration of Canadian music alongside other Canadian performers including country singer/songwriter Colleen Peterson and bop/rap/jazz group the Shuffle Demons.

Timed neatly to support the release of her next album, *Home I'll Be*, Rita appeared as a guest on the CBC radio show "Swinging on a Star" shortly before Christmas. As well, her first Christmas television special was broadcast on the CTV network a week before Christmas of 1990. The theme was a family Christmas in Cape Breton, with musical guests the Men of the Deeps, the Cape Breton Chorale and country/ rock singer Matt Minglewood. Rita sang traditional carols as well as songs from her own Christmas album including the title song *Now the Bells Ring*. While the musical content of the show was solid and well arranged, especially an episode filmed at the church in Big Pond, reviewers panned both the stilted acting and the dramatic premise of the show. Television reporter Lois Legge, writing in the Halifax *Chronicle Herald*, commented on the plot and sequences which included Rita greeting guests and talking with children about the meaning of the season. Legge called them "…both forced and unbearably hokey. And the acting—well, let's just say Rita and Matt shouldn't give up their day jobs." Columnist Henry McGuirk, writing in *Country Music News*, remarked, "Rita's Christmas show on the CTV network received mixed reviews with some suggesting that the Rita that Canadians know and love was not the same one who was presented to them on the TV show."

Not that she had any reason to worry about her popularity. In December of 1990, *Entertainment Network* magazine bestowed on her the title of "Canada's country sweetheart," and mentioned not only that her four album releases by Virgin had gone double platinum, but also that *Reason to Believe* had reached the number one position in Australia.

But not all was well. Illness, and perhaps some of the changes and stress in her band and professional life were reflected in her latest work. If *Home I'll Be*, her major release in 1990, was a barometer of her feelings, the mood of the music suggested that Rita MacNeil was experiencing a jumble of inner feelings of regret and loss that was spilling over into her music.

Compared to the brightness and energy of *Rita*, *Home I'll Be* felt somber. The cover photo was decidedly unflattering—it showed Rita wading ankle-deep in water against a backdrop of forested hills. If the intended message was that she was frequently homesick, it came through loud and clear on the title cut. With a soulful introduction on the Uillean pipes (Irish bagpipes), and the Men of the Deeps coming in on the song's chorus, the mood was of aching, almost unbearable sadness. Many of the other cuts sustained that mood. *You Taught Me Well* had a sparse, darkly hued instrumental backup with rumbles like thunder from the synthesizer. Occasionally the mood lightened up; Rita belted out *This Thing Called Love*, with an arrangement like a screaming rock-and-roll song complete with electric guitar solos of mid-'60s vintage.

The love songs, always a particular strength of hers, also seemed to imply tiredness and resignation. *Watch Love Grow Strong*, despite the cheeriness of the title, was an ironic outline of love going astray right in front of one person's unbelieving eyes, and the pent-up anguish in the lyrics was played up by a piano solo added as a tag at the end. The album also contained a different rendition of *Southeast Wind*. The first version, on *I'm Not What I Seem*, was a pensive memory of Rita's marriage and divorce. This second version began with a descending bass line which quickly switched over into a heavy rock beat. It was followed, whether intentionally or not, by a down-tempo ballad about disintegrating love called *The Hurtin' Kind*.

Both fans and reviewers appeared to be somewhat puzzled by the reflective, frequently sad moods portrayed in the album. CHFX country radio host Paul Kennedy, in his December, 1990 column for *Country Music News* praised the album as "ten quality songs" but added cautiously, "The only thing that seems to be missing from this collection is a few more up-tempo songs." Yet *Home I'll Be* netted MacNeil a second Juno in March 1991, this time as best country female vocalist.

MacNeil travelled to Great Britain again for a month of concerts and an appearance in a BBC film that was being made about her. Michael Cope, London correspondent for the Halifax *Chronicle Herald*, reported that her concert at the 3,000-seat Royal Albert Hall played to a near-capacity crowd. Back in Canada that spring, Rita appeared on Dini Petty's CTV talk show and chatted about her recent trip as well as her recording and concert career. She admitted, not for the first time, that she disliked being interviewed, that she was uneasy in formal situations, and that she sometimes found her increased fame difficult to handle. MacNeil told Petty that the questions asked by London interviewers were often prying and personal. (It is not only London interviewers who should plead guilty to this complaint. When CBC "Fifth Estate" host Eric Malling did a feature on Rita, his questions about her weight, her cleft palate and her divorce were widely perceived as going past the bounds of fair comment. Rita held her own; when Malling commented over some old photos that, "you used to be pretty cute," Rita's spirited retort was, "I'm still pretty cute.") Petty's studio audience, largely female, responded with the same kind of reaction—a combination of pride and protectiveness—that many Canadians had already displayed towards their newest international star. One audience member, nearly overcome by emotion, blurted out, "I think you're one of the loveliest ladies I've even seen. TV doesn't do you justice!"

Later that spring, Brooks Diamond gave an up-beat interview to Nancy Gyokeres of *Probe*, the monthly newsletter of the Canadian performing rights organization SOCAN. The interview focused on Diamond's success promoting Rita's career. Diamond told the interviewer his often-repeated maxim: "...the best team is [in place] when the manager's business sense reflects the artist's philosophy." Later, when the writer observed that commercial success was not the only kind, Diamond told Gyokeres, "Artists have to be careful about this. One of the tricks in the game is to be what you are, to create a niche for yourself." The impression left by the article was of a solid, stable relationship between manager and client.

But the Canadian music business, and the general public were shaken up by the news in late 1991 that Rita MacNeil had decided not to renew her management contract with Brooks Diamond Productions. She was reputedly considering offers from a variety of comers. The reason was, perhaps, simply a practical one. Despite enormous success in supporting Rita's career in Canada, Australia and England, Diamond had never succeeded in breaking her into the American market. This, despite Rita's solid musicianship and proven audience appeal, may not be as self-evidently easy to do as it looks. Major U.S. record labels were interested in her, but dropped out when they discovered that American radio stations couldn't fit her into any of their formats. It is yet another indication of the only too-familiar predicament Maritime artists find themselves in and many have complained of: their music is fine, even outstanding, but what is it—country, pop, adult contemporary, roots, traditional? The answer is, often, "all of the above." They simply don't fit into commercial radio's pigeon-holes. That is their weakness, alas, but artistically at least, it is also their strength.

Rita's critical accolades from Australia had been outstanding; during her tour in the fall of 1990, reviewer Keith Urban, writing in *Big Night Out* magazine in Brisbane, almost ran out of superlatives. "The lady simply defies conventional descriptions or pillars of praise.... Her performance leaves one speechless, grasping for words, groping for rational appraisal, lost in a sea of literary inadequacy." The praise was matched by the record sales. But being a smash hit in Australia and Great Britain is still, in most people's minds, only a preamble to scoring a major success in the United

States. The potential of the American market is enormous; some industry people put it at between 40 and 50% of the total world market. The market for country music alone is enormous: it's popular enough to warrant its own exclusive international channel, the Nashville Network.

At the annual Canadian Country Music Awards held in September of 1991, Rita was named the Bud Country Fan Choice Entertainer of the Year, and won the award for top-selling album in the foreign or domestic category. Late in 1991, Polygram Video released her first video, titled *Rita MacNeil in Concert: Home I'll Be*. The video consisted of clips from her concerts in Britain earlier that year, and a new song called *The Crossing*, about her ancestral home in Scotland.

Eventually it was announced that Rita had signed with the Balmur company. Discussions had proceeded quietly; apparently Balmur president Leonard Rambeau had visited Rita at her home to discuss business, and Anne Murray herself was very much in favor of the move. Many observers felt that choosing to move over to the Balmur company was an intelligent and timely move, that if anybody could break Rita MacNeil into the American market, it was Leonard Rambeau and Balmur.

But it is going to take imagination as well as effort. Rita MacNeil is a stellar talent, but she's one of many Canadian country artists who defy categorization. She may face the same problem as does singer k.d.lang. Lang's initial impact on the Nashville establishment was favorable, but her idiosyncratic singing style and personal appearance—punk haircut, militant vegetarianism and refusal to wear makeup—was hell on radio programmers, who couldn't figure out who lang's potential audience might be. "We don't play anything by k.d.lang.... She's got a great voice—it sounds like Patsy Cline—but she just doesn't do well with our research," said Jim Tice, quoted by writer David Browne in the March 20, 1992 issue of *Entertainment* magazine. Tice is an influential man; he's operations and program director at station WZZK in Birmingham, Alabama, one of the highest-rated country stations in the States and if lang can't make it past his scrutiny, she will have a hard time getting radio play on any other country stations. Perhaps with this in mind, lang's new album *Ingenue* is being aimed at the adult contemporary stations instead.

That may be MacNeil's best strategy for penetrating the American market. "I want to take the music as far as it can go" has always been her unofficial motto, but at some point she will have to choose. Will she continue to write songs that satisfy her own artistic needs? Or will she tailor her image and alter her music to fit into other formats? MacNeil's friends and colleagues have always said that underneath her gentle exterior, Rita knows what she wants, and won't do anything she doesn't want to do.

Rita's wide-brimmed hats are her trademark.

Bibliography

Carter, Wilf. *The Yodelling Cowboy: Montana Slim from Nova Scotia.* The Ryerson Press, 1961.

Ferguson, Max. *And Now…Here's Max.* McGraw-Hill Ryerson, 1967.

Foote, Steve. *Stompin' Tom, Story and Song.* Crown-Vetch Music Ltd., 1975.

Grissim, John. *Country Music: White Man's Blues.* Paperback Library Edition, Coronet Communications Inc., 1970.

Guest, Bill. *Canadian Fiddlers.* Lancelot Press, 1985.

Kallman, Helmut; Potvin, Gilles; Winters, Kenneth eds. *Encyclopedia of Music in Canada.* University of Toronto Press, 1981.

Large, Betty and Crothers, Tom. *Out of Thin Air—The Story of CFCY, the Friendly Voice of the Maritimes.* Applecross Press, 1989.

Livingstone, David. *Anne Murray: The Story So Far.* Collier Books, a division of Macmillan Publishing Co. Inc., 1981. Published in Canada by Prentice-Hall Inc.

MacGillivray, Allister. *The Cape Breton Fiddler.* University College of Cape Breton Press, 1981.

Malone, Bill C. *Country Music U.S.A.* Revised ed. University of Texas Press, 1985.

Sadie, Stanley ed. *The New Grove Dictionary of Music and Musicians,* 6th ed. Grove's Dictionaries of Music, Inc.

Sakol, Jeannie. *The Wonderful World of Country Music.* General Publishing of Toronto, 1979.

Sellick, Lester. *Canada's Don Messer.* Kentville Publishing Co. Ltd., 1969.